Love Locked Down

Love Locked Down

A Novel About Women in
Relationships with Incarcerated Men

R. Satiafa

Are you in a locked down relationship?
Tell us about it!

lovelockeddown@mail2me.com

cover photo by
Rich Green Photography, Wash DC

To order additional copies of this book, contact:
Xlibris Corporation
1-888-795-4274
www.Xlibris.com
Orders@Xlibris.com
60849

Chapters

This book is dedicated to the artist in us all.
The part that heals us and knows that

Love is not just found; It is created.

★★★★★

◆
Prologue

From the Desk of Regina Jackson

Researcher and Curator of African Art, Mirathi Foundation of Fine Art

On the real. This is what we are dealing with here. And this might help explain why I did it. How I got so caught up!

The brothers call it "hugging the rock," "crushin' the block," "the hammer," "the slammer," "taking a dive," "doing a stint," "the cement doghouse," "drillin' concrete," or just "paying the man"—all euphemisms to describe the life of over three-quarters of a million black men in this country who are doing hard time. During the last decade the U.S. Prison System has become Club Med for niggas.

Sistahs, we call it "losing the dick," "walking the straight line," the "big disconnect," "my man's real job," "3-square heaven," "my nigga's vacation spot" or the FSA (food stamps again) tango—these phrases all describe the life of the woman that is left on the outside alone. Our numbers are off the chart, and the number of women stepping into relationships with incarcerated men by choice is rising.

With the new polygamy (let's face it, sistahs, we have been man-sharing for a long time) creating multiple households for each able-bodied African-American male, several generations of black females have been forced to make difficult choices concerning their lifestyles and love lives. Our mothers and grandmothers routinely chose to bite the bullet—living sexless, hardworking lives that enabled them to bring home the bacon and keep their self-respect—their neighbors never suspecting that their men had been "sent up." But in this new millennium, African-American women are making choices that are stunning the sociologists, baffling the psychologist, and causing the nation to look twice.

I was sitting in the gallery café, thumbing through my regular magazine when I ran across this! I damn near spilled my latte.

"With the shortage of black males becoming critical on college campuses, black women are more likely to date within their gender than outside of their race."

Which means, ladies, the statistics indicate that we will "do" each other before we will "do" the white man. Incredible! Don't believe it? Read the paper. The phenomenon of lesbian girl gangs is prevalent in our inner cities among minority teens and in our schools—girls "takin' care of they business" and fighting over the bitch they love. After years of lynching, sexual harassment, and the American Welfare System, black women still do not feel like the white man's prize. Imagine that! Welcome to a world of ebony pubescent little Xena Warrior Princess that fit the historical and sociological mold!

"Women dehumanized by slavery will not readily embrace their captors."

Hey, don't yell at me! I read that somewhere, too.

We are becoming a race of bronze Amazon women—stronger, better educated, self-supporting, and independent—willing (and expecting) to buy homes, raise families, start college funds, maintain our own automobiles, climb the corporate ladder, and retire in Florida by ourselves.

But is "girlfriend" happy?

Even the pain of watching the black man chase the white woman hasn't made us want him any less. Yeah, we all laugh at Chris Rock's jokes, but it still hurts. And a sistah can hardly get a decent unit in one of our many government sponsored "ghetto condominiums" without bumping into a white girl. And guess what? She's got two nappy head kids in tow and her own story to tell. She is looking for "my man," too.

Try the state pen.

So here it is—we can earn our own money, self-titillate and stimulate, struggle at raising our kids, and hold it all down ourselves. But we can't replicate, duplicate or imitate that hard, warm masculine embrace that smells like Old Spice on a jungle gym and feels like stone black licorice on a hot summer day. You know what I'm talking about. That bumping, grinding, fit-so-fine, blow-my-mind-like-candy-wine revelation that is the black man! In the wee hours of the morning, there is no substitute. We can get paid, but we can't get laid without him. When they make a vibrator that can do all that, you let me know. I'll buy stock.

Then there are the other things that bear mentioning:

— *Nobody wears a suit, styles a ride, throws that line or works that hustle like a black man.*
— *Nobody commandeers it, negro-engineers it or Baby Mamma fear's it like a black man.*

— *Nobody kneels down on the side of a road to change my tire in the pouring rain in the middle of rush hour like a black man.*

— *Nobody comes back for more after I have put a good cussing out on him about nothing like a black man.*

In the immortal words of Chaka Khan, "Cain't nobody love me betta."

And absolutely nobody can put it on me so good that I will deflect and withstand centuries of violence, poverty, torment, ridicule, slander, misuse and abuse to walk by his side (feeling like an erected Egyptian queen!) like a black man.

So when faced with separation, what is a sistah to do? The walls of our prisons are high and hold many. Our fathers, brothers, sons, boyfriends, husbands and lovers are either taken away from us, or follow paths of destruction, and leave us to fend for ourselves. With more African-American men locked down in correctional institutions than on college campuses, we are becoming a nation of uneducated and economically challenged fatherless/husbandless people.

I don't mean to go 'Barbara Walters' on you, but . . .

According to a national statistic provided by the Federal Bureau of Prisons, one-quarter of African-American men between twenty and twenty-nine years are either locked up, on probation or on parole. That is more than the total number of black men in the armed forces at any given time. This is also the age when most of their white counterparts are training for a career, buying their first car, saving for their first home, and choosing a wife. And it doesn't get any better. The median age of the incarcerated black man doing hard time for a serious offense is thirty-eight years—the age he should be helping his kids with their homework, celebrating ten years of marriage, and getting his third promotion on the job.

We are quickly becoming a sorority of lonely, bitter, overworked and under-loved women with our men locked planets away from us, some never to be seen again. But can we embrace those men who have gotten caught up in the criminal justice system? Let's face it, every brother who swears he's innocent, ain't. We have got some real bad boys behind bars. Can the prison system clean them up better than our embrace, and can we accept them back into our arms?

It is an intrepid bridge to cross. To be in love with a man and see him sent up can be difficult. A woman's affection just doesn't dry up when the cell doors clang shut. He takes a piece of her with him—locked away with him. Locked down! She's doing her own time—no probation, no parole.

Then there are the others. Women on the outside looking for love on the inside. They go to jail, for whatever reason—visiting a relative, prison ministry, and so on—and find themselves a man! Like they going to Hecht's and shopping for shoes! I try to be objective, allowing myself to wonder just how a stable-minded, levelheaded, self-assured woman could end up "caught up" in a jailhouse fling. How can that happen?

There is only one reason. Only one!

I remember after my daddy left, how my mother wrapped her life around me and my sister. We were her world, and other than what she did for us and with us, we witnessed little else that gave her any identity. Until one night, I picked up the phone and heard the monotone voice of a female operator on the other end asking if I would accept a collect call. I was sure this was a wrong number because my mother did not accept collect calls on her phone and would whup anyone who did, so I politely prepared to hang up. Suddenly, my mother appeared from out of nowhere, dried her hands, pulled off her apron and all but wrestled the phone from me.

"You go on downstairs with your sister," she said as she waved me toward the door. She accepted the call, smiled and nodded at me, and quietly closed the bedroom door. The next night it happened again, and the following night when the phone rang, I raced to answer it. I heard the monotone voice, three clicks and a pause. I listened carefully to the operator and was shocked.

"Mamma, this is someone calling you from the city jail," I said with all the righteous indignation a fourteen-year-old girl could muster. "Do you know this man?"

Mamma looked at me and smiled with that pained look in her eyes I noticed sometimes and said, "Yes, baby, I know he's in jail, and no, I don't know who he is, but I sure know how he feels." And again, she closed the door and left me standing frustrated and disapproving in the hallway. She was too trusting, I thought, too kindhearted and vulnerable and much too smart to let some "jaily" take advantage of her like that.

The calls continued sporadically for years, and I shook my head at how such a sensible and rational woman like my mother could get involved in an ass-backward-going-nowhere-fast relationship like that. How could that happen?

There is only one reason. Only one!

Years later, after my graduate school burnout, a failed marriage, a torturous custody battle, and a nervous breakdown, I found myself stepping into the life my mother lead—building a life and raising children without a man. I didn't even see it coming. Back in my college days, I was voted the girl most likely to have or do anything I wanted. I had planned it all so well, done all the right things, and still I ended up alone. After all the rhetoric, it wasn't a black chick thing or a white girl thing. I didn't feel like a statistic, either. If anything, I wasn't feeling much at all.

Like I said, this might explain why I did it. It might give reason to why things went down the way they did.

But then, there is only one reason a woman would make such a choice.

Life has a way of spinning you around, throwing you for a loop and making your choices very difficult. It can leave a woman punch drunk with disappointment and regret to the point where her only salvation is the ringing of a telephone.

So when my phone rang that night, I answered it. I answered it, and made the only choice my heart knew how to make. I heard the monotone voice, three clicks and a pause. Like a silent invitation to dance, and took that first metaphoric step.

"Will you accept the call, ma'am? Do you accept . . ."

CHAPTER 1

◆

Night Callers

I was in the middle of this terrible nightmare. I dreamt that I was sealed in a cardboard box and left in the middle of the Woodrow Wilson Memorial Bridge during rush hour! It was scary as hell. I could hear the cars whizzing past me doing 100 miles an hour—folks just going about their business, not giving me a second thought. I was overdressed because my office is always too cold, and I started sweating like one of the wrestlers on the TV show *Friday Night SmackDown*. I could smell my relaxer and knew I would have to get my hair redone before Dennis got back from Africa. Damn! My new suit was beginning to reek of Dark and Lovely and . . . BAM! Somebody just sideswiped my damn box and sent me reeling about ten feet to the left! That was close! I ripped my hose and broke two of my acrylic nails. God! Forty more bucks and another hour in the chair! This IS a nightmare!

It got quiet, then traffic started to back up. I overheard whole conversations of people in convertibles planning their dinner, deciding what movie they wanted to see, and trying to remember if they'd taken their Xanax or not. I kicked and screamed, and nobody heard me. I started to use my remaining eight luster polished tips to break the seal on the box. I had to escape; I had just gotten voted Frederick Douglas Middle School PTA Mighty Mom of the Year; my life was perfect. Suddenly, I heard someone outside putting more packaging tape on the box! I bet it's that bitch, Tina! I hate her!

Just then, the flow of traffic increased, and a huge semi wailed pass me so fast that my box bounced like a bobble head! I imagined myself falling into the Potomac! Another few feet one way or the other, and it would all be over. And just when I was about to get that promotion at the museum! Lord, please, if I die out here, don't let that bitch Tina get my job! *My name* is supposed to be engraved on the office door—Regina Jackson, Chief Researcher and Curator of Central African Art. Engraved in raised black gothic letters! Oh Lord, is that my tombstone? Am I dead? Wait, the box is moving. Is that bitch Tina pushing this damn box over the edge of the bridge?? . . . Oh, God, my head is ringing! Oh . . . uh . . . no . . . it's the phone!

"Hell . . . hello?" I rolled over in the bed, realizing that I was tangled up in my Dior sheets. I had wrapped myself up like some Egyptian mummy and couldn't free my other hand. I dropped the phone twice. When I finally picked it up, the operator was talking to me—in that monotone drone they all have—asking if I would accept the call.

"Yes, of course," I said. It must be Dennis calling from the continent, I thought. I shook my head trying to free it of the cobwebs and understand the telephone operator's request.

"Dennis? Dennis?" I heard a series of clicks and a long pause. I hope I have not lost him, I thought. Dennis abhors incompetence. My eyes rolled to the back of my head as I waited for him to respond.

"Hello? Is anybody there?" I tried again.

"Yeah, hi."

"Oh, thank God! I thought we had lost the connection. You know these transatlantic calls. So how are you? It's amazing just to hear from you. What time is it there? Are you still on The Nile or have you crossed over into Israel?" There was no response. "Are you still there?"

"I'm here. What are you doing?"

"Oh, you won't believe it. I just had the worst dream. I am so glad you called."

"For real? Tell me about it."

"It was insane. It was about the curator opening," I took a moment to breathe, amazed that he would even ask what the dream was about. The dig must not be going well at all.

"Dennis, I really want this job."

"Not feeling good about it? Don't sweat it. Your stuff is tight."

My stuff is tight? I laughed a little to myself. Dennis must be spending way too much time with the crew. It has affected his speech.

"No . . . well, yes. You know I have been preparing all my life for this."

"No, girl. I thought you had been preparing all your life for me."

I sat up straight in my canopied four-poster bed. Dennis didn't sound like himself at all. Something terrible must have happened. Maybe the entire excavation team quit, or the relic he so desperately wanted to acquire for the museum was lost in the Mediterranean.

"Hey, are you alright? Did you find what you were looking for out there? Did you find the blood stone thing?"

He paused for a moment. "I'm good. Just glad to connect with you! To hear your voice! Its been tough here, you know, and I just needed to talk." I heard other male voices in the background—hard voices—like trouble was brewing. I started to get very scared.

"Do you need to come home?" I heard him breathing on the other end, but he said nothing. "You know, you can always come home."

"I want to," he said. The male voices in the background said something else, louder but inaudible. "But, hey, its all good now! Just talk to me! You were telling me about your dream."

"Yes . . . I was trapped in a box . . ."

"And you couldn't get out . . ."

"Right, and people were pushing me around . . ."

"And you didn't have any control. No direction."

"Right!" I said a little too loudly. I checked to see that my door was closed. I didn't want to wake the kids. Then, it occurred to me that Dennis hadn't asked about Rakim and Zeta. This trip must really be stressing him out. But strangely enough, he had heard me—heard my fear and apprehension from so far away. We had not connected like that in months.

"I couldn't see my way out. It was like I was closed up tight . . ."

"In a dangerous place . . . yeah, I've had that dream before. A thousand times! Wish I was there to make you feel better!"

His voice sounded as smooth as butter, and I squirmed in the sheets feeling warm and relaxed. He was dry cognac at midnight, and I felt his low baritone ooze through my head like a song.

"I do feel better," I cooed.

"No more bad dreams?"

"No more bad dreams." I slurred, hugging my pillow.

"All the ghosts gone away?" he teased.

"All the big bad ghosts gone," I answered, content to play the little girl.

"Then I've done my job, sweet thing. Hey, you know what I do when I can't sleep?"

"What?"

"I lay down in my bed and think about you."

"What?"

"Yeah, one part at a time."

This conversation was getting pretty weird. I mean, this was *Dennis*. Dr. Dennis Dickerson was a well respected curator for the Mirathi Foundation, one of the wealthiest fine art consortiums in the world. He specialized in Mediterranean antiquities, traveling all over northern Africa and the southern most tip of Europe. As well as being a generous patron of the arts, he was one of the most successful and revered black men in the nation. He could make million dollar deals, but the term "sweet thing" just was not in his vocabulary. This really didn't sound like Dennis now at all. His voice, his inflections! I thought it was just a bad connection but . . ."I start at the top of your body and think about your hair. How soft and sweet smelling it is."

"Who is this?"

"And then I think about your skin and how smooth and chocolaty brown it is. uumm . . . tastin' real good, baby . . ."

"I said, who is this?!" I yelled into the receiver.

"And let's not forget your eyes. But in my mind, they are closed and your head is back and my tongue is on your neck, and you are enjoying me touching you . . ."

"Answer me. Is this Dennis? Answer me, damn it!" I screamed in confusion.

"No, baby, this ain't *Dennis*."

"Well then, who is this?"

"I'm the man who found you in the middle of the night when you needed a man. This is the man who just made you feel better. I chased away the ghosts, didn't I, sweet thing?"

I was flustered now. I had been talking several minutes to a complete stranger, I think, and had been enjoying it. "Look, you pervert . . ."

"Hey, baby, you accepted the call. You knew I was calling from the joint."

"Hey, who the hell is this?"

"This is Rayboy, baby."

"Who?"

"Rayboy! You know, girl!"

"Rayboy? No, I don't think I could possibly know anyone by *that* name."

I am one wide-awake bitch now and mad as hell wondering if I can put this freak on hold and call the police.

"You remember, I'm Cecil's friend. You remember that time don't you?" He's talking really fast.

"I'm sorry. No, I . . ."

"Look girl, you sound really nice. I'm gon stop playin' you. We ain't never met. I just got your number and . . ."

"Got my number?!"

"Hey, stop trippin'. I just picked a number," he slows down and mellows out. "I picked your phone number out of a million . . . and got you."

Then it hit me—the operator asking if I would accept the call. The clicks and the pauses! This was some thug calling me from *prison!* Oh my God!

"Yep, you are oonnneee in a mmiilllllionnnn," he sang to me like Larry Graham. I heard the smile spreading across his face. "And a chaaanncce of a lifettimmee . . ."

A jaily with jokes, I thought. This was just the kind of day I had been having. I had to admit it was kind of funny. He called me "one in a million," and I felt a blush raise up to my cheeks. Why the hell was I feeling flattered? This was some jailbird wasting my time (and my dime!) because he had nothing but time—and my taxes were paying for that, too!

"Look, Rayboy, maybe I should not have accepted this call. This was a mistake."

"Don't hang up! I don't get no redials, and there's a thousand niggas on this block trying to use one phone. I only got fifteen minutes. Just hang with me awhile. Please?"

I say nothing but do decide to hang up. This gangster-thug-criminal calls me in the middle of the *x%#@* night . . . doesn't he have family to torture or something? Why would a man call a woman he doesn't know . . . and why should I even bother to even . . . *x%#@* . . .

There is only one reason.

I remembered my mother taking calls from the city jail when I was a girl. They are just lonely men, she'd say. They can't hurt you. I stared at the phone. This one had even managed to make me feel better . . . and kept me from falling into the Potomac.

"Let's just start over. You still there, girl? Like I said, my name is Rayboy."

I got up, closed the door to my room and sat back down on my bed. I would give him his fifteen minutes. I'd keep this short. After all, what could it hurt?

"Okay, uhh . . . ?"

"Rayboy."

"How you doing . . . Rayboy?"

"Its all good. Its all good. Did I disturb you? You busy?"

"No."

"What you doin'? Tell me something about yourself."

I say nothing for a while and I'm not sure why. Perhaps the question is too personal! Or maybe this is my chance to be someone else, too. I can say I am preparing dinner for my wonderful husband, who is a neurosurgeon. Or I am composing a new piece of music for the National Symphony Orchestra. Or I can just say I am lying in my bed alone, listening to the sounds of my kids sleeping and wondering how my life got so "like it is" and if I can stand another minute of it.

I just say nothing.

"You still there?"

"Yes."

"Well, let me ask you an easier question then. What's your name?"

I decide to go with the truth on this one. After all, what the hell! He's a jaily. No harm, no foul.

"Regina."

"*Regina*. That's pretty. I always liked that name."

Then, he says nothing for a while, but it is a calculated silence. I know he is thinking hard about what to say next. He wants to be correct with me, as if we were on a date. Not too much too fast. That is, he might want to ask what color panties I have on, but he knows he can't because I might hang up. Then he's lost his one call and whatever fantasy he might need tonight.

"You married Regina?"

"Huh . . . no."

"Gotto man?"

I say nothing.

"Who's Dennis?"

I said nothing again.

"Don't answer. Don't matter," *I am your man right now. At least for fifteen minutes!* Rayboy didn't say that, but I heard it in the silence. That made me nervous.

"Look, I gotta go."

"Hey, wait up, girl! I don't want nothing." He paused. "Well, that ain't quite true. I need you to do something for me."

Here we go, I thought. What is it—money, cigarettes, drugs? I must be crazy.

"I can't . . ."

"No, it ain't like that. I am just missing a part."

"What?"

"You know, I'm just missing a part of you, Miss One-in-a-million. I just . . . I just need to hear you . . . laugh."

"What?"

"Laugh . . . just a little bit."

"What?" and I couldn't help it. I laughed because I thought it was a funny thing to ask. And he laughed a little, too. Like a man really satisfied with himself!

"Yeah, that sounds real nice. Real nice . . . like jazz," Rayboy crooned, rich, warm thick like Remy. Intrusively, I heard the same hard voices in the background and knew his time was about up.

"Hey . . . uh . . . maybe you be willing to do that again for me sometime, Regina."

He wanted to call again. Rayboy was looking for a phone pal—someone to help him pass the time. But I had a life, a great career, two wonderful children and friends. Why should I encourage him? That would be cruel. After all, what could we possibly have in common? This was my opportunity to say no. End something that hadn't really started. Play it safe.

"Maybe."

"Which is it, girl? Whatever you want, I can give it to you. Is there a chance I can call you again?"

"There might be a chance . . . one in a million," I said.

The next morning, I woke up rather refreshed. Better than I had felt all week. I contributed that to a good night's sleep and less worry. After all, *my stuff was tight*; I was "one in a million." I smiled and played with the radio all the way to the kid's school. Rakim and Zeta had made the digital controls off limits to me—for my own good—so they were surprised to hear me sing the Larry Graham ballad loud and strong like it was the national anthem or something. When I stopped the car, they practically ran to the school entrance. Zeta, my eleven-year-old, caught up with her friends and entered the building while Rakim, now fourteen, took a moment to watch me pull off. My son, who was the spitting image of his dad, was always more protective of me, vigilant of my every move and emotion. While Zeta was too young to remember the divorce, Rakim was ever mindful of it. He seemed to work harder at everything now, school, chores, and so forth. He desperately wanted to prove to me and the world that he was a man—dependable, responsible. The kind that wouldn't leave his family! Rakim was my rock.

I pulled into the museum parking lot and passed the space marked *Employee of the month*. I saw that bitch Tina's cherry red vintage Mustang parked in it. I parked my Volvo wagon soooo close to her driver's side door that I knew she would never be able to open it. She would have to squeeze her big fat ass through on the passenger side. Yes, today was going to be a good day! I walked into the gallery cafe and sneaked a peek at the pastry line. Two cherry danish, an assortment of cream puffs and a delicious little lemon tart—the last one! I reached for the tart just as a red nail-polished claw cut across me, swiping it from out of my grasp. Tina Benchford was standing beside me in line.

"Morning, Regina. Sorry to push you along but I'm on the move today," she said as she actually took a bite out of the tart in front of my face! A discerning look passed over her as lemon excellence nestled in the corner of her mouth. She grimaced.

"A bit too sweet for me! Would you like the rest of it?"

You bitch! I kept my composure. "No, thank you, Tina. Dennis and I are planning a fabulous welcome home dinner at the Plaza tonight." I took the time to look her square in the eye so my meaning would not be lost. "I don't want to spoil *any* of my appetites on anything less." Interception! Score! Scowling, Tina wiggled away with her tart.

I entered my office, full of plush furnishings and stunning art. Signed giant *giclées* by Muzi Branch and Sir James Thornhill hung on either side of the door as if you were entering a shrine, and a Diane Hayes original was poised over my desk, bursting with color and life. Dennis had had the office redone for me when talk got around about the possible promotion. *You have to feel the part,* he said. *Be the job,* he said. And that had meant a new wardrobe, new hair, and an elevated circle of friends. *You have to bring the job to you,* he said. Pity that motto did not apply to the man himself. Dr. Dennis Dickerson spent his days traveling the world over in search of the most rare and most beautiful.

I never felt I was either.

During the day, I felt honored that he would be with me. Dennis could have had his pick of women in DC, but every evening, when he was in the

States, he made his way to my door for a quiet dinner, a thorough perusal of *The Post,* and a quick lecture to my kids on the rewards of staying focused and working toward their full potential. Dennis was everything a woman could ask for—handsome, wealthy, and devoted. Yet he was, as my Aunt Betty would say "slow out of the gate." No one could accuse him of *trying* to get me into bed. I doubt if he had ever had a "one night stand" in his whole life. Then there was the other thing! Dennis had a few "questionable characteristics" that lead some people to believe that maybe he was gay. After all, what straight man chooses "The Minute Waltz" as the ring tone on his cell phone? Still, everyone at the foundation thought we were an item, and I would never tell them otherwise. Especially not that bitch Tina!

I was surprised to see there were flowers on my desk—a huge bouquet of white lilies probably from Jerusalem. Jerusalem! A card fell out and I opened it immediately. It was from Dennis.

> **"Trip running long. Will have to cancel for tonight.**
> **Will call when I can."**
>
> —DDD

He wasn't coming tonight and he wasn't going to call. I knew that! The relationship was all smoke and mirrors. I had no idea what he wanted and absolutely no clue what he wanted from me. I threw the card in the trash. Half the museum staff thought Dennis was gay, and maybe he was. I touched the soft petals of the classic flower. White lilies—the universal symbol for death! The flowers soon followed the card!

That evening, I drove home, cooked a mediocre dinner, helped Zeta with her homework, and turned in early. At about quarter to nine, the phone rang. Zeta and I picked up at the same time. She was expecting one of her girlfriends to call, and I told her it was too late for her to receive phone calls. As she pleaded her case, I heard another voice on the phone—the operator asking me if I would accept the call. Oh, what the hell! It would keep the line busy, and Zeta would get off the phone.

"Yes!" I said as Zeta complained that she was no longer a baby and would not be treated like one. She hung up screaming. That little . . . I would deal with her later.

"Hello?"

"Hey girl, like, you know . . . I know you got a life and all, but I was thinking about you all day and not talking to you was kinda like not seeing the end of a movie and . . ."

"What?" I asked. He was rambling.

"I wanted to know how it turned out today."

"How what turned out?"

"The job! Did you get it?" This guy, Rayboy, had remembered. I sat on the bed and looked at the clock on my night stand. He remembered! I could give him fifteen minutes.

"No word today," I said trying to sound hopeful. "But I feel real good about it. I should hear any day now."

"That's great, girl. Just remember you the shit . . . oh . . . I'm sorry, you probably don't cuss or no shit like that. You sound like a good girl church-going mamma and everything."

"I do okay," I said.

"No, for real! You need to take your praise, Regina. I know how hard it is out there. Shit, that's why I'm in here. It hard to take care of a family—be around for them and still pay for everything."

I took a deep breath and realized how exhausted I really was. And I wasn't just thinking about today. My life had been a treadmill-run from start to finish. I mean, I love my career. I worked hard at Brown for my anthropology degrees. I make more than three times what my father made working for the DC Metro. I take care of myself, and kept my figure after two babies and an ugly divorce. And men were no issue for me. I always got plenty of attention and was never hard up. But now at thirty-four years of age, nothing is as easy as it use to be. Every morning, I look at myself in the mirror, and see my mother's face staring back at me and recognize the pain etched in every line.

"Hey, Regina?"

"Yes, Rayboy?"

He says nothing. I repeat myself, "Yes, Rayboy?" I hear him laughing under his breath. "What is with you?"

"I like how you do that, girl."

"Do what?" I didn't know what was funny, and he was still laughing.

"The way you always say "yes". You know, like never "yeah" or "uh huh." Always a real Y. E. S. like you sure all the time. Like everything is always good where you are, and you large and in charge! All confident and in control and shit! Are you?"

"Am I what?"

He hesitated, and his next words came out silkier and strategized like he was my shrink.

"Are you always in control?"

This time I hesitated. The question sounded loaded as if my answer would tell him too much about me. More than I wanted him to know.

"You like being in control, Gina? On top . . . of things?"

He called me Gina like he thought he knew me. Rayboy was fishing for something, and I wasn't going to take the bait. So to lighten the moment, I screamed into the phone.

"YESSS!!"

He laughed real big—a powerful sparkling sound, a rich baritone that reminded me of the seasoned men in the barbershop where my daddy use to get his hair cut every other Thursday afternoon. Rayboy had the hardy laugh of a good man, and I wanted to tell him so. But I didn't! Instead, I asked a question.

"Rayboy, how old are you?"

"Old enough to have not got my ass back in this place," he joked.

"No, really. How old?"

He got quiet and paid close attention to my question as if he were trying to find a legion of reasons why I would ask it. "Old enough to be your daddy, sweet thing."

"That old? You don't sound like . . ." I heard the remnants of a song in the background coming from a cheap radio.

"Hear that?" he said as he tapped the rhythm line out on the phone. "Oh, that's butter from the duck, baby girl. Yeah, the Yardbird's out tonight making magic."

"Yardbird?"

"Shhh, listen." Rayboy was caught up in the music and I could tell his eyes were closed as he inhaled every note.

"Gina?"

"Uh uh?" I asked, dreamily, instead of saying YES. I was getting into the flow.

"When I say I'm old enough to be your daddy, I just mean I'm old enough to teach you a few things and still young enough to teach it to you real good. You know what I mean?"

I knew what he meant, and it made me feel all warm inside. He was trying to seduce me.

"Girl, listen to me," the timber of his voice changed, and I closed my eyes, too, to hear him better. "This is what's real and as old as time. Me and the Yardbird, well, we live somewhere that time don't exist no more, Gina. We are timeless. Just listen."

With my eyes closed, I imagined Ray laying beside me—the Ray of my fantasies—all tall, dark and shiny with sweat from making love to me. He was also safe. In the dark over the phone, I could make him into anything I wanted. The melody gave him shape, the harmony gave him a soul, and the bass line was his heartbeat, pounding through me. I imagined he was my lover since the man I wanted was nowhere to be found.

Ray started to hum and scat a little to the moody sounds coming from the old radio. "After a man been locked up for any real length of time, baby, he get a whole new concept of time. I am as old as the ocean and as young as a raindrop."

I laid down on my four-poster, embracing the dark, and the notes took me up to wherever Rayboy was until it was time for him to go.

The next night, Rakim and Zeta had karate, and we got home very late. After doing a load of laundry, I dragged myself to bed. But, before I turned out the light, I hit the flashing button on my answering machine. I heard the three clicks and a pause and then the dial tone because the call was not accepted. Something inside me was a little disappointed I had missed Rayboy's call. I closed my eyes remembering the sweet rhythms we shared in the dark the night before.

It took Rayboy four days to call again, and I was amazed at how bothered I was by that. I had gotten the promotion, and I wanted him to know. When he did finally call, I told him about me getting it. He was stupid happy! A week later, he called again. I'd had a stressful day and needed a diversion, and so I accepted the call. That was my rationale. We talked about much of nothing—what I was cooking for dinner. What was in *The Post*. He said he had been thinking about me a lot, but he didn't want to be "all up in my way," so he tried not to call me for a while. Give me some time. He said I sounded like an interesting person he would like to get to know better. Interesting, huh? I guess I was interesting compared to the batterers, perverts, and crack dealers he was use to. I never asked Rayboy for any details concerning his incarceration; I figured he was calling me to escape from all that. By the same token, that was the reason I accepted his calls. It was like playing "Mystery Date" over the phone, accept this time, I could never lose. We were both becoming professional escape artists via telephone.

A few days later, he called again. We talked about all kinds of stuff this time. It turned out that Rayboy was pretty smart. On Monday, I told him about some new acquisitions for the museum and in our next conversation; he talked about postimpressionist art. The following Thursday, I said something to him about the Harlem Renaissance (trying to really let him know he was out of his league with me), and the next time we talked, he proudly compared the works of Zora Neale Hurston and Langston Hughes.

I mentioned I liked James Weldon Johnson, the poet, and the next night he called, he read to me with mellow jazz in the background flowing from the same cheap radio. It felt like an evening at Carnegie Hall.

> *The glory of the day was in her face*
> *The beauty of the night was in her eyes.*
> *And over all her loveliness, the grace*
> *Of Mooring blushing in the early skies.*
>
> *And in her voice, the calling of the dove,*
> *Like music of a sweet, melodious part . . .*

I closed my eyes. This was nice. I let myself get carried away by the music . . . and the words . . . and a little bit by the man. *A man in jail!* My whole body stiffened at the realization of it.

"Look, Ray, I have to go."

"No, don't go. Baby, I . . ."

I hung up, shaking. What in the world was I doing? I was spending my evenings on the phone with a complete stranger who was locked up for doing God knows what! Part of me was sure I needed to end this relationship, but part of me didn't want to let go.

He kept calling, and I kept on answering. I talked to him like he was an old friend. And Rayboy listened well! I realized that he was picking up books in the prison library about whatever I mentioned. I should have been creeped out by that, but I liked it. He was studying me. Trying to be what I wanted. I could not remember a man caring that much about what I liked or what my interest were—ever. Art. Music. Poetry. Politics. It didn't matter; Rayboy stayed on point, and our fifteen minutes started to become an event.

Rayboy started to call more frequently—three or four times a week. I found myself planning my evenings around the telephone. I started to daydream about the sound of his voice. Then later, Rayboy's voice started to take shape in my head with more detail. He was kinda lanky. Smooth, dark complexion with heavy eyelids and a bright smile. His lips were full, and he wore a mustache and his hair was sorta wavy like this guy who sat in front of me in Spanish class back in the eighth grade. I gave Rayboy the body of an action figure, like my son's old G.I. Joe—not too muscular but toned, with long fingers. And big feet! In my head, I knew him well, and every night, I would wait for his call. Dinner, homework, a quick goodnight to the kids and then fifteen minutes with Rayboy on the phone.

However, one night my routine was broken. Seconds after I came upstairs and sat by the phone, I heard a car pull into my driveway. It was Dennis. He was back from Israel and surely full of news about his trip. I needed to get downstairs to let him in. Just then the phone rang! I answered already knowing who it was—operator drone, click, click, click, pause.

"Hey, Gina,"

"Hey," I said, pulling the curtain to one side so that I could see Dennis' progress. He was filing threw the trunk of his platinum BMW—S Class, obviously looking for something rather important. I smiled; it might be his toothbrush, I thought. Dennis carried three things with him at all times—his black leather briefcase, a daily copy of *The Washington Post,* and his one-out-of-ten-dentist recommended toothbrush complete with personalized travel case.

"Hey, Gina, I got a good one tonight, girl. My cell mate—we call him old man—he be cracking us up all the time. Listen, listen—a black man, a Jew, a Mexican, a Arab dude and a stripper get caught in an elevator, see . . . and the elevator gets stuck, see . . . ."

One of Rayboy's buddies, maybe this "old man" character, is feeding him the joke and doing a terrible job at it. I need to get off the phone before the doorbell rings, I thought. Not because I need to let Dennis in but because I didn't want Rayboy to know I was entertaining guests this late at night. I was shocked at my reasoning—I didn't want this inmate to know I had a man!

Dennis is still looking in the trunk of his car, and now he is talking on his cell phone. What was he doing?

". . . So the girl gets up and says "I ain't no taco, paco . . . to the Mexican dude, right? . . ."

Rayboy keeps talking, and Dennis keeps looking in his trunk as if he lost something. He looks worried. Now he is checking his breast pockets and looking on the ground around his feet.

". . . So the black dude says "fuck all ya'll . . ." Rayboy's voice fades as if he has covered the receiver with his hand. He says to his friend, "Man, I can't say that shit to my girl. I thought you said this one was clean, nigga."

He called me *his girl* and for a moment, I forgot Dennis was even outside. Finally, the doorbell rang, and I heard Rakim, jump out of bed to get it.

"Rayboy . . ."

"Man, sorry about that, Gina. I don't want to fill your ear with a lot of junk. That shit was funny in the mess hall and I . . ."

"Rayboy, I have to hang up," I said, trying not to sound hurried—or like I was going downstairs to see a man.

"Oh, its cool. Its cool. I know you got business, a fine thing like you."

That startled me a bit. "How do you know how I look?" I asked.

"Oh, I know you got to be gorgeous. I can hear it. And every night, when I close my eyes in this ugly place, I can see it. You're my peace, Gina. Didn't you know that?"

I swear I stopped breathing for a full minute. I didn't know what to say, and he heard that.

"You ain't got to say anything. Just understand that's how it is for me, okay?"

"Alright."

"Goodnight, baby girl."

"Goodnight." I hung up the phone and started breathing again. *Gorgeous*, he said. *You are my peace,* he said. I turned around and ran smack into Dennis. He was standing in the threshold of my bedroom door, and I almost bit his head off!

"Dennis! Why are you in my room?!" I yelled. I got myself together, smiled and added more calmly, "I wanted to greet you properly downstairs."

Dennis stared at me as if I had lost my mind. The stern posture of his chin suggested I was about to get a "look, bitch" response but that was not the man Dr. Dennis Dickerson was. He collected himself and took two steps backward.

"My apologies, Regina," he began, looking genuinely remorseful. "I took liberties, but I was anxious to see you, dear. Rakim let me in." With that, he took three steps forward and kissed me on the cheek. In an odd way, I was disappointed. I wanted him to get angry. I needed him to get passionate about something that wasn't already centuries old and buried under a ton of rock.

I looked at him standing there in all of his manly perfection. He was tall, sharp, sophisticated with deep-set eyes and a facial structure that reminded me of a black conquistador. I sighed! Dennis Dickerson was every woman's dream. He was everything, including my boss. That only added to our problems!

We spent quiet evenings together discussing dead empires and lost dynasties. Dennis was going to make our little fine art foundation as great and notable as the Smithsonian. He could do anything!

Dennis was content to read to me while sitting back on the lounger as I sat across from him on the love seat—alone. Everything in me begged for more from him, but I was not going to rush him. After all, I was already a two-time-loser. What did I know about men? I would try to play this hand loose and straight, letting Dennis take his time. After all, he was a gentleman! Refined and well educated, and he wanted me to know that he respected me.

Just the same, I would have done anything for him to rip my clothes off, throw me on the bed and lay it down on me so hard that I would sing Aretha Franklin songs for a week!

Dennis crossed the room, removed his suede silk-lined jacket and fashioned it over the back of my dressing table chair. He expertly pinched the shoulders to insure the jacket would not lose its sharply tailored shape.

"Regina, we have started badly," he said. "Let me make amends." He reached into his pocket and pulled out a royal blue velvet box with Hebrew lettering on it. "This is for you," he said simply as he sat down on the queen-size bed, waiting for my reaction.

I slowly opened the small jeweled case already knowing whatever he had chosen for me would be fabulous and one of a kind and much too expensive. I was right. It was a gold bracelet, encrusted with pure ivory and expertly carved with Egyptian symbols. The ivory and gold were braided together encasing six perfectly cut emeralds, the last of which were bigger than the rest.

"There's a story behind this piece," he said, removing his shoes, carefully placing them side-by-side at the foot of the bed.

"I know the story," I said, still mesmerized by the bracelet's beauty. "There was a pharaoh, thirteenth century, who had five daughters by a Surinam princess given to him in marriage . . ."

". . . and one daughter by a Nigerian slave girl," he added, propping the pillows behind his head. He stretched his legs across the comforter, crossed them at the ankle and then corrected the creases in his slacks.

"The Princess believed he favored the slave girl's child over all the rest, so she had her killed."

"Right," Dennis said, "And the pharaoh made all of the other five daughters slaves to mourn her memory."

"Such a sad story," I said, walking toward the bed.

"Yes, but such a beautiful piece," Dennis and I held it together, admiring its luster. God, it was stunning!

My head popped up and I looked him in the eye. "Where and how did you get it?" I asked. Dennis began to fidget with his tie, loosening it and releasing the top buttons on his shirt.

"Let's just say it came to me."

I knew what that meant. This bracelet was another of the many dozens of antiquities that Dennis "found" on his trips. Curators were notorious for making unscrupulous deals in exchange for rare artifacts. I was sure most of Dennis' findings were legitimate—acquired on digs and loaned to him by creditable art traders. But, sometimes pieces just "found" themselves part of the museums holdings through untraceable paths of ownership. Dennis counted on me to "recreate" a believable path so that our prized collection would not come under unnecessary scrutiny.

I sighed. "You know, Dennis . . ."

"Just give it the proper pedigree, that's all. Wear it for a while. It will speak to you," and he placed it on my wrist clasping it shut. I felt regal and grateful. I sat down in the middle of the bed and finished unbuttoning

Dennis' shirt. He watched my fingers at work then closed his eyes, letting his head reel back.

"I missed you," I whispered, and I truly had. Perhaps, if he had been here, I would not have seen the need to play on the phone with potential mass murderers. "Did you think of me at all during those nights on the *beautiful* Mediterranean?"

He looked at me dreamily. "Of course, I thought of you! Regina, in my mind, you are the beautiful Ceylon, and I am the Moorish king coming to claim you."

I laughed. "Dennis, what are you babbling about now? Another African princess?"

"As a matter of fact, yes! And a blood thirsty king and a warlord from Sri Lanka!" His body was relaxed, but his mind was always working.

"What were their names?" I asked, knowing he was dying to tell me.

"Who cares? This was during the reign of the Moors. They were fighting all the time. What is important is the woman."

"The woman?"

"The woman *and* the necklace." He crooned. Dennis was such a romantic—at least, when it came to his history. "Ceylon, named after an ancient city, was a stunning Egyptian princess that belonged . . ."

"Belonged?" I teased.

"Don't interrupt. She *belonged* to a great Sri Lankan general. Legend has it that she was captured by the Egyptian king. It was a civil war—Moors fighting Moors, and many men died. It was very bloody. The king had a necklace made for Ceylon that symbolized her worth. A brilliant piece made of diamonds and the rarest rubies. The rubies represent the blood of the Moor. And that's what it is called."

"What's called?" I was hardly listening now. I only had one thing on my mind. I slid in closer.

"The necklace—it's called "The Blood of the Moor." I want it, Regina, and I am going to get it."

I asked him again. "Did you miss me?"

"Uh huh," he said as I leaned forward, playing with the hairs on his pecs. I drew imaginary circles, one after the other, getting smaller and smaller until my fingers rested on his nipples. Hard to the touch, I felt my own respond, and my tongue made its way to his chest. I began sucking, kissing, pulling and squeezing until I was warm and wet, and I reached for his hand, guiding it to the center of my desire. On contact, I heard him moan and felt his fingers move beneath me, then finally delving inside me as deeply as he could.

"Yes," I said, aching for more. I grabbed my shirt at the waist whisking it over my head, unveiling two firm and ripe C cups ready to be fondled. I was so ready I could hardly stand it. I needed to feel the weight of him on top of me. I came closer, bathing his neck with kisses, but careful not to mar the creases in his pants.

"When you were outside so long, I thought you were deciding to leave," I moaned, feeling his hard erect warmth beneath me.

"What did you say?" Dennis' hand stopped moving, and I screamed inside. I had done it again. "You saw me outside? You were watching me?"

"No . . . not watching you . . . I just heard you pull up and . . ."

"It doesn't matter. Look, I'm tired. I really should go." He sprung unceremoniously off of the bed, scooping up his jacket and his shoes. He headed for the door like the house was on fire!

"Dennis?!"

"Reggiinnnaaa . . ." he said in that maddening tone I hated so much. I knew what was coming next.

"Sweetheart, it isn't anything you've said or done. You are wonnnddderffful," and he pinched my cheek as if I were a nine year old.

"It's just that it's late; I've had a long trip, and I am sure I have a lot to do tomorrow." He was already heading down the stairs while I was still searching for the shirt I had tossed.

"Dennis!" I yelled after him.

"Goodnight, sweetheart! Coffee in the morning," and he was slamming the door closed, always careful to check the lock, making sure it was secure.

Not again, I thought. I collapsed in the middle of my bed trying to replay what exactly happened to make him bolt. After almost a year of him coming to my house, at least four months of him entering my bedroom, I had yet to see this man's penis! How was that possible? I have lost my touch, I thought, kicking my legs in the air in frustration. That man must be crazy or I am cursed. Cursed!

I sat up in the bed, poised and ready to dial his cell and make him come back to finish what we had started. Was that what I wanted? Was he even who I wanted? It didn't matter. *He* couldn't treat me like this! What was wrong with him? What was wrong with me? *Too hot in the pants,* Mamma would say. *Don't no man want no woman who coming after him Like that!* I slammed the cordless back down in its cradle. I was so tired of chasing love and getting absolutely nowhere.

Tomorrow, I would face Dennis Dickerson and give him a piece of my mind. But tonight, I wanted to feel rare and beautiful and sought after and priceless. I didn't feel like trying to figure anybody out or wonder what I had done wrong. I wanted to be the princess.

I walked over to my night stand and lit my scented candles—the ones I had been saving for "a special occasion." I turned off the lights, slid out of my clothes until I stood naked in the dark and watched the candles' glow reflecting off the jewels hanging from my wrist.

Then, I laid down on my bed and waited for the phone to ring. Prayed that it would because I longed to feel close to somebody! I wanted a second chance to feel like somebody's sweet baby girl.

CHAPTER 2

◆

Righteous Family Secrets

Dr. Dennis Dickerson didn't show up for work the next day. Instead, he had Starbucks deliver a double latte and fresh lemon tarts to my office. I wanted to scream!

The day lagged on. It occurred to me that I hadn't even had a chance to tell Dennis about my promotion. I tried calling him a couple of times during the day, getting no answer at all. He was just busy getting settled, I told myself. No mystery there at all! One day without hearing from Dennis turned into two. Then three! He was hiding from me.

But where Dennis was missing in action during the day; Rayboy was on active duty at night. And after a few more weeks, it all started to feel like a game. Rayboy and I talked every evening, laughing and joking about anything. Everything seemed more electric as the mundane occurrences in my routine were heightened by his nightly input. I'd associate the simplest things with Ray—

Buying a dress—I'd choose his favorite color—green
Driving to work—I'd choose his favorite route—through Rock Creek Park
My car radio—goodbye, top forty—hello, Charlie Parker and Thelonious
   Monk.

He was slowly becoming a part of my daily life as bits and pieces of him fell into my brain like sprinkles on an ice cream cone. Then, one day, I did something bold. I went seventeen miles out of my way to drive by the DC jail. I don't know why I did it! It was stupid! I just sat in the parking lot for a few minutes looking at the massive stone building. It was everything jails look like in the movies—high fences with barbed wire and uniformed officers standing around. And there were families—women with children coming in and out, going up and down the many stoned steps leading to the men they loved. I frowned. If jail looked this bad, prison must be terrible. Strangely enough, Ray had never invited me to visit him. Never urged me to write to him. Rarely even mentioned anything about his life "inside" during our fifteen minutes. He was content to talk about the things I liked and almost proud to show me how he spent his time—in pursuit of my pursuits.

I drove around the block again, staring up at the barred windows and wondering what life was like in there. Did cells even have windows? Of course, they must! I suddenly realized how little I knew about this man that I was spending more time with than my own family. It could be hell in it. Would he tell me? I started the engine of my Volvo wagon. Pulling out of the lot slowly, I took another look at the correction facility. Maybe it's not so bad, I thought. Suddenly, I was startled by a loud beep from the car behind me. The light had changed and I'd slept through it—an unforgivable sin in the DC drivers get-the-hell-out-of-my-way rule book. I pressed the accelerator, rounding the corner for what I hoped would be the last time. As I did, I took a final look at the people in line. Could I be one of those women? Could I wait at the door, waiting for visitation, waiting to see my man?

Pleeeaasse! I am not that desperate!

Still, I hesitated. I stared at the building so hard that a young woman in line began to stare right back at me. She was petite and slender, with braids pulled tight in a ponytail that swished down her back. She looked strangely familiar. Or maybe just her look was familiar—the look of a woman who was waiting for love to happen to her. I'd seen that look in the mirror a thousand times. We caught each other's eye. She waved at me, the line started moving, and she turned away, taking two more steps closer to the inmate of her dreams.

I've got to get a grip, I thought. I need a distraction. Luckily, today was Friday, and I was going to Righteous' house for dinner. Righteous was a beautiful half West Indian woman who lived in the corner luxury unit on the fourth floor of the newly renovated Clifton Terrace Apartments in upper Northwest. She was stately, standing over six feet tall, with the build of an Amazon. At sixty-two years, her long shiny black hair was her trademark: not a strand of gray in sight. She was a cross between June Cleaver and Wonder Woman. She was also my mother, and I often wondered how my sister and I survived under the rearing of such an icon. As far back as I could remember we never called her mother; she was always Righteous to us. And in the neighborhood, it was the name that best suited her. On any given day, she could either beat you down with The Word or give you a righteous cussing out. Her bark was always worse than her bite, however, and on Friday, her kitchen was neutral ground for the Clifton Terrace Bid Whist Club. It had been that for over twenty-five years.

My aunts Betty and Hazel, along with Sister Dora gathered around seven for cards, "a little something to eat" and sloe gin. My grandma actually started the circle years ago and when she died, Sister Dora, who was my mother's best friend, asked me to sit in. I was honored. I spent a week studying the game, proper card table etiquette and reading up its history. When that first Friday night came, I was ready to take up Big Mamma's hand. I am still ready. That was over nine years ago, and I have yet to see the first card fall! I have never seen them play one hand of cards! The combination of lively conversation, Otis Redding, curry chicken, and gin take hold. That's the real winning hand.

When the elevator door opened, I knew I was home—jerk chicken and rice with hot and spicy greens assailed my senses as I entered the apartment door. Righteous stood alone at the helm, stirring multiple pots and adjusting the flames beneath.

"There's my girl," she said with a twist of her head, already sensing my presence. I circled her waist, kissed her cheek, and let the aroma build my appetite. I was the first to arrive because Righteous had asked me to come early. I knew what was coming next.

"So how have you been?"

"Fine." I wasn't going to make this easy.

"Are you sure? Rakim has been worried about you."

I laughed trying to make light of it. "That boy always worries."

"He called me last night . . ."

"Last night? When?"

"After he heard you and The Doctor arguing." Here we go! Cut to the chase! My mother wanted to know what sane woman argues with a man—a *doctor* no less—that she should be marrying.

"Righteous, I can explain why Rakim would think . . . ."

". . . And this morning, I received another phone call. From the good doctor himself." Her West Indian accent getting thicker and louder. "Him sayin' he don't know why his Regina is so jumpy and "not herself." Righteous' head turned all the way around like a snake.

"For the life of me, I say to him, I don't know what would make her so crazy. It could only be her need to get married IMMEDIATELY!"

I couldn't believe that Dennis had actually called my mamma! The kitchen seemed to be getting hotter as Righteous stood before me, full frame, hands on ample hips, ready to speak her mind.

"Now darlin', I know he be gone too much but you keep a steady head, ya hear." I sat down on the cushioned chair in the corner she had backed me into. This was going to be hard.

"Now, I can only tink of tree reasons a woman would throw away a good man . . ."

"Mamma . . ."

"One . . . she be a crazy fool—and everybody know I ain't raise none o' dem."

"Righteous . . ."

"Two . . . she be tinkin' he ain't good enough. Let's see . . . he got arms and legs and a well payin' job. Nope! Tat ain't it! He damn well perrrfect!"

"Will you just give me a chance to . . ."

"Ah . . . then it must be reason number tree. She got some other man looking her way." Righteous returned to the simmering pot and stirred it ever so slowly, waiting for my answer.

"It's tree . . . I mean three, I think." Boy, I felt stupid, but if anyone would understand about Rayboy, it would be my mother. I told her everything. I told her about the nightly calls, and the things we talked about, and how interesting he was, and how he made me feel, and how Doctor D didn't come close to that, and how weird Dennis actually is. None of it mattered!

"*A jailbird?!!* You wasting *my* precious remaining days on a *jailbird!!?* You are throwing away my two little angels' future on a jailbird?! *Lord God, have mercy on my soul*!" Always having a flare for the dramatic, Righteous fell to her knees before me. "Lord, baby, ain't you learn nothing during them years I was scrubbing floors putting you through school?"

This was going to get bad. I got up to close the door so the whole fourth floor wouldn't hear the show. I could hear my Aunt Betty coming out of the elevator so I had to make this quick.

"Mamma, actually I talked to him the first time because of you. I remembered how you would take the time to talk to the inmates when they called."

Righteous looked at me as if I had grown two heads. "Girl, your life ain't nothin' like my life. I saw to that. I didn't have no education and no future when your daddy left. No choices for me. Dem men on the phone were company. I had two little girls I had to stay home for." She cradled my head between her hands. "It ain't like that for you."

Aunt Betty sailed through the door with Aunt Hazel in tow, both carrying bags from the corner market. We all exchanged kisses and Righteous gave us her back as she tended her pots. Betty and Hazel, sensing the tension in the room, eyed one another as they emptied the contents of the bags on the table. The kitchen went deathly quiet. I prayed Righteous would let the subject drop, and we could have the traditional hen party that Friday night was suppose to be.

"Hey, is any body here?" came a loud, slurred voice from the door. Dora stumbled into the midst of the kitchen, nearly knocking the fried apples and plantains from the table. Hazel embraced her, mostly to keep her from falling.

"How ya'll doing. It was so quiet in here, I thought maybe it was Thursday and I was a day early," Dora said, walking all the way over to the stove, peeking into every pot.

"You smell like you started something a little *too early,* girl," said Righteous, smelling the gin on Dora's breath. She knew her friend was not an alcoholic; Dora just never bothered to wait for anybody. Dora had her own rather liberal views on everything. She said she was blessed with the gift of sight and could see the future. Therefore, was not subject to certain rules of propriety. She was quite a character. Dora ignored her best friend and came to join me at the table

"So how you been, sweetie?" Dora smothered me between her fat arms. It was more than Righteous could stand.

"She is ruining her life!" Righteous yelled.

"I knew something was wrong," said Betty, who was the purveyor of all the neighborhood gossip. "Tell Auntie all about it."

"There is nothing to tell, Betty." I said throwing my hands up.

"She is marrying a jailbird," Righteous wailed!

"A jailbird," Aunt Hazel echoed. "That nice doctor going to jail?"

"Noooooo," I laughed, shaking my head—and wanting the lock my mother in a closet.

"Oh my God, Regina. Where are the children?" asked Hazel.

"Matter of fact, they are with Dennis right now. They went to the mall for new shoes and Dennis is dropping them off here later," I said calmly, proving that everything was fine.

"You left your children with *a criminal*?" Betty questioned as she frantically diced the plantains, shoving every third piece into her mouth.

"Aunt Betty, I . . ."

"No, you got tings all messed up. My daughter got a good man waiting on her hand and foot, AND she got a mass murderer waiting to rob her blind!"

"Oh Regina, I seen a story just like this on that news show," said Dora, taking the mixer glasses from the cabinet and passing them all around. "This conversation definitely needs gin. You see, the inmate escaped from jail and . . ."

"Oh! Don't tell me," Aunt Betty yelled, holding her heart. "He killed the woman."

"No, he married *her boyfriend* instead," Dora said, laughing hysterically.

"Dora, tat isn't funny!" Righteous spat, coming around to the table with a plate of hot cornbread and greens.

"Oh no, it ain't funny at all," injected Betty. She turned toward me with a look of concern plastered on her face, and grabbed my hand in hers. "Regina, you know I love you. You and your sister mean the world to me. So I tell you from my heart—don't let one of them jailbirds give you an *FTD*."

"What?" Echoed through the room!

"I'm telling you, one of them *FTD's* can kill you dead!" Betty said woefully.

"They can send flowers that can kill you . . . *from the prison?*" a confused Dora asked.

Righteous wanted to beat Betty with the spoon. "Noooo, she mean *STD,* a sexually transmitted disease!"

"Oh mercy, child, you got one of them!?" cried Aunt Hazel. Now I wanted to beat myself with the spoon for bringing any of this up in the first place.

"Listen, everybody, I just kinda met a man who got my attention, that's all. That hasn't happened in a while." I spoke the words slowly and calmly, realizing that I had never really said them out loud. "His name is Ray, and we talk on the phone. I like him very much. And yes, he is incarcerated."

My Aunt Hazel was nearly seven years older than my mother and liked to think she was the matriarch of the family since Big Mamma passed on. She worked hard to maintain protocol, shedding the West Indian accent she thought marked them all as foreigners. She never married and had no children but forced her motherly wisdom down the throats of her sisters until they wanted to choke.

"Regina, I am sure I speak for all here who love you when I say, don't do this! You will only bring shame and embarrassment down on this family."

I was through! And I definitely could not let her get away with that. I forced a smile and said, "Auntie, I assure you, I would not do anything *one of you* wouldn't do."

No one said anything for what seemed like a full ten minutes. They were all waiting for the other shoe to drop, and it soon did. Still scowling, Righteous turned to serve the meal, the spoon from the greens fell from her hand and squarely into Hazel's lap.

Hazel screamed at Righteous, "This is really all your fault! You can't blame the child! You brought those girls up thinkin' they could do anything they wanted. Big Mamma always said so. Now it's come back to bite you in the ass!" She preached as she cleaned greasy greens from her dress.

"Oh I see. *You* tellin' Me how to raise my children when you never had none!"

"I could have . . . *any dog* could have! Lay down long enough . . . or enough times . . . like *You* did!"

Me, Aunt Betty and Dora all held our breaths. Righteous raised to her full height and got right into Aunt Hazel's face.

"Yes, ma'am, you coulda had anyting you wanted if you hadn't been waiting for Jerry to come home!"

Aunt Hazel's eyes got as big as saucers at the mention of Jerry's name. He was the love of her life. She dared Righteous to say more.

"But we all know tat Jerry couldn't stay out the slammer long enough to have nuttin' wit you!"

Aunt Hazel rose to her feet and headed for the door. But my mother was on the attack. "Everybody knew, including Big Mamma, that Jerry preferred being in jail to being with you!"

Betty looked back and forth at her older sisters like they had lost their minds. "Righteous, that can't be right. Hazel told me Jerry just worked too hard and wouldn't marry her until he had earned enough money to give her a proper lifestyle." Betty chuckled to herself and placed a helping of jerk chicken on her plate. "No man would prefer to go to jail."

Righteous was on fire now. She says to Betty, "They did in those days when they preferred the company of *men*, being with *men* . . . sleeping with *men*. Yes ma'am, that's the lifestyle her Jerry was talking about." Hazel looked mad enough to spit. Righteous blinked, knowing she had crossed the line.

Laughing, Dora poured herself another gin straight and teased out loud, "Well, well, Miss Hazel, *Witch* Hazel can she be talking about? Sssssurely not you, ha, ha, ha!"

Hazel turned steel cold eyes on Dora, "I know you not talkin'! What about Amos? Your own husband? Nobody goes to visit their sick brother for *two years!* We all knew he was stuck up in Greenville County Prison doing time."

Dora sobered up quick. "I never made a secret of it. Just didn't think everybody needed to know my business, that's all." She looks at me apologetically. "You see, Regina, in those days, women were ashamed to let folks know their man was in jail. We made up all kinds of stories to explain why they weren't around."

"Like 'they job transferred them," said Righteous, still cutting her eyes at Hazel.

"Or the doctor said they needed a drier climate," said Dora.

"Or maybe they were taking care of a sick relative," Hazel dug at Dora who totally ignored her.

Righteous looked at me, and I saw the face of the woman that I remembered her to be years ago, "Truth is, Regina, there was hardly a woman around tat hadn't lost a man to the system. Colored men were arrested for little of nuttin', and incarceration times were ridiculously long. Down South, men were put on the chain gangs and suffered the cruelest kind of treatment. They never came back the same as they left . . . if they come back at'all."

"Or maybe men just disappeared," Betty said quietly, staring at a picture she had taken out of her wallet. It was of a man I had never seen before. Betty's eyes started to tear up as she handed the photograph to Righteous. The mood in the room changed and Righteous knew it was time for a long overdue conversation. Betty looked in my mother's eyes and sought the truth.

"Is . . . is . . . that what happened to my Vincent?"

Years ago, Betty had a fiancé named Vincent. They were madly in love. One day, Vincent told Betty he was going out to get her an engagement ring, and he would present it to her that night over a grand dinner at Big Mamma's house. She was so excited. Betty spent all day getting everything ready, but time passed and Vincent never returned. No one saw or heard from him again.

Hazel forgot her own pain long enough to reach for Betty's hand as Righteous spoke. "Baby, Vincent did go to get you that ring, but he didn't have enough money to buy you the one he wanted you to have. The best one! So he made a mistake. Made a bad choice, and the police caught up with him that night on his way to find you."

"That's right, Betty," Hazel's voice trembled as she spoke. "I saw the police come and get him right as he got to the door. I will never forget the look on his face."

Righteous continued, "We would have told you then, but he didn't want you to know. Didn't want you to know his shame."

"You mean, he would prefer she thought he was dead?" I asked.

"You have to understand the times were different then. People worked hard for reputations. Black folks had little else." Righteous turned back to Betty who looked like she had just been slapped in the face.

"His *reputation?* All these years, and he was concerned about his *reputation*! What about me?"

The room fell quiet, and all that could be heard was the sound of the steam rushing out of the food filled pots. Dora twisted the cap off of a new bottle of Hennessy, and every hand reached for a glass. We had reached a new plateau tonight. A sad level in our sisterhood that no group of women who love one another want to go. There was pain there, loneliness, and regret.

There was a soft knock on the door, and all the women rose to answer it. All but two! Dora sat across from me, smiling to herself. "Did you bring the cards tonight? Let's play some cards."

My eyes popped out in astonishment, and she laughed. Perhaps, I had graduated tonight: finally ready to fill Big Mamma's shoes. Dora took the deck from me and began to shuffle as Fanny was welcomed to the table.

"Fanny Mae, where you been, girl. You late," Hazel said jokingly, trying to lighten the mood.

Fanny reached for some fried plantains and poured herself a ginger beer. She didn't drink hard liquor. "I would have been here sooner but Clydell, you know, my new boyfriend, called and told me them white folks on his job were transferring him wwwaaaayyy somewhere down south . . . tomorrow! Have you ever heard of such madness? Giving a man no notice like that . . . he says he will be gone a real long time and I can't go because . . ."

Hazel, Righteous and Betty all got busy loading up their dinner plates and lifting their forks.

"Regina," Dora said reflectively while staring into her glass. "Maybe you should tell Fanny a little bit about your new friend Ray."

About that time, Dr. Dennis came in with Rakim and Zeta, and all other conversation was forgotten. The ladies awed over the children, how much they'd grown, and how they looked more like their grandmother everyday. They all fussed over Dennis, saying he had lost weight and rushed to fix him a heaping plate. He thrilled them with stories about his adventures in Africa and told them all about the priceless bracelet he had given me. Righteous beamed and gave me a look that said "See, *He is the one for you. Please see that.*"

We didn't play cards that night, either!

Later that night, as I sat on the bed and I waited for Rayboy to call, I knew something in me had changed. I had thought this was a game. Just something to do! It had never occurred to me that this man had a life that had somehow gotten interrupted. This fifteen minutes I spent with him was merely fifteen minutes out of my day, but for him it was more. It had to be. He gave me his tenderness in the only way he could.

The phone rang, and I listened with irritation to the drone of the operator. She was standing between me and the voice that I really wanted to hear.

"Yes, I accept. Hello?"

Click, click, click, pause.

"Gina?"

"Yes, Ray, I'm here. I'm here."

"How ya doing, baby?"

"Fine, I had a great time tonight. I spent the evening with my folks." The statement rolled off my tongue naturally like I was talking to an old friend.

"Oh, that's cool. Your mamma . . . and your old man," Rayboy asked hesitantly. We both felt uncomfortable with the familiarity of the question. It was a little too personal for people who hadn't officially met. I had never mentioned Righteous to him, and I never talked about my father with anyone. Ever! Ray got quiet; he was probably wondering if he had crossed the line.

"I was with my mother." I answered.

Ray caught the omission immediately and dared to venture where all of my "real" friends were afraid to go.

"So what about your dad?" Ray asked. "I bet you are a real daddy's girl."

"And why do you say that?"

"Because you are so polite and so proper, and I bet you smile all the time. Bet you have him wrapped around your little finger."

"I don't smile all the time," I said feeling the night's levity leaving me. It always did any time anyone brought up the subject of my father. Ray had called me a "daddy's girl"; I was more like a wounded house pet. My father was little more than a collage of memories that halted abruptly at the age of five. That was when he decided to leave me, my mother, and sister alone to live without him. We were probably better off.

"He wasn't around." I said simply.

"You mean tonight?"

"No, I mean, ever!" I spat.

Ray chose not to respond to the pain in my voice by asking me a lot of questions. That wasn't his way; instead, he went about trying to make the pain go away.

"That's all right, baby girl. It don't make no kind of difference because you got me now."

And I believed him because I wanted to. I laid back on my bed as if it were an examining table. Then I closed my eyes as the doctor went to work.

"Baby, I got more for you tonight. More for us! This Weldon guy sure do know how to bang some words together. Like piano keys, you know? Listen, baby, listen. You ready?"

"Yes, Ray, I'm ready." And I heard the pride in his voice. He was reading to his sweet baby girl.

> *"The glory of the day was in her face*
> *The beauty of the night was in her eyes*
> *. . . And in her smile, the breaking light of love;*
> *And all the gentle virtues of her heart . . ."*

CHAPTER 3

◆

Hard Facts about Hard Time

Oddly enough, the circus that was my life was finally starting to make sense. Dennis and I found common ground as we leaped head first into the plans for the new exhibition. He kept me busy researching all the new pieces from the dig, and I was grateful for the diversion. I threw myself into my work, and we spent long hours during the day cataloging the finer antiquities and unraveling their pasts. I loved it!

That is, all but the paperwork. Dennis kept miserable records, and whole columns of numbers rarely made sense. To my frustration, he spent exorbitant amounts of money on trinkets that were not worthy of the museum collection. I often spoke to him about it, and he laughed it off. *"I am a slave to my art,"* he would say.

Dennis hated leaving anything behind. But it was things like that that made me appreciate him even more. Those times reminded me why I was first attracted to Dennis. He was so at ease in the throws of his real passion—ancient art—and I was in awe of his brilliance. In the evenings, there was less stress surrounding our relationship. It was defining itself as what it already was—a friendship—and I was growing comfortable with that.

In fact, I was cultivating two relationships, both strangely dependent and independent of each other. Where Dennis was fascinating, Ray was funny and comfortable. Dennis was always introducing me to new things, making me reach higher and want more, while Ray always kept me down to earth and real. Dennis was the classics and opera while Ray was old school jam and progressive jazz.

But most importantly, Dennis was my day—the man I was seen with in the light. But Ray was my night—my thrill in the darkness, my secret lover, and my goodnight embrace.

The three of us fell into a routine. And I started to get good. My timing was always perfect. With Dennis, it was dinner by seven, a little TV or *The Post* until nine, then a quick goodnight kiss between friends.

Sometimes my timing was slightly off. For instance, the other night! The phone rang, and while Dennis helped Zeta with her social studies homework, I excused myself rather formally and sprinted like a track star up the carpeted stairs to my bedroom. Downstairs, I left them all debating the legitimacy of the electoral college and the significance of the Voting Rights Act. They would never miss me!

"Hey."

"Hey."

"You sound like you out of breath. I catch you at a bad time?"

"Uh no . . . I . . . uh" I stammered, checking behind me to see if the door was closed.

Rayboy laughed, the kind of laugh that makes a woman's head roll back expecting to be kissed. "Hey, Gina, you ain't got to front with me. I mean you ain't in the joint. You got business."

"Well no, its just that the kids and I . . ."

He cut me off, "No Gina, I said you got *business.* I mean you got a man there with you."

How the hell did he know these things? "No Ray, I . . . it's not . . ."

"And it ain't the first time he been there when I called, either," Rayboy said matter of factly. He laughed again. "I ain't worried about him. Don't matter. Know why? He ain't your man."

"Ray . . ."

"I know he ain't your man because you on the phone with me, and any man let his woman get on the phone as much as we be on the phone . . . well . . . that nigga can't be getting his rap on. He ain't your man."

I remained silent for a while as Rayboy's words sank in. Sure Dennis was "my man." Why else would be here all the time? Ray just doesn't understand!

"Our relationship is built on communication, structure, and balance," I said. "And Dennis is a gentleman. He appreciates finer things."

"Hah!" Rayboy almost scared me to death, he reacted so loudly. "He got a dick, don't he? You women kill me with that shit."

I rolled my eyes to the back of my head. I really did not want to discuss Dennis with Ray. Instead, we talked about the new Walter Moseley book, Miles Davis verses Winton Marselis, and the impact of the thong on American fashion culture. Ray had some very passionate views about that last one.

Soon, Rayboy was giving *me* a reading list, and my days began to fill with his suggestions—restaurants he liked, playing the lottery (something I would have never done on my own), and learning about foreign cars. Ray had even owned a classic Porsche that he had detailed himself. He liked Italian roadsters, too and from then on, every time I saw an Alpha Romero, I would get excited. I had a man in my life who was giving me something I needed, and he enjoyed doing that.

I should have known he'd want more. And I really should have known things would get complicated.

The next evening, I rushed through homework with the kids, sucked up dinner and retired early with the cordless in my hand. It had been a great day! My promotion at the foundation was working out; the new position suited me. I had even gone out on a limb and proposed a more contemporary exhibition—Classic Caddies—featuring prominent black people who drove Cadillacs. The board loved it! They thought it would bring a younger audience to the museum as well as the mature crowd who knew that Cadillac was the black man's quintessential car of choice. I was so proud of myself and wanted to tell Ray all about it. When he did finally call, I droned on and on about my presentation until I noticed how quiet he was.

"Ray, are you okay?" I asked.

He said nothing for a long time and then cleared his throat as if his unspoken words were choking him.

"Gina, you ever think about me?" he asked.

I wrinkled my forehead in confusion. "Think about you? Ray, I think about you all the time. Like today, I thought about you all day long when I was doing the research on the cars and . . ."

"No, not like that. I mean really think about me. The way I think about you."

I got quiet, not knowing how I should answer him. I knew what he meant, and I had thought about him in that way a thousand times. That was ironic considering I had never seen his face, and we had never touched in a physical sense. But in so many other ways, we had touched and were intimate, and I was definitely aroused.

"Yes," I said. "I do think about you." Ray didn't respond immediately, and I heard the hollow echo of men's voices in the background. Ray switched on his radio, and I imagined he closed his eyes, blocking out everything around him except for the sultry tones of the Queen of Soul. Aretha was singing "Ain't No Way" like only she can.

"Yes," I repeated.

"Good," he said.

We were both quiet now, and the tinny sound of his cheap radio filled the void of silence between us, creating a bridge for something. I reached over, grabbed the remote and searched for the FM station he was listening to. In seconds, we were connected by sound, listening to the same moody blues, swaying to the same frequency. We were close! Very close, and I closed my eyes, leaning back on my bed.

"Gina?"

"Uh huh?" I moaned giving myself over to the music.

"Let the music touch you," Ray said. "Let it touch you where I want to touch you."

"Ray, I . . ."

"Don't talk, and don't be afraid. Just pretend that I'm there with you." And I did. He spoke sweet words to me until I swear I could feel his hot breath kissing my ear. The music swept over my body, and my hands followed until he was everywhere—over me, under me, inside of me. Then the music swelled and I came—hot pulsing, liquid fire. I was lost, then Ray called my name, bringing me back, and it sounded like a goodnight kiss.

"Bye sweet baby. My sweet baby girl," Click! He was gone but amazingly, he was still there with me as the radio played on and on. Moments later, I smiled in the dark and fell into a deep satisfying sleep.

The next morning I was feeling especially confident. I walked into the gallery cafe wearing my newest power suit with chunky heel pumps and matching bag. My hair was swept up in a very relaxed french braid that said *"I always wear $800 suits in the middle of the work week for no reason, don't you?"* My earrings and necklace were custom beaded by a popular local artist whose trademark style read clear across the room. And everybody saw me walk in, make a beeline for my table where Dr. Dickerson was waiting for me with a sweet lemon tart, a smooth double latte, today's copy of *The Post*—and that bitch Tina sitting in *my* chair to his right!

"Good morning, Regina," Tina slurred as she sipped her espresso, pinky finger up. Dennis rose to meet me, kissed my cheek and pulled out my chair. I kissed him back, giving him that extra little hug Tina needed to see and sat down to his left.

Dennis winked at me through bedroom eyes and crooned, "Sweetheart, you look beautiful and so rested . . . even after *last night*."

I felt like *I had* gotten some. I wondered if I had and didn't remember! Dennis smiled devilishly. Tina damn near dropped her cup. I looked askance at him and realized that he often said such things in front of people, inferring that our relationship was more intimate than it was. He loved the appearance of impropriety and, for Tina's benefit, I had to play along.

"Oh, Dicky, you just don't know. It was all I could do to drag myself in this morning." I leaned into Dennis, he leaned in toward me, and I said a little too loudly, "Honey, either you have got to come earlier or we need to come to work later."

Dennis' eyes twinkled. "Maybe I can make you *come* earlier."

Tina and I both blushed! I was feeling like I had sex with *two* men, and I had not had any with either one! I never imagined the great Dr. Dickerson could lower himself to such erotic banter. Very kinky! I would have to tease him about it later. Tina however, failed to see the humor in it. She grabbed Dennis' newspaper and buried her face in the sale section.

"You two. *Reeaallly*! You flaunt your relationship so unprofessionally like nothing else in the world mattered. I thought better of you! I mean, surely you two could find some other way to occupy your time."

Surely, you could find some other table, I thought. Bored with the sales section already, she tossed it aside, and a column in the editorials got her attention.

"Like this . . . read this . . ." and Tina points to an article in the paper. The headline read *Black males overpopulate U.S. prisons.* I bit my lip instead of my tart. Tina's eyes got big as she read to herself and then aloud to us.

"Listen to this, will you. Dennis, this article mentions that horrible prison you visit all the time, Montgomery. This is terrible. "*Although African Americans only make up 12 percent of the nation, 47 percent of the prison population is African American.*" Could that possibly be true? Are there that many black men locked up?"

"Why do you ask, Tina? You shopping for a man now?" I jibed, not believing my rotten luck. Of all the articles in the damn paper, she had to stumble across THAT one!

"No, I was worried about *you*, Regina and that teenage boy you have at home. He is probably quite the hoodlum by now," she implied wickedly, *since his mamma is fucking her boss every night!*

"Oh no, Tina. Rakim is quite the young man. Regina does a great job with both of her children." Dennis smiled at me, and Tina fumed, not wanting to back down.

I watched her head scroll down the column as she continued. *"In fact, the U.S. Department of Justice indicates that nearly one out of three African-American males, who were born in the year 2001, will go to prison in his lifetime.* Can you believe that? Brothers are becoming extinct out here. Soon, Regina, you'll be stuffing them and putting them up in one of your exhibits."

"Then, I guess you'll have to start robbing the cradle if you ever want another date," I laughed. Dennis looked at me. That was a low blow, even for me, but I was nervous and wanted Tina to stop reading. I cast angry eyes at her.

"Tina, why are you reading to us about prisons? Shouldn't we be looking in the Art and Leisure section? Find out what the other museums—you know, our competition—are doing this weekend." I really wanted to change the subject and she totally ignored me.

"Dennis, doesn't the museum donate the staff's time, books, and lesser valued pieces to the prison?"

"Uh, yes, for the betterment of the inmates. I deliver them myself . . . sometimes . . . to make sure they are properly stored and cataloged. I even conduct lectures. Right now, we are studying the Moorish dynasties." Dennis tilted his head clockwise as he stared at her. Tina batted her eyes flirtatiously at him—as one of her falsies came unglued. Dennis watched curiously as the hairy accessory traveled south. It hung precariously from her eyelid like a swordfish hanging from a cliff. When she blinked, it looked like it was waving at us!

"Well, that's my point! She tried to read more while she fixed her lash. *The research also states that approximately one out of four African-American males aged between twenty and twenty-nine years are either in prison, on parole or on probation on any given day."*

Dennis' head popped up on that one. "Let me see that," he said as we watched Tina's lash take a final nose dive into her coffee! All of a sudden Dennis' head was leaning in toward that bitch Tina as he read the paper—and she was leaning back! She smiled *bitchfully* at me as she fished her soggy lash out of the cup.

"What's wrong, Tina. You looking for a man and can't find one *anywhere?"* I asked. "Are you that *desperate?"* She shot flames at me across the table. Dennis ignored us both and started reading where Tina had stopped.

"Listen to this, Regina! *In the US, the 1990's was called "The Punishing Decade" because we have incarcerated more people in that ten year period than any other decade in recorded history."* He looked up from his paper. "You know what that means, don't you?"

While Dennis waited for Tina to answer, my mind drifted to Rayboy, an intelligent man who was wasting his life behind bars. We were reading national statistics that were actually the sum of a man's life. So many of our men are locked up! These facts were the answer to the question on every black woman's lips—"where are all the black men?"

"Uh, no, I don't know what that means," Tina admitted coyly sounding like some love-struck thirteen-year-old, who needed a big strong man to explain it to her. Then, she scooted her chair closer to Dennis. I struggled to keep my composure. I wasn't going to let her see me sweat. They wanted to talk about prisons? Fine!

"Well, one thing it means is," I said, "putting folks in jail has become big business. Somebody must be making some money. It also means that before long, a significant number of black men will not be able to vote." Tina looked at me in confusion. "You lose that right when you go to jail."

"Precisely, Regina! The kids and I were talking about civil and voting rights last week. *Thirty to forty percent of the next generation of African-American males will permanently lose their right to vote.* It says so right here," Dennis plowed through the paper for the continuation of the article.

"That's awful, Dennis. Thank God for *wonndderfull* men like you," Tina mooed as she rubbed up and down Dennis' arm like an oversexed massage therapist. Who does she think she is? Note to self: Tina needs a beat down out in the parking lot today.

"Dennis, you need to stay out of these prisons. They are full of dangerous men." She pointed a french-tipped finger at me. "How could you let him risk his life like that?" That bitch Tina was really getting on my nerves now!

"Tina, it is a fact that we have more black men in prison than we do on college campuses. It would be criminal for us to ignore that. The least we can do is educate and rehabilitate them while they are locked up," I said, knowing that I wanted to add more to that statement. I wanted to say "we need to love and respect them, too, just because they are our men." But I didn't say that! I was too much of a coward. Ray had become my friend, and I never talked about him in "polite company." I never asked to visit him, and I never talked to him around my children. I was a hypocrite!

Tina peered at her watch, then rose from her chair. "Gotto go, kids, it's been fun. Dennis, I will see you later! Did I mention how nice it is to have you home?" and she rubbed his arm again. How pathetic! She was almost gone, then turned to face me with a thought.

"Oh Regina, I hate to mention it, but please take more care when parking your car. I can barely get in when you park that big clunker of yours next to my "little red devil." Thanks, honey! Tootles," and she was gone. I watched Tina waddle away in her Vera Wang knockoff, two sizes too small, her butt cheeks swinging like twin pendulums across the café floor.

How do you walk around with that big clunker of an a . . . Dennis was still filing through the paper when Tina left. "You know, it is no coincidence that the highest incarceration rates for blacks is in states that rally around big business. Private industry is dropping their workload on America's prisons; it's cheap labor. It's the new slavery and people are cashing in."

I eyed him suspiciously. "Dennis, you don't mean that!" Dennis started to hum as if he were waiting for me to wise up. I looked at him in amazement.

"Don't tell me you think it is all some big conspiracy, Dr. Dickerson."

Dennis put down the paper, folded it up and looked me straight in the eye,

"Regina, everything is a conspiracy if you're not winning. Remember that."

I stared at him wondering just where that statement had come from. He sensed my attention and brought his eyes back to mine.

"I like to win," he said, his words, slow and deliberate. Then he rose from the table and walked away.

I returned to my office and decided to tackle the paperwork from the Israel trip again, but I could not concentrate. The prison statistics kept bouncing around in my head. This prison thing was an epidemic, and it affected so many other things like the rise in single parent families among African-Americans, the dating pool for women and the availability of marriage partners. No vote, no change! No dating, no screwing—no wonder there were so many evil sistahs everywhere!

I was deep in thought, chewing on the third pencil I had ruined that day when I had a visitor. With so much on my mind, no wonder I did not hear her come in. All I heard was a voice that came out of nowhere. How she got pass Patti, our bulldog of a receptionist, I will never know.

"I seen you,"

"What? Excuse me?" A young woman, one of the café workers downstairs, stood in the door of my office looking around as she spoke to me. She entered meekly, as her eyes scanned every object, from my classic Queen Anne mahogany desk and coordinating executive lounger to my jewel encrusted Faberge' egg enshrined in the far corner.

She ran her fingers along the crystal edge of the eighteenth century Hebron vase just flown in from Israel, and I flinched, wondering if she had any idea of its value. Finally, her eyes rested on me, taking a mental inventory of my Mary McFadden vintage custom tailored suit and my Amalfi alligator shoes.

"May I help you?" I attempted again, and I tried to force a smile. Perhaps I had left something downstairs and she was coming to return it to me. She ignored my question, intent on finishing her virtual tour, and then slowly lifted her eyes to mine. I had seen those eyes before, and then it hit me.

"I said I seen you. In your car the other day. You was at the jail . . ."

I froze! This was the girl I'd seen in line and thought looked so familiar. She had been familiar because I had passed her everyday at work in the serving line. That day, she had been in street clothes and not the hair net and gray uniform she wore today. Funny how I had never really looked at her, never really noticed her, but she obviously knew me well. Well enough to know my name, find it on the administrative marquee and follow the maize of hallways to my office. I couldn't imagine what she wanted, but whatever it was it couldn't be good.

"I'm sorry," I said, lowering my eyes and turning my head toward the window. "You must be mistaken."

The young woman smiled devilishly and plucked the $4,000 crystal vase causing it to ring through the room. I almost fainted. "Nah, it was you. Last

Thursday—the same day I go visit my brother," she grinned askance at me and nodded her head as if to say "you bad bad girl. I caught you!"

"Perhaps it was. I . . . I had business there. The museum often donates books, tapes and lesser antiquities for study for some of the inmates who . . ."

"Don't bullshit me, lady. I seen you driving 'round in circles. I know what that's about. You was thinkin' about coming in and seeing a man." She didn't sound coy or judgmental, just matter-of-fact. She was letting me know that she had me pegged. She would do the talking, and I would do the listening.

"You ain't got to admit it . . . at least not yet," she moved on from the vase to the Egyptian stone relic on the bookcase. Not sure just what it was, she apprehensively poked it with her left pinky finger. "To tell you the truth, I was glad to see you at the jail. Me and CeCe always watchin' you and that Dr. Dickerson everyday at lunch. 'Cuse me for sayin' so but he ain't nothing but the white man's stone cold nigga." She faced me, wide-eyed, for the first time. "Ain't he gay, anyway?"

I stared at her wondering where this was going, and she giggled at my confusion. "Anyway, me and CeCe . . . CeCe is my ace G down in the kitchen . . . anyway, we be thinkin' what a stylin' got-it-all-going-on sistah like yourself doing with *that*?" Shit. *Pleeaasse*. I'm glad to see you getting it real, girl."

Uninvited to do so, she sat in the blackberry stained captain's chair and crossed her legs as if she were planning to stay a while.

"What do you want?" I asked, now very suspicious and ready to go.

"Who? Me? I don't want nothin'. I come 'cause I thought maybe *you* need somethin'."

I tried to laugh to relieve some of my tension but it didn't work. "I need something from you? Hah! What could that be?" I picked up my lizard-skinned shoulder bag and briefcase and headed toward the door.

"Oh I'm not sure but I think you uptown girls call it "discretion . . . unless you want everybody at the foundation who comes through my line to know about your jail dick, why don't you just calm down and rest yourself."

"Excuse me?"

"You be diggin' on him like you do them lemon tarts?" she asked slyly.

"What do you want?" I repeated.

"Look, you got me all wrong. I like you. In fact, I want to be you. Trouble is you think you all that and can't talk to a sistah." She turned sharp eyes on me. "We really got some things in common. We not as different as you think."

I forced a laugh again trying to play hard. She gave me the wide-eyed look again.

"For instance, one—we both single mammas trying to get our baby daddy to act right." I looked at her hard wondering how she ever knew that. "Sorry, ya'll talk loud in the lunch room 'cause you think ain't nobody in there listenin'. We listenin'." She continued: "two—You tryin' to play a nigga you know ain't the right nigga for you 'cause you need a man, and three—the man you really want is locked up. Ain't that right?"

"Look . . ."

"My name is Trisha . . . Trisha Lawrence."

"Look, Trisha," I said, nervously fishing for my wallet. I would just pay this little bitch off and pretend this didn't happen. Trisha jumped out of the chair and threw up her hands.

"Hey, Mssssss. Jackson you really got me all wrong. I do need somethin' but it ain't your money. I need you to write a letter for me."

"A letter?"

"Yeah, to the warden of the Bakersville County Correctional Facility. Me and my man want to get married, and we can't do that without the warden's permission. We have to petition for it." Trisha's eyes softened as she spoke. "See how you got me wrong? Well, I come off like that to most people, especially on paper. I need somebody to help me get this letter wrote good so me and Sam can hook up right. He has been inside for four years." Trisha plopped back down in the chair as if she were exhausted.

"A letter," I repeated.

"That's all. Nothin' else. You write me a good letter that says all the right things, and I'll help you get out of the parking lot and in to see yo man."

I had to smile at that. This young woman, who could not have been much more than twenty-one years of age was trying to fix me up with a con—my con.

"Alright Trisha, I'll help your write your letter."

"And you have to come with me to Bakersville."

"Why, for heaven's sake?"

"'Cause there are other papers to fill out. I need you there."

"But Bakersville is at least four hours away."

"CeCe is coming, too. It will be fun," Trisha squealed as if she were planning a field trip. She rose again and headed for the door. "I know its a long ride but we can talk about your man . . . and my baby." She patted her stomach, indicating the new life inside.

"You're pregnant? Does Sam know that?"

"Of course he do. It's his baby."

"But, how . . ." I stopped short, not willing to show all of my ignorance in one afternoon.

"Boy, for such a smart sista, you got a lot to learn," Trisha smiled and took a step into the hallway. She stopped short, leaned back in and said playfully in a whisper. "Bring your laptop. You can take notes on our way to Bakersville."

CHAPTER 4

◆

Trisha's Story
Time to Saddle Up

Trisha pulled into the east corner of the museum parking lot in her all-black showroom-new Cadillac Escalade. Her giant tires and dazzling platinum rims seemed as tall as my windshield, making my Volvo look like a dwarf in comparison. Her windows were tinted black and I only knew it was her by her personalized plates—SAMS QT. She was obviously driving Sam's car while he was sent up, or it was a gift to her from him. The latter would definitely require some explanation considering the newness of the automobile and the apparent length of his incarceration.

The engine continued to purr as the driver's side window came down and a smiling Trisha greeted me.

"Good Morning, Mssss. Jackson," she teased. I was starting to feel more comfortable about making this trip and spending this time with Trisha. We both realized that we were an unlikely pair. Let's face it, other than in the serving line at the museum, or possibly on the Metro, our paths would never cross. I sincerely doubted Trisha Lawrence had season tickets to the Kennedy Center, and I knew I would not be attending the next "bootie fest" at the DC Armory. Still, she did not make me feel out of place or play that "you snob bitch" role with me. In fact, it was obvious that Trisha thought we had a lot in common, and today's trip would show me why.

"Good Morning, Trisha, and please call me Regina," I said as another head peered from the passenger side.

"Alright, If you say so," Trisha smiled and pointed her index finger at me like she was picking out a pair of shoes in a display window. "See!," she said, to the other girl, "She ain't as bad as we thought. Mssss. Jackson, this is my friend, CeCe Brooks. She stay over in Alexandria in the apartments near me, and she work in the cafe kitchen."

"I work lunch shift," said CeCe leaning toward me. "How ya doing?" She was a plump older girl with a round face, not nearly as attractive as Trisha but obviously pleasant.

"Oh, right, you're Dr. D's lady," then whispering to Trisha, "*Ain't he gay?*" Trisha shrugged her shoulders and checked her lipstick in the rearview mirror. CeCe's head pivoted around in the SUV. "I can move to the back."

"Oh no, I would prefer to sit in the back. I brought my laptop as you suggested, Trisha. We will work on the letter on the way," I said, and Trisha beamed. I climbed up into the vehicle, and we were off. CeCe and Trisha sailed immediately into conversations about TV shows, tampons, and "flaves." They were obviously girlfriends from way back, and I was content to be the invisible "Msss. Jackson" in the back seat.

Trisha talked about Sam all the way down route 95. She had actually met him when she was a teenager. Trisha Lawrence was the kind of girl my mother never wanted me to be. She was loud, wore her skirts much too short, and her necklines much too low. Her jewelry was too big, and so was her mouth addressing life with a boldness meant to shock and offend. I liked her. For even with my manners and lack of protocol, she was big enough to accept me. She was the kind of young woman who was never intimidated and always in charge and could look beyond society's rules to find what was real. As attractive as she was, I am sure she could have had her pick of men in Northwest DC. Still, she chose an inmate to settle down with and an "uptown girl" like me to confide in. Trisha was indeed special! I made myself comfortable, set my laptop down in the seat and listened to the story of how Trisha Lawrence met her con.

★★★★★

When she was a teenager, Trisha's mother would take her to visit her father at a minimum-security prison near the Tennessee state line. Sam was in the same block, and when Trisha would come see her father, he would ask who that little cutie was.

Trisha's dad was called Nickel because he was the king of the nickel bag score on the street back in the day. He always said if things had been different, he could have been a Harvard MBA. But he came into this world through the womb of a dope fiend down in Anacostia, and there were no metro passes to Harvard from there.

Nickel was a bona fide hustler, so it was quite natural that when Sam, a respected player in the game, wanted to know who the little cutie was that came to visit him every other week, he saw an opportunity he couldn't let slide.

Sam was a career criminal, already spending half of his thirty-eight years on this earth in some kind of correctional institution, starting in "juvy" when he was thirteen. His first hard run however, was over a sex offense charge with a minor when he was twenty-three years. After that, he became a "cowboy"—meaning he specialized in armed robbery—quick, fast and dirty,—but his appetite for young girls didn't cool. He had a craving for "pink"—underaged tail. Nickel had Sam right where he wanted him. He convinced Sam that Trisha was only thirteen years old and then sold her to him for $100,000.

A week later, Trisha came back to the prison—without her mother. She signed the visitation book requesting a visit, not with John "Nickel" Lawrence but with Samuel "Cowboy" Reynolds. And she had done everything her father had instructed; she wore her hair in two long pigtails tied with lavender ribbon, and a tight low-cut blouse with no bra, and most importantly, a loose fitting skirt and no underwear.

Sam met her in the visitation room and slipped something into the guard's hand as he walked by. He smiled boyishly telling Trisha that he had actually been nervous for the last few days, anticipating Trisha's arrival. He looked her up and down, admiring her soft smooth skin, round breast and her behind, small but firm. She smiled shyly (which was hard for Trisha because she did not have a shy bone in her body) and looked down at her feet. Nickel told her that she had to appear innocent; if she could pull this off, neither she or her mother would ever have to work another day in their lives. On impulse, Trisha grabbed Sam's hand and laid her palm down on his. Weighing almost 200 pounds and standing almost a foot taller than Trisha, Sam's hand appeared humungous in comparison.

"You're so big," she said quietly, and he looked startled by the chiming sound of her voice. "I am Patricia, but everybody calls me Trisha. What do you want to call me?"

He licked his lips. "Trisha is fine, little girl. Just fine. You can call me Cowboy."

"Cowboy!?" she giggled, and he laughed, too, rather devilishly. Sam hardly looked like a cowboy, with his gang symbol branded into the dark skin of his arm, a deep gash in his neck, three gold teeth showing and low-cut fade.

"My daddy said that I am supposed to be nice to you, and do what you say." She straightened, and the V in her blouse revealed a hard erect plum-colored nipple pressed firmly against the starched pastel blouse. Sam licked his lips again and cast a stern look over at the guard, who immediately got busy earning Sam's money. There was a couple sitting at a secluded table and bench at the far side of the visitation hall. This corner was understood to be for conjugal visits, and Sam had just reserved it for an hour. The guard nodded his head, walked over to the bench and rudely escorted the man and woman away. Sam led Trisha to the bench and sat down beside her.

Sam stretched his long legs under the table and folded his hands behind his head as he studied his new acquisition.

"Plump and fine, still got your baby fat," he said as he watched her squirm around on the bench trying to get comfortable.

"You know my daddy long?" Trisha asked.

"Just inside here. He's cool. I give him much respect . . . but he sure got a fine daughter. Nickel been keeping you a secret and I can see why."

She blushed, and Sam seemed to like that, but he kept looking at the clock. He was very conscience of the time. Trisha rattled on for what felt like a half hour about school and "daddy said this" and "daddy said that" while Sam kept an eye on the big clock on the opposite wall.

"Daddy said he like my hair like this, but I like it on my shoulders. Did you meet my mamma? Daddy said I look just like her. Daddy . . .

"Trisha . . ." Sam said, his eyes blazing from wanting her. "There something you need to understand real good." Trisha leaned her head in to him as if he were about to divulge an earth-shattering secret. Sam eased his hand beneath her pleats and said, "I'm your daddy now."

Little Trisha looked back at him with the knowing eyes of a woman. She had played this role many times before (her daddy had taught her how), and now it was time to give this cowboy what he had really paid for. Trisha opened her legs, and Cowboy's hand slid into the soft wet piece of property he'd just purchased.

"Oh yeah, baby . . ." he moaned as she licked his lips. Trisha slipped her small hand through the arm hole of his sleeveless shirt and slowly massaged the rock hard nipples of his chest.

"You like that . . . daddy?" she whispered as her tongue spiraled slowly in his ear.

"Oh yeah," he said again, his temperature rising as they continued to tease each other on the bench.

It was two o'clock in the afternoon; the visitation hall was full of people—children, grandparents, even preachers—but this was Cowboy Sam's time on the bench, and he intended to use it right. Sam placed both of his big hands on Trisha's behind and brought her closer to him. The four-foot wide waist-high table served as a poor shield for their activity, but it would have to do. He turned Trisha's face to his and kissed her passionately in the way a lifelong lover would—as if he were making a promise to her. He was upping the anti and wanted to offer her something more than money. And Trisha understood—her father had been wrong. She wasn't just pussy bought and paid for in the joint—she was Sam's fantasy, his freedom, an erotic investment, and the embodiment of the only youth he would ever have. Trisha nuzzled his cheek. Perhaps she could find the man in him that she could never find in her own father, the-five-dollar-bag man. At least in buying her, he knew she had value and to Trisha, that made Sam priceless.

She threw both her spindly arms around his neck and hugged him as if he was a giant stuffed bear won at the state fair. He gently hoisted her up, pulling her leg over his thigh so that she faced him on his lap. Trisha watched as he played with the pleats in her lollipop skirt, spreading them out to completely cover his crouch. As he did, she unbuttoned three buttons on her shirt, releasing two small perky breasts ready to be sucked to distraction.

Sam looked at her with eyes glassed over with hunger. "Now, little lady, its time to saddle up," and she felt his fully erect penis plunge between her legs. Trisha began to rock as Sam's massive hands cupped her butt cheeks, moving her up and down. As she rocked, her nipples kissed his face, and he sucked one into his mouth loudly causing the guard to notice, then discretely walk away. Trisha moaned and buried her face in the top of his head. It was good. It was real good.

"Suck me, daddy, harder. Fuck me real good," she moaned, and she forgot everybody else in the room. All the prison preachers in the world could not pull her away from this cowboy.

Sam watched her pigtails bounce around her shoulders as she melted like hot chocolate around his dick. She was delicious, and he slowed up a bit just to make it last a little longer. She whined.

"Don't stop. Please. You ain't hurt me or nothin'."

"Oh, you like that hard ride, don't you, ma'am?" he grinned all gold.

"Just giddy up, cowpoke," and she clicked her teeth twice and spurred him with her tiny foot. Sam almost lost his rhythm. He seemed surprised at her sense of humor and her willingness to play.

"Nickel Man's a sucker," Sam said. "I would have paid more for you." He brought her down hard on his member, and Trisha boar her nails into his chest, trying not to scream. She came with a shudder, collapsing into his arms as he took her harder—all the while keeping his eye on the clock.

"This was going to cost a fortune," he said. "We need more time." He told her he had visions of her leaning over the table, her nipples crazing over the Formica top as he took her from behind then licking the milk from her thighs.

"Next time, daddy. I'll be back . . . soon."

They talked easily in the afterglow of their first time together. The dreary gray of the prison walls, the armed surveillance, and the sea of uniforms seemed far apart from them as they sat quietly at that far corner bench. As they talked, they realized there were things they actually liked about each other. There were things they had in common that only people who lived by the law of the streets would share. They had a parallel history. They shared a few laughs, swapped a story or two, then after a while, he took her again in the way he had imagined. Much slower, the second time. After all, all they had was time.

Trisha was content to rest on his chest and listen to him talk about his life inside; Sam had been incarcerated practically all of her life—never holding down a real job, owning a home, or voting in a presidential election. She decided in that moment that she would live whatever life she could for him. She would give him all the life she could.

And, someday she would tell him she was really eighteen, but by then it wouldn't make a difference.

★★★★★

By the time we got to Bakersville, I was a wreck. Trisha had given me an earful about Sam "The Cowboy" Reynolds, and I didn't feel I could go in and meet him without dying of embarrassment. Trisha was not the least bit uncomfortable sharing everything about her and Sam. She felt it would help me write the letter they needed to tie the knot. She needed the letter to be convincing because she could not tolerate any delays, with the baby's arrival a few months away.

"I will have a wedding," she declared. "This baby will have parents who are *married*. That ain't never happened in either one of our families," and she clip clopped up the stairs, ponytail dangling.

We all three signed the log, had our purses searched and were told to remove our shoes. The guards checked the soles for weapons, and when Trisha bent over to put hers back on, I noticed she was not wearing any underwear. Dear God in Heaven! I know she isn't going to . . . I tried to get Trisha's attention as our names were called and we were shown into a holding room. My eyes scanned the long hall. I was too curious not to look around like a tourist but too afraid to get caught staring. I saw the hard faces of hard men that live in a hard, gray, cold place. Even surrounded by family and friends, their sentenced isolation prevailed, leaving a menacing presence over the room. Seconds later, we were quickly escorted into the visitation hall and almost immediately, a medium height, medium build black man with a gash in his neck and a serpent branded on his left bicep crossed the length of the room, headed in our direction. I had to admit, Sam Reynolds was very handsome, in a I-might-just-beat-you-to-death kind of way. Trisha patted my hand and led me over to *the bench*. My heart started pounding. I realized that all of Trisha's babbling was to prepare me for what was to come next. I felt my knees wobble and CeCe slid her arm in mine for support.

"Hey, baby," Trisha said in a giddy schoolgirl voice. It was already beginning. Trisha sat on Sam's right and CeCe sat on his left, leaving me to sit on the opposite side of the table. I was relieved except it put me directly in front of this cowboy who was probably wondering if I was on today's menu or was I there to keep him from getting it.

"Sam, this is Ms Jackson," Trisha began as she slipped her hand inside his shirt. "She is going to help us get the warden's permission to get married." A smile spread across his face as he nodded toward my laptop.

"Alright then, Ms Jackson. Glad to meet you," Sam said, and the four of us made small talk about the wedding, the baby, and the house Trisha had all picked out. Apparently, Sam had an inexhaustible supply of money stashed on the outside, and his baby girl knew exactly what to do with it.

I had done my research and had brought along the petition form of request for marriage. We were moving along very smoothly. I leafed through the documents, reading to them the fine points. "Well, the law is very explicit here. You have to still get blood tests but luckily that can be done here in the prison infirmary. And, of course, there is a license which can also be obtained with a little effort. And you will still need witnesses but that should not be a problem either. All we really need is the letter and we can start that process now . . ."

It was about then I heard Trisha purr and noticed that her hand had moved from inside Cowboy's shirt and was now deeply rooted down inside his pants. His eyes volleyed between me and the big clock on the wall; it was his way of telling me that we were going to have to "multitask" in order to get all of our business conducted today.

"Trisha?" Sam's voice was husky with need.

"Yes, daddy," she cooed, already unzipping his pants and lowering her head into his lap.

"Time to saddle . . ."

It was all too much. I jumped from the table like I had been snake bit! My laptop went crashing to the floor, sending a sonic bomb through the room. All eyes were on the far corner bench, and my embarrassment was paramount. A baby started crying, and her mamma screamed at her to shut up. A man that looked like my first Sunday school teacher looked at me and shook his head woefully while another man asked the guard if he had to wait until Sam fucked all of us before he got his turn at the bench. Overwhelmed, I grabbed up the pieces of my laptop, apologized to everybody and nobody and headed for the door.

In the holding room, I cried uncontrollably. I imagined myself as being any one of those women in that room—waiting to see Rayboy. Could I do it? Could I enlist in such a sordid love affair that would force me to give up so much? What would I be getting in return? And would it be worth it?

I felt CeCe's hand on my shoulder as she tried to console me. "That's alright, Ms. Jackson. I know this was hard for you. It was hard for me, too at first. When I first started making these long trips with Trisha, I thought she was crazy. But she ain't. She just in love with a con." She paused for a while, gathered the pieces of my computer and attempted to fix the mess I'd made. "I didn't tell you, but I am dating an inmate, too."

"Dating a . . . in here?" I asked trying not to sound so shocked.

"No," Ce Ce said and pointed to my mangled laptop.

"Here." Ce Ce read the confusion on my face and laughed. "You don't have to come all the way out to no prison any more. You don't even have to leave your house. I met my man on line. On a site! Inmates.com."

That night, I had dinner with Dennis and the children. I told them nothing about my day. I helped Rakim with his social studies essay, and I thought about how great the odds were that one day he might be locked away from me. I held him tighter that night. After Dennis and I did the dishes, I brushed and combed Zeta's hair, and when she asked for pigtails, I refused.

After they were tucked in, Dennis began to read *The Post* to me like always, and I told him "not tonight—I had work." He more than understood and said he'd see me tomorrow.

Then, I sat on the bed and waited for the phone to ring. I knew that it would. Operator, click, click, click, pause.

"Hey sweet girl, what's going on?"

"Hi Rayboy. Glad you called tonight! You would not believe what kind of day I have had."

"What you mean, baby?"

I opened my mouth to tell Ray where I had been, and what I had been through—about my trip to Bakersville—but nothing came out. All of a sudden, telling him about the trip just seemed wrong, like I had peeked into his medicine cabinet.

"Gina, you still there?"

"Yes Ray. I . . . I . . ."

"So what happened?"

"I . . . won the lottery today!" I blurted out! I don't know where that came from!

"For real, Gina? For how much?"

"Oh, not that much! About three hundred dollars." I lied.

"Three cheese! Man, that's all right."

Rayboy was so excited for me. He went on and on about how he would win all the time, picking obscure little convenient stores all up and down the beltway, trying to choose a winner. He picked the places randomly but there was always a science to picking out his number. He laughed to himself, recalling those days. I was almost glad I told him the lie because he was enjoying it so much.

He got quiet for a moment as if he were reflecting on a thought. Perhaps I had caused him to think too much about his days on the outside. His tone changed, and his words came out slower, like the music he loved so well.

"Hey, Gina, you know I'm still good at that."

"Good at what?"

"Picking a winner! The right number! You *are* one in a million, girl."

His words were like a gift, and they implied that I had given him so much of whatever it was he needed. He was telling me how much more he still needed from me.

I thought about telling him the truth. Maybe he would understand why I went with Trisha. Of course, I would not tell him *everything* that happened. I could not possibly bring myself to describe Trisha's sexual antics over the phone. I cleared my throat.

"Ray, I . . ." All of a sudden, there was a commotion in the background. Rayboy obviously covered the telephone receiver with his hand and spoke to several men standing close to him. He sounded calm but cautionary.

"Gina, baby, I'm gonna have to go. Things getting a little crazy in here tonight, and I'm gonna have to see what's up wit these niggas." Rayboy was already finishing his conversation with the other men when I responded to him.

"Okay, okay, we can talk later." A chill ran through me as I thought what could be happening in that place. I remembered the hard faces I had seen that day on the inmates and the guards. Society uses words like *correctional facility*, *rehabilitation center*, and so forth. Prison was hell on earth, and Ray could hear the fear I tried to hide in my voice.

"Don't worry 'bout nothin', Gina. Everything's cool. I am king in here. You ain't know that?" he chortled. "Gotta go!" He said and he hung up. I nodded to myself, reassured that he was probably fine. He was home.

I took a shower, went to bed but couldn't sleep. Instead, I thought about Trisha and her five-year relationship with her cowboy. She probably had spent many nights worrying about him just like I was worrying about Ray now. Then, I thought about CeCe, and how content she seemed to be clicking away at her keyboard corresponding with a potentially dangerous man. What would make a woman, *attract* a woman, to a lifestyle choice that could be so destructive?

Today had opened many doors for me, taking me down a path of unexplainable abuse and erotic sexual behavior. It had opened avenues to a world that I could only fantasize about. I felt it pulling me like a magnet. I had to know more, and the answers were only a web site away.

The phone rang again, and I just let it ring. Instead, I went downstairs and sat in front of my desktop. Tonight, I decided to log on.

CHAPTER 5

◆

Date-a-Con.com

"Regina, I am beginning to get jealous."

"Excuse me?" Dennis was standing over me at my desk with my morning cup of coffee. He had every right to be jealous, too. I had been rushing him out of the house in the evening so that I could talk to Rayboy and spending less time with him during the day because I was always on-line. I was obsessed with this internet prison dating thing CeCe had introduced me to. It was a whole new world!

There were dozens of sites dedicated to matching women with the perfect convict. There were even live open chat lines going on 24/7 for anyone who wanted to talk about their relationships and seek advice. Some of these women had been dating inmates for decades. Sometimes, women changed jobs and relocated to be closer to their man. In other cases, inmates relocated to different prisons to get closer to their women on the outside. In any case, these women were making love connections quicker and easier through the penal system than could possibly be made anywhere else.

Most sites suggested people answering ads posted by inmates use an alias and not too much personal information to start. On most sites, inmates actually posted their photographs; web surfers could pick out the ones they wanted and actually put them in a "shopping cart." A minimal fee was charged for each selection.

I never contacted any of the convicts, but I read nearly a hundred ads and letters posted from inmates looking for Ms. Right. I was fascinated with prison life, and through posted letters and chats, I learned a lot about life on the inside. I even started to probe Dennis about his occasional visits to Montgomery. It was a maximum-security prison about an hour and a half outside of DC. That was a long drive for a museum curator to make, but it made sense for Dennis who was also a trained educator and speaker. He loved talking about his work. There were "lifers" there—men destined to spend the rest of their days behind bars—who had been rehabilitated and developed an interest in art while incarcerated. Privately sponsored foundations, like Mirathi, of which Dennis sat on the board, donated its time and materials to convicts as a community service. Such service translated into tax write offs for the organization and an inflated sense of humanitarianism for them.

I lived in the chat rooms, sitting in on live talk going on about women on the outside in relationships with men on the inside. Even though I talked to Ray every night now, I did not want him to know about this obsession I was nursing. He would think I was crazy. Anybody would! So again, I was harboring secrets, secrets that were starting to take over my life. And now Dennis was getting suspicious. Did he think he had competition? That was funny—all this time I had been jealous of his passion for old world relics. Now he was jealous of my fascination with new world tech. How delicious!

"I'm sorry, Dennis. I know I have been distracted. It's just been all the work," I said as I turned my computer screen slightly to the left. I swiveled my chair toward him to block his view, and the high slit in my skirt revealed more than I intended. Dennis' attention was momentarily captured by a juicy brown thigh. For a second, I thought he salivated.

"I have been having a terrible time getting these figures of Tina's to jive."

"Figures?" he croaked, trying to bring his attention back to my face and our conversation.

"Yes, mostly your expense account. All the paperwork from the Mediterranean trip is botched. Even your travel vouchers. All screwed up."

"Yes, she spoke with me earlier about that very thing," he admitted rather sheepishly. He sat the cup of hot coffee down on my desk and came closer. I pressed the sleep key on my computer keyboard so that the monitor would display gold fish swimming in a bowl and not the prison pen pal of the month.

"I'll do better . . . sweetheart," Dennis leaned over toward my cheek and then hesitated. Instead, he rested his palm beneath my chin and brought my lips to his in a rapturous, devouring kiss. His tongue circled my mouth seductively, swirling around, pulling me into him, and then he delved into my mouth with a passion I had never experienced. His other hand caressed my neck gently fingering my hair as if he were trying to show me just how gentle he could be. Then his fingers moved lower to cup my breast, awakening my desire. I gasped at the shock of it, rejoiced at the feel of it and thanked God for whatever revelation prompted his need to touch me. Because there was a need! I could feel it, smell it and see it in his eyes. His want of me blazed like fire, and his tongue seared me with its heat as he left my mouth and traveled down my neck, burning me with hot kisses. I couldn't breathe—couldn't move—I was so overwhelmed by this show of emotion that I backed away from him. Dennis' head rose up, and he looked at me like a tiger whose meal had just been interrupted. I stared back at him in a daze, wondering where THIS Dennis had been. I knew he was there lurking inside the quiet man that sat at my dinner table night after night. Suddenly, my phone rang and the receptionist voice boomed through the room.

"Ms. Jackson, your 9:00 appointment is waiting. Shall I have him come . . ." As Patti spoke, Dennis wrapped the telephone cord around his left hand and ripped it out of the wall!

"Dennis, what are you doing?" I stood up, knocking the coffee everywhere but Dennis never took his eyes off me.

"Like I said Regina, I am going to do better," and he pulled me into his arms, pressing my body against his, letting me know just how much he wanted me. I was speechless but it was obvious, this was his time. There were things he wanted me to know. As he let his hands roam freely over my body, he whispered tenderly into my ear.

"Sweetheart, I . . . I have to go away again but only for a few days. To Egypt," Dennis teased my nipples through my light wool blended suit. "I want you to know if all goes well on this trip, things will be different when I return. I will be the man you need. Be the man you want."

I brought my head back enough to look at him. There was a note of trepidation in his voice that frightened me.

I cupped his face between my hands and forced a smile. "Of course, darling!" I said. "We can . . ."

Just then, Patti tapped on the door. "Regina, the phone went dead. Foster from accounting is here at your request. He wants to see you immediately."

I scrambled to pull myself together as Dennis straightened his tie and fell back into that guise of cool composure that he was known for.

"I have to take this meeting," I said painfully.

"I know. We can talk later," Dennis said as he strolled to the door. "And hopefully, pick up where we left off." He gave me a wink, "But it will have to be much later. My plane leaves in an hour, and I just wanted to see you before I boarded. Be good while I'm gone." He smiled a smile of promise that said *I'll be back,* and in the next instant, he was gone. Patti's eyes followed Dennis down the corridor, then back at me in disbelief. She looked mortified and then tried to suppress her laughter.

"Patti, what's gotten into you?" I asked, expecting her to send Foster in with due haste.

"Well, Ms. Jackson, a better question would be *who* has gotten into you?" And Patti's eyes traveled down to my chest. I followed her gaze and saw that my satin blouse was unbuttoned down to my waist and my nipples were hard and pressed erect against the soft fabric. I got busy pulling myself back together while she reached past me, straightening the Hayes piece that had somehow gotten pushed askew in my efforts to stay upright. Then, she just stood there, obviously still amused.

"What?" I barked, frantically tucking in my blouse.

"Oh, nothing. But well," she fumbled. "I guess we know now, Ms Jackson. Dr. D is definitely not gay."

My meeting ran over by almost an hour. Foster was livid about the shortages and the overages in the monthly expense vouchers. Heads were sure to roll behind this one. Normally, that would have unnerved me but after Dennis' kiss that morning, nothing seemed to matter. Later that afternoon, CeCe met me at the corner hyperlink coffee bar on Massy and M to personally tap me into an ongoing conversation she had been a part of on the internet. I felt comfortable enough to tell her about Rayboy and our telephone relationship. She encouraged me to give Rayboy a chance. What could it hurt, she asked.

CeCe's screen name was "Solemate" because she thought she and her convict pal were a perfect pair. I thought that was cute. We sailed into the ongoing conversation like we were diving into a pool.

Solemate: Hey, sassy! how are things with your newest PP?

Brashandsassy: Girl, Tony T is so fine. I g2g back and get me some of that. He wrote me a letter that made me want 2 holla! I was reading it at work and almost embarrassed myself in front of my boss. My only problem is that he still seeing Asha, and she be sending much stuff 2 him. I can't compete.

Solemate: Spending all her $$ on a man in the joint. She making an investment. Tony T better go straight 2 her crib when he get out.

Goodmansgirl: I hear you. She buying that man, girl. My man told me she sent him 2 pair of Tims and $200 last month.

N-O-cent1: How she get Tims up in the jail? And what Tony gonna do with them?

Brassandsassy: He gonna sell him for what he really need. He say he ain't keeping nothing she send him because he don't want her. He want me.

N-O-cent1: Bet he keep that money though, girl.

Goodmansgirl: For real. lol

N-O-cent1: For big real. lol. Hey, sassy, go back and tell Tony you need $200 to pay your light bill. See what he do.

Goodmansgirl: Do it! Do it! See if he give you Asha's dime. She want 2 play like that, let her pay like that.

Brassandsassy: For real, girl, that be the real hustle right there.

This was the best soap opera going, and it ran all day and all night. I could tune in anywhere—at home, at my desk at work, on my laptop during boring PTA meetings, or the coffee bar. I could hear about Sassy and Tony—and Asha. I could "listen in" on Smoothgroove and Brownbabe who were both planning prison weddings this fall. And I could get caught up in NC-Cures problem of trying to choose among three cons she was crazy in love with.

Of course, to enter a chat room and be a part of the action, I had to have my own screen name. I chose *Lovelocked2*. Most times, no one ever acknowledged me. The women were so caught up in their own conversations, they never saw me enter. But one afternoon, my handle got the attention of a woman from the Bronx, and she asked me to introduce myself to the other women in the room. I did, to be courteous, making sure I did not reveal my real name or Ray's or any personal information about us. Bronxtail asked me about "my man," and how long I had been in love with him. I started to explain to her that I was truly *not* in love and that I had no need to initiate a relationship with a man in the pen. Then, it occurred to me I didn't know what to tell her. I couldn't say "I was doing research" or that "I was just curious to why rational women would get involved with criminals." So I told them the truth—at least, the truth as I saw it to be then. I said I had made a friend and didn't know if I wanted to pursue the relationship.

Bronxtail: LOL!! Lovelocked, are you serious?

EbonyQ: LOL. what she mean *pursue* the relationship?

Sugababy: U better wake up, sistah.

Bronxtail: U trying 2 fool yourself, girl. Be lucky. U got us. We can help u out with that.

LoveLocked2: I don't understand what you mean.

EbonyQ: Are u a white girl or something? Married 2 a bank president or some shit like that?

Sugababy: Lovedlocked, ignore EbonyQ . . . pleeaasse.

Bronxtail: Ebony, leave LoveLocked alone.

Bronxtail: Sweetie, we have seen u in the chat room enough 2 no u got it bad 4 somebody locked up somewhere.

EbonyQ: Yeah, LoveLocked, u got it bad.

Bronxtail: Hey, but u don't have 2 feel bad abt it. It's just a new thing 4 u. Roll with it.

Roll with it, she said. I wasn't sure I could. There were parts of me that enjoyed, even needed, to have Rayboy in my life. I had to admit that. Until recent events, he had given off more warmth over the phone than Dennis did five feet away. But still there were other parts of me—the stay-on-the-high-road-because-you-can-do-better-because-you-are-better part of me that resisted any notion of a real relationship with Ray. Bronxtail could sense that, and she tried to make me feel easy about the whole thing. She even sent me an instant message so that she could chat with me privately about the course I was taking. And when we did, she shared with me her own story of dating a con over the Internet, and how it triggered a series of events that would change her life forever. I saved that conversation on my computer and in my own tangled memory. Her real name was Sophia, and I called her story Date-a-Con.com.

★★★★★

Sophia had been dating over the Internet for years, but not for the reason most people would imagine. She was a very attractive woman, who earned a good living as a private duty nurse. Most of her clients were wealthy and came from the ritzy section of Central Park. She was what people called a night nurse—working from 8 p.m. to 8 a.m. In the morning, Sophia would return to her small efficiency apartment in the Bronx, where she took care of an aging mother. Her apartment was cramped, so there was little privacy. There was only a thin screen that separated Sophia from her mother and the nearby kitchen.

Sophia's mother suffered from an acute liver disease. She rarely went out and would threaten suicide when Sophia would suggest she go to a nursing home. "Why should we hire a nurse for me when I birthed the best nurse in all of New York? Besides, I'll be dead soon enough, she would say.

So between working the graveyard shift at night and living the graveyard shift during the day, Sophia had little time for anything else. Her mother was so cranky that she rarely ever brought friends home. Sophia found the perfect escape through the Internet—men she could cybersurf for and have cyber sex with at any time of the day or night. Things would be perfect for months until they wanted to meet her and step into her world.

Sophia was always afraid to cross that line so she would end the relationship quickly. One day, she happened upon a dating site devoted to helping death row inmates foster relationships with women on the outside. That is perfect, Sophia thought—I will never ever meet any of these men. She carefully read through the ads and chose "Wildbuck"—a lifer with no possibility of parole—to be her prison pen pal. Her added rationale was that since he had been incarcerated for so long, the SOP (sex on paper) should be fantastic! How could you go wrong with someone named *Wildbuck?*

Sophia paid the nominal fee for Wildbuck's information and wrote him a letter of introduction. He immediately responded, and they ventured off into a stimulating pen pal partnership. He was locked up in Morgan County Penitentiary, originally from Colorado, married once, no kids and had worked on farms most of his life. That is, until he brutally killed his boss for not keeping a promise concerning his requested vacation time. Wildbuck admitted to being a little hotheaded but felt that the years behind bars had settled him down. Sophia felt quite at ease writing to Wildbuck, telling him about her life, personal interests, and dreams for the future. Since Wildbuck virtually had no future, he concentrated on helping Sophia stay focused and directed on getting her advanced nursing degree. He even helped her study by referencing information in the prison library for her. He was learning right along with her, and it helped to occupy his time.

Wildbuck, whose real name was Wayne, was encouraging and sensitive, writing several letters a week—all to help keep Sophia centered. Not to mention, he was quite a romantic, writing pages and pages about what he could do to her given enough time, a can of Cool Whip and a bed that took quarters. In no time, Sophia was sending Wayne little gifts. Sophia and Wildbuck were the perfect couple. For Sophia, it was heaven.

Several months later, Sophia earned her degree and got a better paying job at a local hospital. It was one of the best days of her life, and she wanted to share it with Wayne, whose support had made it all possible. She decided to take a chance and ask to come visit him. Much to her surprise, Wayne told her not to come. In fact, he was trying to transfer out of Morgan County because he had gotten into some trouble on his block. Apparently, he had made quite an enemy of a notorious criminal named MaCray Boden, and things were getting out of hand.

In the months to follow, Wayne's letters got more and more desperate. He had even petitioned the warden to relocate him. Boden had threatened Wayne's life on more than one occasion, and an altercation was inevitable. Sophia grew afraid for her Wildbuck as each letter got more terrifying.

"Surely, there must be something I can do, Wayne," she asked in all her letters.

"Just keep being my ray of sunshine," he wrote. "And promise me you will be there for me when I need you."

"I promise," Sophia wrote back.

In the months to come, Sophia's work schedule got very hectic. Between her ill-tempered mother, the few private duty clients she kept and her job at the hospital, Sophia had less time to write. Wayne continued to write, keeping her informed on his efforts to get transferred. Sophia apologized for not writing as much.

"I understand," he wrote. "Are you still my sunshine? Remember, you promised."

"Yes, I promise, Wayne."

Time went by and gradually, Wildbuck's letters stopped coming. Sophia tried not to worry. After all, she was the one who didn't want to get attached. Maybe, he had just moved on. She also realized that she might not have been the only woman he was writing. Wayne may have had several pen pal relationships going on at one time. Perhaps, he was pursuing another. It even occurred to her that maybe her gifts weren't nice enough, and Wildbuck thought she had not invested enough into the relationship. He was probably stockpiling packages from lonely women all over the country!

Regardless of the reason, Sophia was deeply saddened not to hear from him, and the days that followed seemed to drag on into the next. Until one day when she was leaving the hospital at the end of her shift, the strangest thing happened. Sophia was standing at the elevator door when it opened, and there stood an inmate surrounded by three armed guards. He wore a bright orange uniform, black boots, and a wool hat. His arms and legs were heavily shackled, and his face was worn and tired. He must be terribly sick, she thought to herself. Inmates were routinely brought to the hospital when the prison infirmaries could not handle an illness or life threatening injury. Sophia remembered Wildbuck, and his fear of an altercation with Boden. She wondered if this inmate had been wounded in a prison fight or riot. Sophia gasped as the realization hit her. Wildbuck might be dead! No one would ever know to notify her if something had happened to him. She was not family. She had never even signed a visitation book to see him.

As if in a trance, Sophia followed the armed procession down the hall to the examination room and showed them all in. She watched the guards talking to the prisoner. They seemed to know him well. In fact, they seemed to actually like him, being far too at ease around him. He must have been in the New York State Penitentiary for a very long time, she thought. Two of them sat in the far corner of the room eying the younger nurses at the nurses' station while the third spoke with the doctor about the inmate's condition. The doctor on call told Sophia to take the patient's vitals while he consulted with his interns. She really should be leaving, but the hospital was short staffed so she decided to stay.

The prisoner sat still, his head down, as Sophia reached for his wrist to check his pulse. She felt a jolt shoot through her body as she held his hand. His skin was almost white as hers yet his features were those of a black man's. Sophia removed his ill-fitting hat and was compelled to touch his hair, a nappy salt and pepper. He raised his eyelids to look at her, and for a moment it felt as if they were the only two people in the room. The two corner guards were seriously flirting with the floor nurses now, and the other guard had actually walked out of the room to hear the doctor give his chart evaluation to the interns. Nervous now at being so alone with the convict, Sophia dropped the blood pressure band, and the inmate reached down to retrieve it. When he gave it back to her, he clasped her hand tight in his and stunned her with his words.

"You still my *ray of sunshine?*"

Sophia blinked. She had not heard or read those words in months. And even then, from only one man!

"Wildbuck?" she whispered.

"In the flesh, sunshine," he whispered back with a twinkle in his eye. Sophia thought of the photograph that had been posted on the web site. He didn't look much like his picture but then, neither did she. People are rarely that honest on the internet. That withstanding, she had no doubt it was him.

"Wayne, what are you doing here," Sophia asked, a little too loudly.

He coughed for the benefit of all in the room so no one would get suspicious. "Not so loud. Act normal," he looked around to make sure no one was listening. "I got my transfer, sunshine. Right here to New York just to be with you! I had to do something. Boden was going to kill me over nothing. Prison ain't much of a life, but it is MY life, and I don't want to die screaming and bleeding like a stuck pig."

Sophia ambled around him, standing between him and anyone else in the room, as he continued. "I wanted to be with you. So I faked an illness so they would have to bring me to this hospital." He brought his face closer to hers as if she were checking his eyes and ears.

"One day, it hit me. All that talk about internal medicine while you were in school. I started coming up with a plan. You helped me do this, sunshine."

Wayne was trying to flatter her, but instead, Sophia was scared to death. Wayne was here with her in the flesh! She envisioned explaining this to her mother. Oh my God!

"Wayne, I am touched you would come all this way to be close to me but . . ."

"No, sunshine, that ain't why I'm here," his face lit up like a Christmas tree.

"Sophia, I came to be *with you*. You are going to help me escape!"

Sophia felt faint. Wayne reached for her arm to steady her. When she caught her balance she said, "I can't possibly do this. How could we . . ."

His face turned stern with malice as he dug his fingertips into her flesh. "What you wasting your life away for anyway? Waiting on sick rich bastards and a mamma who ain't never gonna die! What you living for? You might as well be in the cell next to me!"

Tears began to stream down Sophia's face. It was all true—she was alive yet afraid to live. All these years, she had been hiding in her tiny apartment, her own kind of prison. Wayne was the key to set her free. He had brought her this far, making it possible to find the confidence she needed to finish school. He wanted his freedom, and he was opening the door to hers. But it had to be now!

Wildbuck searched Sophia's eyes as she weighed the consequences. He knew she was a smart girl, and she was quickly calculating her predicament. She realized that she had been writing to a convict for almost two years, giving him the necessary tools to fool the prison doctors and the guards. She had told him what diseases could not be treated in the prison infirmary and which ones would get him a free pass to the hospital where she worked. Whether Sophia liked it or not, she was an accomplice.

"Wayne, I can't . . ."

"Yes, you can. All you have to do is decide if you want to be free or not." Wildbuck pierced Sophia with his eyes. "Free is better, sunshine. It don't matter what the cost."

Wildbuck gently rattled the shackles on his legs then showed Sophia the key hidden in his sleeve. He had planned this for months, and it was going to happen, with or without her. Sophia eyed the open corridor, and the stretcher near by. She noticed again the distracted guards. She knew that if she could get him into the adjoining bathroom, Wayne could fit through the tiny window and shimmy up toward the roof. From there, he could hide in the laundry duct until she could get him a change of clothes and literally walk him out of the side door. It could be done!

Sophia was still deep in thought as he pressed her for an answer. "You promised me, sunshine," he warned in a whisper, reminding Sophia of her words. "You said you would be there for me."

Sophia's hands shook with fright. So many people depended on her! How could she just walk away? She looked into the tired pleading eyes of the convict who sat before her. She imagined his life in a tiny cell, watching the world change through letters from the outside. When she returned her attention to him, Wayne saw a different Sophia. A decision had been made, and right or wrong, she would see it through.

"You are right, Wildbuck," she said, taking hold of the key. "Free is better."

★★★★★

That was the end of Bronxtail's message, and I sat in the coffee bar wondering what happened. I went back to the chat room to see where she was, but there was no response from her. Later, I asked EbonyQ about her.

EbonyQ: Cant say 4 sure. No, 1 really knows what happened with her and Wildbuck.

Solemate: We know Sophia lives with a man somewhere in Colorado—we think.

LoveLocked2: I suppose she really can't tell us, can she?

EbonyQ: Hell, no! she can't! She got 2 protect her man and herself if she ran with him.

Solemate: And on the internet nobody knows where anybody is for sure. They could be across the country or next door.

EbonyQ: Sorry, I can't help you, LovedLocked. I do no that Macray Boden is a real bastard though. Niggas running from him up and down the east coast. Killed some dude in Red Onion with his bare hands.

Solemate: Yep! I heard he knifed a man in Mecklenburg over a cartoon of cigs. He got a real bad rep. You ever seen him, Ebony?

EbonyQ: No, but I heard he is FINE. Looking like he young when he should look old, and he got a nickname in the joint—Rayboy.

Oh my God! I slammed my laptop shut and headed back to the museum. It couldn't be! Ray? Not my Ray, a killer? I began to shake with disbelief. It couldn't be true! No way! He reads me poetry, I thought. He sings me to sleep and tells me I'm beautiful. He loves foreign cars and reads Hurston. It can't be true, I said to myself. Then, the little voice of reason kicked in—Regina, you knew he was a criminal. That's why he lives in a prison. You knew he had to have done something to be in there in the first place. He wasn't just visiting!

I made my way down M Street and onto the Metro. Faces blurred before me as I hurried back to the safety of the museum. I ran pass Patti and into my office, shutting the door soundly. Oh my God! I said aloud, throwing my head on the desk. Who had I gotten myself mixed up with? I picked up the phone and dialed Righteous but no one answered. I made a long distance call to my sister hoping she would be home. She wasn't! Who was I fooling? I was too chicken to call the person I really wanted to talk to call. How could I tell Dennis I had been communicating nightly with a man in prison? I wanted to throw myself into his arms and have him hold me until all my confusion went away. I wanted him to tell me everything was alright. I was just looking for love in the wrong places, and now he would have to give me all the love I needed. I looked at the clock—4 p.m. A whole day wasted! I needed Dennis here, not on his way to Egypt! But what was I going to say—*Yes, Dennis, I have been accepting collect calls from a convict, but now I realize he is a criminal?*

I picked up the phone and dialed CeCe, and left a message on her cell, asking her to come to my office immediately. Then, I noticed the flowers.

Dennis had left me more lilies: this time, in a small glass vase dotted with tiny white pearls. Lilies! I thought they were the flower of death before, but maybe I was wrong. Maybe they stood for rebirth and renewal. A new start! I took a breath, inhaling their scent and read the enclosed card.

> "The glory of the day is in your face
>
> The beauty of the night is in your eyes."
>
> Hate to leave you again.
>
> Can hardly wait to return to you.
>
> Until then—Dennis

I instantly felt better. Everything was coming back into focus now. I tried to call Dennis on his cell, but he was out of range. No matter! He would call soon, and I would put this whole episode behind me. I read the card again. That's funny, I thought. Dennis had paraphrased the same poem that Rayboy had recited to me a while back. I mulled for a second on how coincidental that was but only for a second. I was more impressed with how sweet a gesture it was, how perfect, and how much I was looking forward to him coming home. Things would be different, he said. He would be the man I wanted and needed, he said. Dennis was obviously wrestling with something, and I did not know what it was. Could it have been another woman? Or, maybe just the pressures of the job? That didn't matter, either. I would make him forget anything else that was in our way. I would do better, too. I looked at the flowers again. If Righteous were here right now, she would say "dis be a good ting." I laughed to myself. It was a good thing. Things were moving in the right direction, and it was about time.

"The beauty of the night is in your eyes . . ." I read Dennis' card, but all I could hear was a different voice, smooth and mellow, ringing in my head. I was devastated by the realization of Rayboy's crimes. How could I have been so easily fooled? He sounded so sensitive and loving and *human* all those nights on the phone. Now, I knew he was a monster. I had been deceived, and it hurt more than I wanted to admit.

I pressed the shutdown function on my computer keyboard. I was making myself crazy. Rayboy and men like him, live in a world I knew nothing about. I needed to back away from it before it ate me alive. Just then, CeCe appeared in my office doorway. She looked shaken and uneasy, and I asked her to come in. She probably had made the same connection that I had between Rayboy and MaCray Boden. She was sweet to worry about me, but she didn't have to anymore. I had come to my senses. The ONLY man in my life was on a plane to Egypt, and I would be waiting for HIS call tonight.

"Ms. Jackson, I came to talk to you. It's real important. It's about your man."

"I know, CeCe. You are a little too late! I already know."

"Oh, Lord Ms. Jackson, what you going to do?"

I was still bothered that she would not call me Regina. "I don't know," I said.

"You can't play around with a man like this one. He will hurt you."

"I know, CeCe," I shouted in frustration.

"And you can't go to the police either. They won't help you."

"I know Cece," I repeated. "I know. God, how did I get messed up in this thing? I just have to tell him to back off. I'll just stop talking to him."

"Stop talking to him? He will never go for that! Oh, Ms. Jackson, this man is dangerous. He ain't gon just let you walk away from him. There is too much too lose. And he don't like to lose at nothing. He gets everything he goes after. Everything! Including you."

"But, at least, I have one thing going for me. As long as he is locked up, I'm safe."

"What are you talking about? He comes and goes as he pleases. He practically runs the prison. Just like he do everything around here."

"CeCe, what are you talking about?"

"Ms. Jackson, I think you got tangled up with the wrong man. 'Course, I can't prove anything, but something terrible is going on at that prison, and you are going to have to find out what it is."

"CeCe, you are scaring me."

"You need to be scared! Look, he had us all fooled. Don't blame yourself! So much money and power and influence! Sometimes it just turn a man bad."

"I wish I had never answered the phone that night! I wish I had never heard MaCray Boden's name! Who would think that a man who loved music and poetry and could laugh at bad jokes and rock me to sleep at night with his voice could do such terrible things? I thought he . . . I thought I . . ."

"MaCray Boden!? . . . Rayboy? Oh no, Ms. Jackson, I aint talking about him. I am talking about *our man in the prison*. I am talking about that missing money that folks keep whispering about all over the place. Mr. Foster, the accountant, was talking about it today in the café. I'm talking about the trips nobody can explain. And now, Miss Benchford losing her job over nothing."

"Tina? Fired? What are you talking about?"

"Just today! While you were out. And he done it with a phone call. *A phone call*—to the museum trustees. I heard it myself. He is covering his tracks. You have got to be careful."

CeCe came over to my desk and clasped my shoulders to make sure her words were sinking in.

"CeCe, you are not making any sense! What are you talking about? Rayboy . . ."

"Listen to me," she said, her voice shattering with the impact of it all. "I am talking about *your man*, Ms. Jackson. A very dangerous man who ain't what none of us think he is. I am talking about your Dr. Dickerson."

CHAPTER 6

◆

Anna's Story
The Man I Prayed for

Zeta sat in the far side of the room, scowling at me from the corner ottoman where I had thrown my clothes from the day before. It was early, barely 6 a.m., and she was already up and fully dressed in her girl scout uniform. My head was still buried in my pillow, but I watched her through matted lashes as she whined impatiently under her breath waiting for me to get up. Zeta heard my alarm clock when it chimed forty minutes ago, and she heard me curse and turn it off—twice. She knew I was awake, and she knew I knew that it was her turn to lead Troupe 437 in the Daisy Days Parade. It was time to go!

I laid motionless in the bed, as numb on the outside as I felt on the inside. My thoughts were a mass of confusion. Dennis's face kept emerging in my mind, and his words, promising me that everything would be different. Well, he didn't lie; everything was different now. I had stayed at the museum half the night, going over figures—checking them and rechecking them. I had revisited expense vouchers and acquisition forms from all his recent trips—Egypt, Israel, Nairobi, and the Sudan. None of it made any sense! Even his flight itinerary did not jive with his travel receipts. And to make it worse, artifacts that he purchased on these imaginary trips could not have possibly come from where he said they did. I slapped myself on the forehead for missing that! I was so preoccupied with getting Dennis into my bed, facts that should have been obvious completely slipped by me. Where he said he was didn't match up with where he really was at all. CeCe was right! Something was definitely going on. But why did she feel I was in danger, and what did it have to do with the prison? It just didn't make any sense.

The fear in CeCe's eyes the day before was real, but she was jumping to all kinds of ridiculous conclusions. CeCe was trying to piece together rumors she had heard in the museum cafeteria. Pieces of conversations that just didn't fit together! Nothing fit. On top of that, she was fusing the confusion at work with the trouble that was happening in the prison. Apparently, there was a predator—probably one of a thousand monsters in that hellhole—that was terrorizing the prison population. His name was MaCray Boden, better known as Rayboy.

My blood started to boil as my thoughts drifted to Rayboy—another man I had apparently misjudged. Unbelievable! How could I have been so stupid? If you live in a zoo, you must be an animal. And if you live in the State Penitentiary it stands to reason that you must be a criminal. A sharp pain raced across my chest! Something inside did not want to allow that Rayboy could be the cruel and heartless man that those emails described. He couldn't be, I declared to myself. No way! No way that I could be so wrong about someone I have been so close to for months, even if it was just over the phone. I couldn't be that wrong!

But then, maybe I could. I slowly opened my eyes and stared at the mural of family photographs Zeta had pasted and framed upon the walls of every room in our house. I saw images of me and Jabari, Rakim's dad, on a camping trip in the Shenandoah Mountains. We looked so happy. Then, I saw pictures of Stephen, the man I married, with me and Rakim on the Jersey shore. My stomach was huge; Zeta, my precious baby girl, was due any day. Rakim was only three years old, but Stephen taught him how to swim and make sand castles and listen to the roar of the ocean from inside a horned seashell. God, how he loved that boy! And when Zeta came, his already immense capacity to love seemed to double. Stephen loved being a father. I thought he would always love me that same way, too. I thought he would never leave me. I thought wrong.

I rolled over on the bed into complete consciousness. Zeta loomed over me like a surgeon with a knife, studying my deplorable condition.

"You know we have to be there soon. Are you getting up?" she asked, none too kindly. Her voice was full of frustration and contempt as if she already knew the answer. She was so much like her father, a paragon of expectation and dreams. No wonder he left me, I thought; Stephen wanted to see the world while I only wanted to have it brought to me piece by piece. A sadness engulfed me that pressed my shoulders back down on the bed. Zeta screamed, arms flying in the air.

"You always do this to me! You never do anything I need to do!" Zeta screeched as tears welled in her eyes. Her pain was evident, and I tried again to sit up and wipe the weariness away. It was quarter after six, and the best I could do now was to just put on my shoes and get in the car. I searched for my keys.

"You are not going like that, are you? Zeta was mortified like any preteen would be. Everything I did seemed to embarrass her! Every conversation we had either ended in an argument or her running down the hall crying, cloistering herself in her room. In her estimation, I never said the right thing. I never picked the right video. I never liked her friends, and I only lived to make her miserable. We had a gap between us the size of the continental divide.

"Zeta Baby, I am sorry but I overslept. I had a very long night at the museum," We both looked up at the clock and shook our heads.

"It's too late. We'll never make it. You'll never make it." Zeta marched to the door and glared at me from its threshold.

"I've already called grandma. She said she would take me. She will take me anywhere I need to go," Zeta spat, her little fists pounding against the skirt of her uniform. Even as upset as she was, she looked so cute with her little green tam cocked to the side, bangs peeking out in the front. Her badges were proudly displayed across her chest on the forest green felt sash. I was so proud of her! Some of the badges we had worked toward together—making cookies, mending clothes for the shelter, and reading to sick veterans at Walter Reed Hospital. I sighed and hung my head as Zeta pounded down the stairs. I knew I was letting her down, and she was not going to let me get away with it.

Moments later, Righteous was peering at me through my half-opened door. I braced myself for whatever poison might fly from her mouth. Instead she just stood there, poised like the Mona Lisa as she took account of my drawn shades and unkempt room.

"Good Mornin', baby," she said quietly as she entered, stepping over three days worth of shoes, discarded lottery tickets, and the ledgers I had brought home from last night. Righteous sat on the edge of the bed, straightened the items on my nightstand, then brought her hand to my face. She ran her fingers through my hair, her able fingertips massaging my scalp. She hadn't done this for me in years. I closed my eyes and let the memory of this ritual relax me. It was a mother's touch.

"Regina, you been workin' and thinkin' too hard, girl," her words oozed into my head. "You always had a way of making tings too hard. Even when you was a little girl. But no matter! We come to help today, baby."

"Thank you, mamma," I said, recognizing I had actually called her mamma. Her hands felt so good moving from my temples to my crown, and I remembered sunbaked summer afternoons when the three of us—Righteous, my sister, and I—would sit on the porch and trust our comfort to one another. We would oil each others' scalp first, paving rows with our fingers. Then rub and talk and laugh and holla until the cold dark air, and the mosquitoes drove us back in the house. Rosetta was miles away from us now, leaving our circle broken, yet the bond of our sisterhood was still there.

"My boy Rakim say he not had any breakfast this morning nor dinner last night," Righteous chided.

"Mamma, I . . ."

"No matter," she said. Dora and I gonna take care of some tings for ya. We gonna take Zeta to the Daisy Days Parade, and we gonna take Mr. Rakim—who getting as tall as The Washington Monument—to the waffle house so he can get his fill of anyting he want."

"Thank you, Righteous." I said, rising again from the bed. She smoothed down my eyebrows and checked the arch in her own as she picked up the hand mirror from my night stand.

"You're welcome but dere is more. Today is surely your day because I am feeling very generous."

I should have known something was up. "Yes, Righteous?"

"I brought you a housekeeper."

"A housekeeper?" I tried to get out of bed but she was sitting on my comforter.

"Regina, you know an important woman like yourself need a day woman to help out."

"That's why I had children," I declared.

"Zeta is busy with her scouting, and Rakim is a BOY!" Righteous had very old fashioned ideas about men doing housework. "Besides this lady be a new friend of mind who just moved into the building. She need a job."

"I won't hire her," I said stubbornly.

"Fine den! Just pay her for today. She has already started pulling together that wreck of a kitchen you got down there." On that note, she rose and headed for the door. "Her name is Anna." Righteous looked at the clock and hastened her steps. "We gotta go now. Zeta's late enough as it tis. Ya' know we never gonna get any peace behind dis."

I smiled, realizing that she was saving me in so many ways. "Thank you, Righteous," I repeated. She paused for a moment, furrows creeping to her brow.

"Baby, you got a good life. Fight for it and don't let no mess get in your way," and with those words, she was gone. I stumbled to the window and saw her, Dora and the kids pile into Righteous' SUV. Zeta sat in the back, and as the vehicle pulled off she looked back and waved at me. No smile, just an acknowledgment that we were okay, but we were not through.

As the house fell quiet, I heard the faint sound of running water coming from the kitchen. I went downstairs and walked between the polished french doors to meet my housekeeper. She was an older woman, in her fifties most likely, heavyset and rather short. It has hard to judge her size because she was covered from head to toe, shrouded like a Muslim woman, girded up to her neck in cloth.

"Good morning, Anna. It's nice to meet you. I'm Regina," I said, trying my best to be pleasant. She stood at the sink, washing the dishes, giving each plate a thorough inspection. I took two steps forward.

"Yes, good morning Regina. Pleasure to meet you, too," she said smiling as her eyes scanned the cluttered counter tops. "I wished we could have met sooner."

Her meaning was not lost on me at all. "I've been very busy with work," I said apologetically, taking another step forward and pointing to the electric dishwasher beside her. "You know, you don't have to wash those by hand."

Anna looked at the large appliance with disdain. "I want to *wash* the dishes. See them clean! Not give them a spa treatment."

Good grief, I thought, and I took two steps backward.

"Regina, why don't you just go in the living room and rest yourself. Your mamma told me about how hard you work." She swept her arms over the counter as she rolled up her sleeve. "You don't give this place a second thought. I have got it under control."

I had been dismissed from my own kitchen and relegated to one room of the house as Anna worked her magic, moving from room to room. I had to admit, Righteous was wise in sending her. She was a pro and when she finished, the entire house looked army spit-shined with not a pencil out of place. I actually took a nap, although I did not rest well. The events of yesterday still weighed on me heavily. That was probably why Anna brought me a cup of tea and sat down on the sofa beside me. She looked at the ledgers I had laid on the coffee table and winced.

"I told you to rest," she said sipping from her own cup.

"I know, but I have things on my mind, Anna, that just won't go away," I blurted out, not sure why I would give her even that much of an insight into my life."

"Yes. Regina," she said. "Righteous told me." I continued to go through the financial records, oblivious to her statement. She sat her cup down rather loudly.

"I said Righteous told me . . . everything."

My head popped up, and I looked Anna straight in the eye. "My mother talks too much," I said.

"Yes, she does, and perhaps, you think she loves you too much, too." She reached over and placed the spoon back into my cup, stirring my tea. The heavenly aroma rose in the air, and a smile brightened her stern face.

"Smell that?" she asked while taking a deep breath. "Its my own blend of chamomile, ginger, and rose leaf. Funny thing is no matter how hard I try to make it the same every time, it always comes out a little different."

I said nothing. She continued.

"You see, Regina. Some things we can't control. For instance, I grew this ginger myself. I know exactly where it came from and what went into it to help it grow." Anna took another sip and reflected on its taste. "But that chamomile, well, I got that somewhere else. It was growing wild in a field of weeds. I picked it but I ain't never too sure about it."

I kept quiet, waiting for Anna to get to her point.

"That chamomile come across mild sometime, and sometime it be too bitter. You just never know." I was getting impatient. I started to think up ways I could pay her and get her out of my house without having to hear Righteous' mouth. Anna ignored the smirk on my face.

"Regina, I am trying to say sometimes people are like that chamomile. Even me! Your mamma brought me over here to tell you why you need to leave that con alone."

I took a deep breath and started to rise. She put a steadying hand on my knee.

"But I ain't gonna do that. Instead I'm just gonna tell you a story. A story about me and my man, and then you can judge for yourself." Anna sipped her tea and straightened her spine as if correcting her posture helped her relax. Then, she closed her eyes like a woman in deep concentration. And then she told her story, slow and reverently, as though it were a prayer.

★★★★★

Anna had been a good wife considering she had no husband in the traditional sense. She had married young, only eighteen, and the union had been blessed with two children early on—a boy and a girl. They were happy. Then, one day, Anna's husband "went out for cigarettes" as they say and never returned. All she was sure of was that she was now alone raising two babies, and her wedding band was still on her finger.

The years passed, and the children grew into adulthood. All that time, Anna kept her same job as a maid at one of Maryland's top resorts. As her children left the nest, Anna looked for other ways to fill her time. She became more involved in church, attending services three or four times a week. It became her social outlet. That was important because until she joined the church, her life revolved solely around her children and her immediate family.

Anna was close to her own sisters and brothers. They all rallied to protect her and help her in the raising of her children since she didn't have a man. And she was reminded of that often. At family cookouts and holiday dinners, the subject of Anna's "abandonment" always came up, leaving her ashamed and embarrassed. She was always reminded that her sisters were "good wives" and that is why their husbands would never stray. Her brothers were "well pleased" with their women and therefore would never leave them. Anna would merely sit and play with the ring still on her finger, and when men would show an interest in her, she would simply smile and say: "I'm sorry. I am a married woman."

The two symbols of her life became her bible and the wedding band she still wore. You see, Anna had married her husband before God and in His eyes, she was still very married. The bible said so.

One day, the church singles committee—which she insisted she was not a part of—planned a trip to Kings Dominion, a local theme park. The trip was a fundraiser, so Anna felt obligated to go. With her children away and busy with their own lives, she convinced a good friend to come along. They boarded the church bus, in search of exciting rides and good clean fun.

Even as a child, Anna had always loved roller coasters. Her kids had told her about the Loch Ness Monster, one of the biggest roller coasters in the world, and Anna couldn't wait. Anna and her friend got off the bus and made a beeline for the infamous ride. On first seeing it, her friend took a step back.

"I can't get on *that* thing," she said.

"I can," said Anna, who immediately got in line. She took a deep breath. I can do this, she thought reaching for the cross around her neck for spiritual strength. Then from out of nowhere, a voice answered, "Yes, you can do this. I will help you."

Anna turned around in line facing the man behind her that had spoken. A very handsome man! He smiled and continued. "You don't have to be afraid. We can do this together."

Anna blinked, unaware that she had spoken her words aloud. Slightly embarrassed, she lowered her head and squeezed forward a few feet.

She laughed uncomfortably. "I'm sorry, I was talking to myself. I didn't see you standing there."

"I saw you . . . standing there. I mean . . . trying to get your friend to get on the ride with you. When I saw that she wouldn't, I was hoping you were the kind of woman that would not let that stop her from having a little fun."

Anna wasn't sure she liked that observation, so she turned away as if the conversation had ended.

He persisted. "I was hoping that, ma'am, because my friend was too chicken to ride, too . . . and I don't particularly want to ride alone . . . I was hoping that you would ride with me."

A partner would be nice, she thought. No sense in wasting a seat! So she agreed, and moments later, they were sitting side by side waiting to take the ride of their lives.

Soon the roller coaster started, jerking them forty feet into the air. Anna grasped her cross pendant so hard that it ripped from her neck and went sailing to the ground. The man sitting beside her saw it and the look of horror on her face.

"Don't worry about it. It will be down there when we get off." Anna looked shaken, as if it had been her pace maker and not just a piece of jewelry that disappeared into nothingness on its way to the ground. The man reached for her hand to reassure her.

"I'll even help you look," he offered. He patted Anna's hand and gripped it between both of his own. "My name is Lucas," he said and just when Anna was about to pull away, the Loch Ness Monster began to shoot them through space at record speeds, leaving her breathless. Anna screamed with excitement, like the girl of her youth, as she held on tight to Lucas' hand until the roller coaster came to an unexpected stop. A voice boomed from below, announcing that the ride had jammed and a technician was on the way.

Anna and Lucas sat high in midair, still riveted together, as they watched the ant-size world move below them. She didn't want to admit it, but she was glad to have been stuck up there with Lucas and not by herself.

"Thank you, Lord," she whispered aloud and Lucas smiled at her, squeezing her hand a bit tighter. "Just relax. It'll be okay. They will have us down in a jiffy." Lucas said, and Anna hoped he was right.

But he wasn't! Anna and Lucas were stranded sixty-eight feet straight up in the air for almost an hour. They experienced a slight wind chill factor that caused them to huddle closer together than might ordinarily seem proper. During that time, she got to know him very well. They talked about all kinds of things. Lucas was very open, and Anna felt very comfortable talking to him, more comfortable than she had felt in years. So much so that when he finally asked her if she was married, Anna answered "no."

When the ride was repaired, and when they landed, Anna was a little disappointed. She didn't want to see him go. Being a good woman by any definition, she could not possibly be so forward as to ask for Lucas' phone number. As he nodded goodbye, she just stood there and said a little silent prayer. Anna watched him walk away, then suddenly stop, bend over, shake the dust from his hands and turn to face her again. He waved and ran back to her side.

"We almost forgot something," Lucas said while holding out his hand. The small cross pendant with the body of Jesus welded upon it gleamed in the mid day sun. It is a sign, Anna thought, and Lucas evidently thought so, too. They immediately exchanged phone numbers and spent the rest of the day enjoying the park together.

That night, they said their goodbyes, and Anna boarded the church bus heading home. Lucas was a complete gentleman, never trying to kiss her or saying anything that could be deemed as inappropriate. He promised to call her, and Anna endured the two-hour ride back to Maryland drifting in a giddy euphoria she thought was no longer possible. When she entered her tiny apartment, the phone was already ringing. She and Lucas talked all night. This went on for a week until they both knew they would have to see each other again soon. Lucas lived three hours away and had no car, but planned to take a bus to Maryland to visit Anna the next weekend. She was on top of the world, just the way she felt on that roller coaster. Her family noticed, too and were happy to see her happy again. When the day finally came, she greeted Lucas at the door of her home and knew he belonged there. Lucas never left.

In the months to come, Lucas became a fixture in Anna's everyday life. They quickly fell in love, and Anna soon gave herself to a man who was not her husband. Lucas was a gentle and patient lover. He was an expert in foreplay, kissing every inch of her until she would put her Bible down and beg him for more. Lucas soon got a job at a shipping plant in nearby Gaithersburg. Both of Anna's children loved this new man in their mother's life, and so did Anna's sisters and brothers. The elders of the church approved, too, but urged them not to "yield to temptation."

It was probably at their insistence that Anna blurted out her announcement at the usher board's annual picnic.

"The Lord has known the greatest desire of my heart and has answered me by sending Lucas. I wanted God to send me someone to love. He is the man I have prayed for," Lucas almost dropped his potato salad into the tooty-fruity kool-aid punch. Anna watched his face for a sign of his devotion, and in front of the whole t-shirt clad congregation, Lucas pledged his undying love. It was the happiest day of Anna's life.

Shortly after that, Anna began to work more hours at the resort picking up odd jobs and as much overtime as she could handle. She was putting money away for her wedding. Lucas was spending more time home alone and didn't like it one bit.

"Anna, I like having you home with me. I need you here! I am not the same without you."

"We have got to plan for the future," she said.

Shortly afterward, Anna and Lucas met with the head of the deacon board and picked a wedding day. They told her family, and they all elected to help with the planning.

Anna worked night and day to pay for her wedding and her new life with Lucas. She would come home at night exhausted, but it was worth it. Her life was finally moving forward.

Soon the wedding day came, and everything was perfect. Anna stood in the front of the church in a fashionable yet modest white satin dress, her family at her side. Everything was on schedule, but Lucas had not arrived. He had seemed nervous the night before, but that was to be expected. All grooms are a little jumpy. She had not told anyone that day that she had not seen him at all the night before, After all, she did not want everyone to know they were still living "in sin." Anna watched the door waiting for her man and as time passed, she began to worry. Her brothers assured her, he was just running late. "He is a good man," they said. "Not like that first one," they said. Moments later, a Montgomery County Police Officer walked through the opened door and told Anna that Lucas had been arrested for drug trafficking and resisting arrest. Anna flew from the church to be by his side.

Still in her wedding dress, Anna maneuvered through county lockup to see Lucas. He looked terrible, and Anna begged for an explanation.

"Lucas, sweetheart, what happened?"

"Baby, I am so sorry. I begged you not to leave my side. I just can't spend that much time alone. I can't make it like that," he moaned.

"Lucas, what is wrong?"

"Anna, things happened so fast with us. I didn't tell you some things about me. I should have, but I thought they didn't matter now. Things were different." He wept as he spoke. I do drugs sometimes . . . a little crack . . . a little weed, just to take the edge off." Anna sat motionless for a moment, then took a deep breath.

"We will get through this," she said softly. "We'll get a lawyer. Get you some help. You'll be out of here in no time." Lucas lowered his head woefully.

"Anna, you don't understand. When you met me, I was on parole. I had just finished doing time down in Mecklenburg."

Anna closed her eyes, trying to seal herself off from the shock that was engulfing her. She tried to pray, but Lucas had much more to say.

"I had just finished pulling five years of a seven-year sentence. I had been released early for good behavior."

"Then this is your second offense?" she asked not believing her own ears, but determined to be strong. She plucked her Bible out of her bag and began to thumb through its pages. "We will pray about this and know what to do. You won't do much time. We can . . ." Lucas stilled her hand on the worn book and brought her eyes up to meet his. She looked into the eyes of a man she had never seen before

"This will be my third time in, baby, but my first drug offense," he said coldly slamming the Bible shut.

"And I'm afraid it's for the long haul. They gonna make me pull the rest of the other sentence since I violated my parole plus whatever they tack on here."

Visions of their life together ran through Anna's mind. She saw the two of them in front of a little house with a white picket fence. She pictured them growing old together.

"We can get through this," she declared, finding her resolve. "I don't care about your past. It's your future I want because I have no future without you." Anna rose, her mind set on what she must do.

"I will hire the best lawyer we can afford. Don't worry. We are in this together," she said and headed for the exit. Lucas forced a smile, feeling encouraged. Anna looked like a beautiful avenging angel as she paused in the threshold of the visitation room door. She turned toward Lucas with a puzzled look on her face.

"Sweetheart, you said this was your first drug offense. What were the other two sentences for?"

"Rape," he answered.

Anna hurried home to the bosom of her family and told them what had happened. Her sisters lambasted her for not being able to see the truth about Lucas. "How can you love a man who has committed such a violent crime?" they asked. How can you trust a man who would leave you standing at the altar? Does the church know you were going to marry a drug addict? Her brothers forbade her to see him ever again. Her son wanted to have Lucas charged with breach of promise to his mother, and her daughter said she would never speak to Anna again as long as she had anything to do with him.

Anna looked down at the bare third finger on her left hand—bare except for the shadow of the ring she had worn so long. It was a ring that had no value. It carried no love with it, yet she had worn it her whole adult life. She wanted the real thing.

"Lucas is the man I prayed for. The hell with all of you!"

Anna waited four years for Lucas' release—without the support of her family or most of her friends. During that time, their love grew, and she was surer than before that they were meant to be together. She closed her heart and mind to the monster the world made him out to be, and clung to the memory of the Lucas she had fallen in love with. He had explained those priors—"a misunderstanding" he'd said. "The deeds of an awkward and confused young man," he'd said. "That man died the day I met you," he'd said.

The night he finally came home, they made love like rabbits and talked until the wee hours of the morning, making new plans for their future. But as she lay beside him in bed, Anna knew that prison had changed him somehow. His touch was just as gentle, but his eyes were dull and cold, and it was not long before Lucas was sent up again for possession.

★★★★★

I watched this woman as she told her story. Sitting there with her eyes still closed tight, I watched the contours of her face change as she spoke. She looked pained when she talked about the separation from her family, having to deal with Lucas' incarceration alone. She looked hurt every time she mentioned the husband that left her when she was young; there was still heartache there. But there was only joy when Anna spoke of Lucas. She was truly in love, and perhaps that was worth all the pain.

She opened her eyes rather suddenly, leaned over and carefully picked up her tea cup as if it were still as warm as she'd left it.

"Do you understand why I told you this story, Regina?" she asked.

I cleared my throat; I didn't know there was going to be a quiz. "You want me to know how hard it is to love a con. It's the kind of love that hurts," I ventured.

Anna looked at me sternly and put her cup down again. "All love hurts," she said. "And no, that was not it at all." She seemed irritated with me now. A long moment of silence passed between us while she waited for me to ask her the million dollar question. I instead, decided to pick up my checkbook, pay her and send her on her way. I didn't want a lecture. Besides, I was still very tired and determined to research those ledgers until I found out what was going on with Dennis. I ripped the check out of the book and extended it to Anna. She was not having it.

"You young girls think you have it all figured out don't you," she said coolly.

"Excuse me?"

"You think because you make your own money and keep your kids in designer clothes and drive the newest thing on wheels that you don't need nothing else. You got everything. You know everything."

I could tell I was about to get read, and I was not in the mood. "Anna, I appreciate you coming here today to try to help but . . ."

Her voice raised an octave. "You think love should always come in a pretty package wearing an expensive suit and riding in on shiny custom rims. Well, it ain't always like that."

"Anna, I didn't mean to upset you . . ."

"And even when it does come to you like that, you ain't never in for the long haul. You can't pull the time. The first little bump . . . your first little challenge in your perfect-looking relationship and you ready to jump out."

"Anna, I don't have to sit here and listen to . . ."

"Look at you," she spat. "Ready to dismiss me because I rocked your world a little bit." Anna's head turned to Zeta's family murals on the walls and then cast a knowing look back at me.

"I can already see your life is a dog pile of failed relationships."

"I beg your pardon!" I was getting pissed now.

"We black women always talking about black men not being willing or able to commit. Well, how about our level of commitment?"

"We let 'the other woman' run us away. We let him losing his job be the reason for us to put him out. We let 'not taking out the trash' be the issue that ends a good marriage."

I scooted back on the sofa, feeling very uncomfortable. Anna's temperature was rising, and I didn't know how far this was going to go. She kept right on talking.

"We run to our girlfriends at the first sign of trouble—wagging our fingers and stretching our necks sayin' what we not gonna take and what we not gonna do—what kind of sense does that make?"

She looked at me wide-eyed. Was that a question I was supposed to answer? Would she stuff me in the dishwasher if I didn't? I decided to keep quiet.

"Girl, let me explain something to you. Black women in this country gonna have to start learnin' how to fight for their men. If we don't, we gonna lose them to all the systems they got set up in this country that don't value us anyway."

"We losing our families to the welfare and social service systems that won't help a sistah if she got a man in her house. That's why my husband left." There was a tremble in her voice as she spoke of her husband as if she had never said the words out loud before. "He . . . was a good man . . . a real good man. We were just young and when the babies came, and the factory laid him off . . . well, he just figured we would do better without him."

Anna's shoulders slumped over, her heart heavy with the words she did not speak. *He was wrong. We needed him. I needed him.*

My eyes scanned the cluttered walls of my living room, and I immediately felt burdened by the failed relationships of my life. How could love be there one day and gone the next? Stephen is on the shore somewhere, I thought. Did he take all the love I had for him away when he walked out of the door? My husband had loved me, too, and it had not mattered. My love was not enough to hold us together. Love was not glue.

Anna's eyes followed mine around the room. "Like I was saying, we losing them to this screwed-up social class system that say a black man is worth less if he don't have a white-collar job and a college education. We are losing them early in a school system that has never known how to teach our black boys. Then, after they finish messin' them up, we lose them to the judicial system that wants to lock them away rather than help them."

Anna raved on, lashing out at me but as I listened, I heard the voice of a very frustrated woman, a woman that had sacrificed everything throughout her life for other people, and now she wanted hers.

"You think because I make beds and clean floors for a living I know less than you, but that ain't true. I read and I watch and I listen and I know what I am talking about."

I had no doubt she knew what she was talking about, knowing only two men and feeling in some way abandoned by both. I reached out to Anna, trying to console her, but it was no good. She was determined to see me as the enemy. She knocked my hand away.

"You think because I read my Bible and believe in God's promises that I am somehow weak in the head. But honey, that only makes me stronger. You think . . ."

"Anna, I am sorry about Lucas!" I shouted, trying to bring her attention back to what was really bothering her. It had nothing to do with me. Anna looked at me dejectedly. She was losing steam, and the fight in her was waning.

"Lucas . ." she said, barely above a whisper, tears rolling down her cheek. "Lucas was the man I prayed for. He was the man I asked God for. I can't walk away from him now. I just can't."

We sat together for a long time, drinking our tea and talking about our children—always a safe subject among women. Anna pointed to the pictures on the walls, and I told her about both Stephan and Jabari. I confided in Anna in ways I would have never done with Righteous. Must have been the tea! After we had shared a laugh or two, I drove her to the metro, and she promised to come back in two weeks.

That night, Righteous called and said she and Sister Dora were taking the kids to the movies in town. They would bring them home in the morning. I was relieved! A quiet night at home was just what I needed. I opened a bottle of smooth merlot, picked up the TV remote and threw myself across the bed. Righteous was right—I do think too much. Tonight, I would give my brain a much needed rest.

After watching two reruns of shows I didn't like the first time around, I chugged my glass of wine and closed my eyes. That's when the phone rang!

"Hello?"

Click, click click, pause.

"Yes, I accept," The three words stumbled like cold marbles from my mouth, and I poured myself another glass of wine.

"Gina? Hey girl, what's up?"

"Nothin' mmmuch," I slurred into my pillow.

"Gina, you okay?"

"Yep. I'm real good," I said a little too loudly. I emptied my glass like it was tap water and rose up on my elbows and knees, getting into position. I felt like a lion ready to eat this rat alive.

"Yep? Did you say 'yep'? Nah, something's up. Talk to me, girl."

Then, I started to scream at the top of my lungs. "*You* lyin' bastard!! *You murdering thug! How could you play me like such a fool. I thought we had something. You do terrible things to people. Horrible things! You made me think that you were . . . . I don't know . . . somebody that wouldn't hurt me but you are a . . .*"

"A con," Rayboy said simply. "I am a con. A criminal! That ain't no surprise, is it, Gina? What you think I was calling you from prison like this for? 'Cause my celly get better reception up in here? This ain't no vacation resort. I am a criminal. I have committed crimes against society. That's why I'm in here."

"I hate you!" I said

"No you don't," he said.

"Don't call me anymore," I whimpered, tears beginning to roll down my face.

Ray got real quiet, and then whispered, "Please don't say that. Please don't say that, Gina. You're my one in a million."

I wanted to curse him, but the words choked tight in my throat. I wanted to make him feel like I felt—empty because it was all over. Our secret romance was dead. I was angry. I wanted to kill him. Threaten him with some kind of legal action but all I could do was cry. I thought I was safe; I thought he couldn't hurt me from prison, but he had. Miles lay between us, walls and barbed wire separated us, and still he had touched me. Somewhere between the poetry and the laughter and the music at midnight, I had fallen in love.

"I got to hang up. I have to hang up," I said.

There was a long silence, then the voice in the other end sounded different. It was still Rayboy just another side of him. "Regina, you can't hang up, baby. It's not over. *We* are not finished."

I tried to take the I-am-in-control-and-you-betta-shut-up-and-listen approach, but the wine was working against me instead of for me. I just wanted this to end.

"I'm hanging up now. Please don't call me again. I will block this . . ."

"I don't give a good damn," Ray's voice sounded older, harder, more intelligent and sophisticated. It was still him, just another side that he had hidden from me. It made me think that the Rayboy I thought I knew before wasn't the real man at all.

"I don't need your permission to call, Gina. I was just giving you that. In fact, I don't even need you to accept the call."

I laughed at that. Ray didn't think it was so funny.

"Gina, understand me when I say I am calling you from *my house*. This rock is mine, and I do what I want in it. Do you hear me?" His voice sounded so cold, and I realized that he had been in control all along.

"Don't matta what you want, I need to talk to you. And you're right. I ain't been real honest with you. I didn't call you by accident that first night. I needed to find you. I needed your help. Baby . . . sweetheart . . . you're in the middle of some deep shit and don't even know it."

My head was spinning. I was listening to Rayboy yet I was hearing that same cautious/caring tone that CeCe had used with me the day before. Rayboy was trying to warn me of something.

"Listen, Gina, there is this guy you work for . . . Dickerson. Dennis Dickerson. You know who he is. You need to watch out for him. He's not what you think. He . . ."

Just then, a hand grabbed the phone from me. I turned over on the bed and discovered Dennis standing over me, his head cocked to one side. His face was tight with frustration, and the muscles in his neck bulged with tension as if he was trying hard to control his anger.

"Dennis, what are you doing here? I thought you were in . . ." He ignored my question completely. Dennis slowly raised the cordless phone to his ear and smiled cooly at me as he speaks into the receiver.

"Ray, I am really disappointed in you. I thought I knew you, man. Are you trying to steal my girl?"

"Dickerson, I have had all I'm going to take from you! Leave Gina out of this. You . . ." Rayboy is shouting over the phone, his tone raised to a panic.

"Ray, I would love to talk to you, but I have a beautiful half-naked woman sprawled across the bed waiting for me, and I'm about to rock her world," Dennis said sinisterly. "Wish you were here, but two is company and three is just . . . well, you know the rest. Later!"

"Muthafucka, don't you hurt her! You hear me? You touch her, and your ass is *mine*!" I heard Ray's threats, but they went unheeded. Dennis shook his head and clicked his teeth as if to scold me.

"Regina, you have been a very bad girl. Consorting with criminals now?" Dennis hung up and gazed at me with the countenance of an addict—as if he knew his actions were wrong, but he just couldn't help himself. Like a crazed man, he stood over me while fear and shock engulf every part of my body. This all seemed so insane, yet the insanity was steadily unfolding, and the reality of it all started to gel in my head.

"Dennis, what is happening here? You know Rayboy? How does he know you? What is he talking about? Are the two of you in something . . . *together*?"

"Of course, and have been for a long time. But don't you worry. It's just business." His tone was very nonchalant, like he was reading a menu or transcribing his notes, but underneath, something dangerous lurked and fear rose along my spine. A second later, Dennis began to take off his clothes like it was the most natural thing in the world for him to do in my bedroom. And even more surprisingly, he threw them—his jacket, tie and shirt—*on the floor in the corner of the room*!

"Yeah, Regina. I know Ray. I'm his teacher . . . and now I'm going to be yours."

I stopped breathing.

"You look frightened, Regina. I wasn't trying to frighten you. I'm just trying to give you what you want, my dear," and then he began to unbuckle his pants.

I started to tremble. Dennis was acting like a totally different person. Even though I saw him everyday, did I know Dennis any better than I did Ray? The "bad guy" locked up in prison was warning me about the "good guy" on the outside! Nothing was making any sense. Nothing except the fact that I was living in the dark about a lot of things and had been for a long time!

"Dennis, what is happening? Please baby, tell, me."

"Gina, you're a smart girl. You can figure this out." Dennis kneeled between my legs. Then, he grabbed both of my wrists, forcing me down flat on the bed. Almost effortlessly, he held my arms above my head with his right hand leaving his left hand free to work. He opened my robe and began to knead my right breast, making the nipple hard to the touch. I was pinned down, struggling to get up, but Dennis is much too heavy. I tried to kick him, but my legs were spread too far apart. I tried to fight, but Dennis and the wine I had consumed were both too strong. I screamed, but there was no one there to hear.

"You've been playing me all along. Is that it? This has all been part of some big conspiracy. Some kind of game you been running on me. You,

the prison, the traveling, and all that missing money!" I wanted to scream.
I was so angry with myself for not seeing it sooner. How could I have been
so stupid?

The sound of Dennis' laughter hurt more than anything. "You trusting
me—that was the best part, baby."

"Tell me what's going on!" I screamed. Just then, the phone rang again,
but I was helpless to answer it. Dennis looked at the phone with amazement
as if he knew who was calling.

"Damn," he said, "If I am right, this is the most expensive call ever
made from Montgomery Prison!"

After the fourth ring, the answering machine activated, and Rayboy's
voice blared out of the tiny speaker.

"Gina! Gina! Baby, pick up the phone!" he yelled frantically. Still
pinned down, I laid there astonished. Just like he said—Rayboy didn't need
my permission to come into my world. He was already there. I stared up at
Dennis, who was bearing down on top of me. He grinned devilishly.

"*Dickerson*! Hurt *that woman and i am going to kill you! You hear me,
muthafucka*!"

Dennis cocked his head as if something struck him as being funny. "You
should know that call cost Ray a lot. Since he won't deal in drugs, he had
to pay cash money. Big bucks! You should be flattered, Regina."

Ray was cursing Dennis' name, calling him a liar and a cheat, and all
Dennis did was laugh. He had both me and Ray right where he wanted us.

"Should I answer the phone, dear? Maybe Ray would like to listen while
we make love. Think he might like that?" Dennis asked cruelly. I stared up
at him in horror.

"*God, Dennis! Get off of me*!! *Why are you doing this*!!" I cried.

"Like I said before. You're a smart girl. Figure it out." Tired and defeated,
I whimpered under him as he held my arms tighter. Dennis took a moment
to take the last swig from the wine bottle as he listened to Rayboy, still

cursing and pleading with him to leave me alone over the answering machine. Unaffected, Dennis teased my nipples with his tongue until they were both erect, then lowered his mouth to my ear.

"Don't look so betrayed, Gina. Remember what I said—everything is a conspiracy win you're not winning. You just got played, that's all." Dennis squeezed my wrists even tighter and raised my arms higher until he saw me wince in pain. He smiled and rested his full weight on top of me. He began to kiss my face sloppily, his saliva dripping down the side of my neck. Then suddenly, he stopped long enough to look into my eyes and saw my distress. For a moment, I thought I saw regret and a glimmer of the old Dennis Dickerson that I thought I had fallen in love with. Seconds later, I knew I was wrong.

Dennis reached into his pants pocket and pulled out a small clear baggie containing something that looked like white powder. He dipped his finger in it and held it up to his nose. I turned my head away, not believing what has happening. He inhaled deeply as if it was the sweetest of nectar; he was trying to shock me. Trying to make me hate him! Dennis took his attention away from the bag long enough to see my disgust. He brought his lips down slowly, and again whispered in my ear.

"Don't worry Regina. I haven't forgotten you." He lowered the bag to my nose and I began to buck wildly like a trapped animal. He just held me down tighter, determined to have his way.

"Relax, baby! This Ray thing? You wanted to try something new. I understand," he said. Dennis glanced at the phone as Rayboy continued to pitifully plead for my life. Dennis eyes flared. He looked utterly disgusted with both of us. He came close to me again, his tongue circling the inside of my ear. I chill ran up my spine as his words poured hot and angry into my head.

"Did I bore you, Regina? Maybe I was too gentle with you! But don't worry! That's all over now. If you think you like it like *that*—if you want it a little rough and hard, you're going to like this."

CHAPTER 7

◆

Dora's Story
The Gift of Sight

The phone just kept ringing. It was four in the morning, and it had not stopped ringing all night. From the moment I had heard Rayboy's frantic voice threatening to kill Dennis, then pitifully pleading for him to let me go, I knew that it was going to be the longest night of my life. It had been a nightmare, and now all I could do was huddle in the far corner of my room, too afraid to leave or even move a muscle. Dennis lay sprawled half-dressed diagonally across my queen-size bed, sleeping fitfully, but sleeping just the same. During the night, he'd cried out several times—words, names, places I did not recognize. He sounded like he was being tortured, hollering unintelligibly at times, and I jumped out of my skin at every outburst.

Hugging my knees tight, I listened to his ragged breathing in the dark, not wanting to make a sound. Not wanting to do anything that might warrant his attention. Possessed—that was the only way to describe him, something apart from the man I had loved. I stared at the bruises on my wrist where he had held me down all night—not to hurt me but to keep me beside him. He was afraid of something! Something had gotten hold of him. Something had entered our lives and was now looming dangerously in my room. I could feel it.

When I was a little girl, the preacher had talked about demons—evil spirits that enter your life for no good reason and stayed there until they were furiously prayed away. Or until they got what they wanted. Maybe this was a demon!

Or maybe it was the coke or whatever that stuff was in the clear plastic bag. I was pitifully ignorant about drugs. My education consisted only of what I'd learned at the school's PTA meeting and the little I had witnessed in college when all my friends were supposedly weeding and snorting. Watching Dennis do that, knowing he spent so much time with my kids, made me sick.

The phone rang again, five rings, then the answering machine picked up. For what seemed like the hundredth time, I heard my own voice on the outgoing message then a click. The frustrated caller had hung up. It had been that way all night. Then I heard the muffled sound of bells chiming a familiar song and realized it was my cell phone. "Mamma" I thought and I began to crawl, panic stricken, across the floor looking for my purse.

Funny how we always think of our mothers when we think we are about to lose our minds!

I had to answer it before the last ring. I clumsily pawed through the litter of discarded clothes—mine and Dennis'—until I found my handbag. I grabbed the tiny flip phone and cradled it with both hands.

"Righteous?" I whispered, trembling with tears streaming down my face.

"Gina!" It was a man's voice saying my name. "Gina, baby girl, are you alright?"

"Ray . . . you're calling on *my cell?*" I said in disbelief "How . . . how did you get this number?"

"I keep telling you there is nothin' I can't get in here. Nothin'."

"Ohhh, Ray!" I moaned, my tears uncontrollable now as I tried to whisper, not wanting to wake Dennis. "Ray . . . I . . . he was . . . Ray, please tell me what is going on. Please."

"Oh baby, I would do anything to be there with you." Rayboy sounded tired. He had been up all night, in his way, going through this nightmare with me. I imagined him pacing in his cell like an animal in a cage. I knew he would have done anything to help me. He couldn't be beside me, but his voice held all the tenderness I needed.

But then it changed as he asked, "Dickerson. Is he still there with you?"

A chill ran up my spine, and I held the phone tighter. "Yes, yes," I whispered. "He is sleeping. I . . . I can't let him hear me. I can't . . ."

"Gina, tell me what happened. Did he hurt you?"

"Ray, Dennis was so angry. He held me down. He . . . he had cocaine and . . ." I cried in earnest now realizing that Dennis was probably unconscious and him waking up was the least of my worries. My fear was turning into frustration.

"Ray, tell me now! What is happening? Who are you?"

Ray took a deep breath and started from the beginning. "My name is Ray Boden. I am inmate number 584-57 in Cell block C at the Montgomery County Correctional Center. I have been here for two and a half years serving a twelve-year sentence."

"On what charge?" I spat and held my breath, preparing for the worst.

"Racketeering and drug trafficking," he answered. I exhaled.

"So . . . so you haven't killed people?"

Rayboy paused. "No, I didn't say that."

"Then you have."

"Gina, I'll admit, I've had to make some difficult choices. Most of them in the blink of an eye. If I hadn't made those choices, I wouldn't be talkin' to you now. You were a choice."

"A choice?"

"I needed someone to help me. Someone on the outside and I chose you."

"I don't understand," I said.

"Your friend Dennis is smuggling drugs into the prison."

"You're lying!"

"He makes his connection abroad. The deals are already made. All he has to do is creatively sneak the drugs through customs and bring them inside the prison on his regular visits."

"Shut up, Ray! You're a lying bastard!"

"Listen. Haven't you ever wondered why an important man like that would bother with coming to a shit hole like this?"

"Dennis is concerned about his community. The plight of the black man! He genuinely . . ."

"Gina, wake up! Dickerson could send any flunky to do this shit. He is the great Dr. D—having dinner with the warden and government officials. Nobody questions him, Gina. He gets paid big in here for the load and walks away clean."

My body was racked with pain now as I sat on the floor in a fetal position listening to Rayboy's story. I didn't want to believe it but with every word, the pieces of this convoluted puzzle were coming together.

"Why? Why would Dennis do such a thing?"

"I asked myself the same question. Big man like that! He already got bank. Position! Why would he do some dumb shit like that? Then I find out about his art foundation. He tryin' to build a museum—a global art corporation that will rival the Smithsonian. That shit is huge! He needs to be able to compete. He needs world-class pieces. Lots of dough! Serious funding! He's making deals and short on cash. He needs money."

"Money? But there are grants . . . all kinds of funding. He doesn't have to . . ."

"And not just money, Gina. He needs power and connections. My guess is that your doctor made a raw deal of his own. Traded his soul for a piece of art! Now he is in so deep that he can't get out."

"So what has any of this to do with you?"

"Drugs are like gold bars in here, baby. You buy what, and who you want. There's a nigga in here that's got it out for me real bad. His name is Shaka Blu. He's using the drugs to recruit soldiers for his war.

"What are you saying?"

"He wants me dead. He's using Dickerson to buy my hit."

"All this for you? This guy hates you that much?"

"No, its more than that. Shaka Blu is pure evil. He and I knocked heads a few years back on the outside. It went down so bad between us that we were sent to different prisons. But Shaka bought himself a transfer, and now he is in here with me. He wants to be king of the world—inside the joint and out. I can't let that happen, and he won't rest until I'm dead."

This was all too much. Too hard to believe! There had to be another explanation for the screwed-up itinerary and the missing money and all those trips to the prison.

"Dennis is no drug dealer," I said.

"No, he is an *art dealer*—who helps pay for his collection by moving cocaine. There! That make it prettier for you? Uptown girls like you like to think that street thugs like me are the bad guys. But honey, there wouldn't be no drugs nowhere in America if big boys like your Dennis didn't make it possible. Whether he want to be or not, he in this shit up to his ass!"

"What are you going to do?"

"Stop him and Shaka from turning this place into a battle ground."

"What do you mean?"

"What I said! If Shaka gun-up, I gun-up and there will be nothing left. This rock will be a cemetery when we're through."

He was talking about prison wars and gang violence and things that I thought were a thousand miles away from my suburban world. By now, Ray knew how I felt about Dennis. I tried to hide the fear in my voice.

"What are you going to do, Ray?"

132

"Whatever it takes!" He didn't say it, but I knew that meant killing Dennis if he had to. That was probably his intention from the very beginning.

There was one more question that needed to be asked. "Ray, why did you call me?"

"I was worried about you, baby."

"No. I mean, why did you call me that first night?"

Ray hesitated knowing he was already on shaky ground. "Because I needed you. I needed you to expose Dickerson on the outside for what he really is. While that son of a bitch is tryin' to buy pretty pictures for his walls, he's helping Shaka start a war up in here, and he don't even know it."

"Why didn't you just tell me that first night?"

"Hah! Would you have believed me? Hell no! You woulda hung up."

I couldn't say Ray was wrong. I probably would have thought he was some crazy fool playing on the phone in the pen. Ray took a deep breath.

"Gina, truth is . . ."

"What do you know about the truth?" I spat. He ignored me.

"The truth is, I started to come clean with you that first night. Started to tell you why I was really calling but . . ." Ray hesitated. "But when you answered the phone, you were so glad that I was there for you. Remember? You were having a bad dream."

"I thought you were someone else!"

"Yeah, but you knew I was who you needed! And I needed somebody, too. I still do. I need you."

The sound of his voice was hypnotic, and I hated myself for giving into it. Ray's words were tender, but they spoke a command. His words wrapped around me like silk then wrestled my will into submission.

We were both silent for a while, then Ray asked the question. "Gina, you never answered me. Did Dickerson hurt you?"

I didn't exactly know how to answer that. Men measure pain in the physical. The pain I felt was enormous, starting down in the pit of my belly, winding around my spine, and raging up through the depths of my soul. And there was no evidence of how I had been violated. No assault weapon. No scars bleeding profusely. No gaping wounds laying open that needed to be mended. I had bruises but they were nothing compared to the damage done to my heart. Mine was the pain that comes when love has been offered and refused. When the best love you have to give has been crushed to dust and left for dead. There is no bandage, pill or treatment, only an undeterminable length of time for recovery. Yes, I was hurt deeply, but I was sure Ray would never understand.

"No, he didn't hurt me."

"Don't lie for him."

"I said no."

"Gina, get out of there. Get out of there now." There were voices in the background, hard and threatening, and Rayboy hurled curses at someone behind him.

"Gina, I gotto go. But you do what I say, you hear? Don't try to irritate that fool. He knows he's cornered, and he's looking for a way out. Don't let him use you anymore. You let me handle this. You hear?"

Use me? I thought that was what *you* were doing, I thought to myself and tried to clear the confusion from my head.

"Ray, you don't know Dennis. He . . . he is a good man. This isn't like him. He and I . . . we . . . God, what do I do?" I asked.

I could feel the jealousy mounting in Ray as I again defended his enemy. Through clenched teeth he said, "You a woman, Gina. Do what you been doing with him. Only smarter," and he hung up just as Dennis began to stir.

The light of dawn crept through my bedroom blinds leaving horizontal streaks of light on my pillows and the half-clad man across my bed. Still glued to the far corner of the room, I reflected on the irony of it all. I had prayed so many times for Dennis to stay the night, for him to give himself to me, and make me truly his. I wanted to be the wife of a well-paid and prominent professional who would love me and my children and complete me. I wanted to be Mrs. Dr. Dickerson and have all the perks that came with that job.

I hadn't bargained on this. Hadn't even considered that the job came with any ugly crap like this! I was supposed to be his queen. He was supposed to be my handsome Egyptian king. Not like the Stephens and Jabaris of the world! How dare he turn out to be just *a man?!*

I found my slippers, put on my robe and stood in the morning light. The sun moved again, and the light streaked across Dennis's back like the lashes from a whip. Light and dark! Black and white! Nothing was that simple! There were no good guys and bad guys—just guys making choices everyday. I walked over to the bed, got closer to Dennis and studied him like he was a bug. He was so beautiful—perfect skin, perfect lines and a body to die for. Somewhere in his life, there had been women to guide and direct him. A mother who sacrificed for him, brought him to God, taught him an appreciation for beauty, cared for him and then had to let him go. Then the world had taken hold and distorted those lessons. He was a caricature of the man he was meant to be.

"Regina?" came his voice, and he reached for me. I let him touch my hand, and I winced in pain. His touch didn't hurt: at least, not in that physical way.

Dennis looked down at my wrists, and tears puddled in his eyes. "Damn . . . I'm so sorry . . . I am so sorry! This was not what I came here for last night."

"What did you come here for?" I asked pointedly. Last night with him had been torturous. When Dennis got on top of me, I was sure he would rape me. But instead, he collapsed like he was emotionally and physically drained. I was scared and tried to free myself from his hold, but he only squeezed tighter. I spent the night awake, trapped beneath him, witness to a nightmare.

"What did I come back for? Do you remember what I said to you before I left for Egypt? I wanted to be the man you needed me to be. I . . . I . . . love you, Regina."

Man, how I wanted to believe that! I would have done anything—*anything*—to have heard that a week ago. Two days ago! Twelve hours ago! But now everything was different. I just looked at him. I could tell he wanted me to say some shit like "I love you, too," but life's not always how you want it, is it? He saw the cold stone reflected in my eyes and continued cautiously.

"There is nothing I want more in this world than to be your man and a father to Zeta and Rakim. They are already like my own."

"Keep my children out of this. Don't even say their names." Dennis cringed at the heat of my words.

"I want to love you and build a life with you and share all I have with you."

Is that right, black man?

"Our dream of building The Mirathi Foundation can become a reality. We can do it together."

Nigga, I wrote that part of your speech myself. Give me a break! I said nothing, and he was fishing for whatever he could say that would make me fall lovingly into his arms. It was just not happening.

"Regina, about last night . . ."

"Dennis, let's back up. Let's start with last week."

"Excuse me, dear?" It amazed me how quickly he could fall into that Buckingham-Palace-pinky-finger-in-the-air shit when he was caught in a lie.

"Where the hell were you? Certainly *not in Egypt*!"

Dennis turned over and sat up straight in the bed, looking like a deer caught in my high beams. "Regina, I most certainly was in . . ."

"*Dennis, lie to me again and die*!!"

"Okay, okay. I was in South America *first* . . . and then I went to Egypt."

"So you made your drug deal first, got paid and then went to Egypt to buy the pieces."

The color ran out of Dennis' face. "You talked to Boden," he said flatly.

"Yes, I spoke with him this morning."

Jealousy sparked in his eyes, and his jaw got hard. "I don't like you talking to that thug, Regina. And it seems you've made a habit of it."

"How did you know?"

"*I know*!" Dennis slowly climbed off of the bed and left me sitting there. He stared out of the window and exhaled. "Look, you can't possibly understand what I have been through. But just know all of it has been for you. My dreams for you and the kids! Us as a family! Regina, I have worked hard all of my life. I have come so close to having everything I ever wanted. *Sooooo close*," he brought his hands together in front of him. "You have no idea how it feels to want something so badly and not be able to have it."

I smiled ruefully. "I think I do, Dennis."

"Then you'll try to understand. I only meant to do this thing once, twice at the most, until I got the museum and the foundation to support it up and running. That necklace, 'The Blood of the Moor,' is finally in my grasp. When we get it, Regina, it will open the doors to so much. Trust me."

"So in other words, you're not a career criminal. It's just a sideline for you," I said sarcastically. He looked at me incredulously like *I* was the one who got this thing twisted. It reminded me of Rakim when he was about seven; he wanted a new bike, and I told him we didn't have the money, and he said *but mamma, the banks are FULL of money. Just go get some!"*

Yeah, that look!

I wanted to believe Dennis so badly. I wanted to understand how his *man brains* had gotten him from his 'A' game to possibly serving 5 to 10.

"Reginnnnaaaa . . ." he said in that Sydney Poitier kind of way that irritated me to no end. "This was all for you," and he reached for me. I backed away.

"Dennis, where do I fit into this thing?" I asked. "My promotion! Were you trying to implicate me?"

He looked horrified. "No, sweetheart. Actually, I was trying to raise you up out of it! I saw I was getting in too deep, and I didn't want you to get caught up in anything." He lowered his head and slowly walked back over to the bed and sat down. "That is also why I have been slow to commit to you. Part of me wanted to, but part of me knew it was wrong. I couldn't entangle you in this mess."

Dennis gently took me in his arms, and my whole body contracted with tension. He released me with sad eyes that spoke his regret. "Regina, sweetheart, I would do anything to erase the memory of last night. That man was not me. It was the coke . . . They made me snort it . . . at the buy . . ." I backed away from him again.

"*That's not me*!!" he yelled stung by the look on my face. To prove it, he grabbed the baggie from the bed, ran into my bathroom and flushed it down the toilet. I stood and watched him do it, wondering what its street value was.

"How much was that?" I asked innocently.

"Probably enough to pay off the mortgage on your house," he said.

"Oh," I said blankly. We stood silently standing in the threshold of the bathroom wondering where we should go from here. Dennis' shoulders dropped, and he shook his head. He reached for me for support and this time, I walked into his arms.

"We can get through this, Regina. I know we can."

"I want to. God, how I want to."

He held me close, and I molded my body into his. It felt so perfect. So right! This was just a thing we had to "get over," I told myself. A test! A bump in the road of our love! I thought about Anna, and how she had prayed for the man she wanted. Divinely, her prayers had been answered—or so she believed—but there were still challenges in their relationship. Challenges! We can work those out, I said to myself. But even as he held me tight, I wondered how much of what Dennis said was really true. Was I finally seeing the real Dr. Dennis Dickerson, or was he playing me again? I squeezed him tight. I was just so happy to finally have him. I just wanted to be happy.

Dennis smiled at me, raising my bruised wrists to his lips. "I'm going to make this up to you, sweetheart. You name it. Anything you want," I weakly smiled back at him but worried if he had learned his lesson.

"For God's sake, Dennis, don't spend any more money. We are turning over a new leaf remember? No more drugs."

"No more drugs," he repeated as his tongue circled my earlobe.

"I am serious! I will not tolerate that madness around my children!"

"No more drugs. I promise."

"No more prison visits."

"No more prison visits," he echoed, sliding the robe down to my elbows and freeing my shoulders. "Hmm, It's just so good to hold you," he moaned as he kissed the soft flesh just above my breast.

"Dennis, I mean it," I said, trying to sound firm.

"I know, sweetheart," he mumbled as he gently pushed me down on the bed. Dennis' appetite turned ravenous, and I felt his penis throbbing against me. His hands roamed over me, paying special attention to my thighs.

"I love these big phat legs you got here, girl," he snarled playfully. I laid perfectly still and let him touch me, closing my eyes as he spoke to me. "Hmmm, this is all I needed, Regina. Not the powder! Not any of that! Just you!" His pants were on, but not zipped, and he settled himself down gently between my legs, supporting his weight above, grinding into me.

"So . . . so you like that?" I purred, allowing him to make me feel good.

"Oh yes, sweetheart," and just like that day in my office, Dennis' touch became sensual and masterful. I spread my legs further apart, and he massaged my inner thighs, methodically working his way around them like a serpent .

"You know," he said huskily, "these are what first attracted me to you."

"You can't be serious." I moaned, lost in an erotic trance.

"Drove me wild! At the foundation picnic! You were wearing a pair of washed denim shorts *way too tight* and . . . oh, yes ." Dennis' fingers had reached my mound, and his fingertips were now wet with the measure of how much I wanted him.

"*Oohh,*" I moaned again, easing my hips up as he came down nuzzling my neck. He sucked his teeth hard, and the cool air tickled my ear, driving me crazy.

"I want you so much. Need you so much," Dennis groaned.

"Oh*, Ray* . . ." Oh, my God! No, I didn't! Damn!

Suddenly, I heard the front door fly open and four familiar voices all talking at once. "*Mamma! We're hooomme!*"

Damn! Damn, damn, damn! What did I say!! Had I called him *Ray*? I could hear Zeta romping up the stairs, Rakim taking them two at a time. Righteous and Sister Dora were downstairs in the living room yammering about what a good job Anna had done cleaning the house. "See, I told you tat girl need a housekeepa," I heard my mamma say. Dennis closed his eyes and cursed under his breath as he tried to pull himself away from me. His eyes were scanning my body hungrily, and I didn't know if he had heard what I said. Maybe that was anger and not hunger in his eyes. Maybe he was about to beat me to death. With all the commotion downstairs, maybe Dennis had not heard me call him by another man's name. I had to try to fix it.

"*Ray*-kim and Zeta are home." That sounded ridiculous, but Dennis seemed unaffected as he continued his loving assault.

"I really need you," he said.

"Stay the night," I said impulsively.

"You sure?" he asked.

"I'm sure," I smiled back.

Moments later, we were ascended upon by my entire family. Zeta and Rakim sailed on top of the bed, forcing Dennis and I to move apart, as they talked simultaneously about the martial arts thriller and the Daisy Days Girl Scout Parade. Sister Dora gave us a blow by blow reenactment of all of Jet Li's "killer moves," her arms and legs slicing the air like she was swatting flies. She was hilarious, and it felt good to laugh. Righteous however, stood quietly in the corner of the room, a smile of relief glazed upon her face. The fact that Dennis was in my bedroom looking like he belonged there was confirmation to an affirmation for her. She had gotten what she wanted. Her family was complete now, and she could die happy.

Dennis rolled downstairs with the kids and made pancakes. Then they went out to the trunk of his car where he had presents for everyone. We spent the rest of the afternoon talking about Egypt and other points on the atlas. Dennis told Rakim about the Moors of Northwestern Africa. About how they were great military strategist! He even told them the legend of "The Blood of the Moor" in true Indiana Jones style, about the beautiful princess, the necklace, and the great war. Zeta and Rakim were mesmerized. He promised to someday take them to Africa, and they cheered. We were acting like a real family.

That evening, Righteous, Dennis, and the kids piled back into the SUV and made a trip to the local video store and then for pizza. Dora and I stayed behind. It was late, and she had already poured her nightcap, kicked off her shoes and headed for her favorite lawn chair on my little terrace downstairs. I grabbed a chair and sat beside her. The moon was full and lit up the sky like a rocket casting streaks across the yard. The light played in Dora's hair creating shiny ribbons of silver. She had stopped coloring it years ago, and the highlights made her look mystical like a wizard. She was unusually quiet tonight, so I waited for her to speak first. My head was swimming with questions that I needed to ask my "play mamma" because I definitely could not ask my real mamma:

> *Like what do you do when you find out your man is a drug dealer?*
> *Or is there a way to tell the good guys from the bad guys?*
> *Or what do you do when you think you have yelled out the wrong name in a moment of passion?*

When Dora finally acknowledged me, I realized that the gin bottle was already half empty. Dora had something heavy on her mind.

"Hey Gina," she slurred.

"Yes, Auntie?"

"You know, I can tell the future. I . . . I got the gift of sight, you know."

"Yes Auntie, I know."

"Well what you don't know is that I can tell you some things about the past, too. You want to know?" she slurred.

I didn't know where this was going. "Sure Auntie," I said. Then, for an hour she talked about her husband, and how he had been locked up. Dora was my mother's best friend, and it almost seemed wrong hearing these confessions without my mother present. But, this was for my ears only. Dora had downed the best part of a fifth of gin, finding the courage to speak so the least I could do was listen. Besides, I needed to buy some time; I was so afraid that I would call Dennis "Ray" again. I knew if it happened again, and Dennis heard it, he would walk out of my life forever. So I sat and listened to the incredible story of Dora and her relationship with her incarcerated man.

★★★★★

Amos and Dora had been an item since grade school. They had grown up together on a small cotton farm in Chicken's Peck, South Carolina. This was in the early forties, and colored families were still treated no better than slaves in some parts of the South. They were very poor yet were blessed to go to school, their parents wanting them to have more, be more, than present times would tolerate. They were taught values and the rewards of "living right" in a little store front church down the road. And they were also taught the importance of working hard and keeping the faith and also that the wages of sin was death.

At night, Little Dora and Amos would walk the miles home from the cotton field and talk about the grand lives they would live someday once they left Chicken's Peck. Amos vowed that one day, he and Dora would leave together.

Well, one year, the cow's got sick, and the water went bad. No one quite knew which one happened first. All little Dora knew was that both her ma and pa died and left her alone. Amos walked the two miles to Dora's house to collect her and her few things, and brought her back down the road to live with him and his step pa. Amos also had two older stepbrothers, and every night they would drink to excess and would pick fights with Amos, who was kinda small for his age. Amos would hide Dora in a closet on nights like that. She couldn't see, but she could hear his humiliation. Being so far back in the woods, his screams went unheard by anyone that would care. But then, there was nobody else to care. Dora stayed quiet though because that's what Amos asked her to do. This went on for years until Dora began to "sprout," and Amos's brothers started sniffin' around her. Amos put all her things and his into a flour sack, and they left Chicken's Peck in the middle of the night. He was fifteen years old, and she was twelve years old.

Gradually, Amos worked their way to Virginia where they stayed with a Quaker family. Amos told them they were husband and wife, and from that day on, they were. Life was good, and every night they would giggle and dream about their future.

By the age of twenty, Amos was a skilled carpenter and was ready to take his "wife" and his skill to the big city. They both loved Washington, DC—so many people—and Amos experienced a freedom he had only dreamt about. Amos made friends easily, and Dora found herself spending more time alone. Amos liked being with "the guys" sometimes staying out all night, and since their marriage had never been consummated, Dora thought that was just fine. Amos seemed so happy with his man friends, and Dora truly loved Amos. He was the only friend she had ever had. She wanted him to be happy.

As Dora grew older and more confident, she began to make men friends, too. Amos didn't mind that at all. Then, one day, Amos met a tall lanky salesman named Jerry. He had the face of an angel. Pretty with long sooty lashes and a charming gap in his teeth. Amos and Jerry became inseparable. There was talk, but Dora always squashed it. After all, Amos was her husband and most importantly, her friend. Tragically, Jerry was arrested for . . . well . . . nothing. Some guys beat him up one night as he was walking home, and the police arrested him. It was hard being colored and homosexual back then. To some, that was considered a crime. Jerry was sentenced to two years in prison because of a fight he didn't even start.

Amos was never the same after that. And it wasn't long before he tried to rob a liquor store in broad daylight. Amos didn't even drink! He was off to prison and happy to go. Amos wrote Dora often sending regards from their dear friend Jerry and the many other friends he would make.

★★★★★

"I loved Amos. Still do," Dora said as I stared at her. "Oh, I knew he was gay as you young folk call it now. But he was my friend and in every instance but one, he was my husband. He loved me, honored me, provided for me, and protected me. That's all I ever wanted or needed from him."

Dora looked down at her glass and winced. "I'm dry," she said and poured herself another drink. Looking off into the silver streaked sky, she began to hum to herself, and then she drained the glass she had just filled only seconds before.

"Dora, you alright?" I asked.

"Regina, I love you more than I could possibly know how to tell you. When your mamma and I met, I was like some wounded animal left to die on the road. My man was in jail . . . because it was too hard for him to live out here with me. The world couldn't accept him the way he was. I could, but the world couldn't."

"Do you still see or hear from him? Amos, I mean."

"No. When he got out, he came home for a while, but it was never the same. I think he's dead." Dora turned toward me. "Regina, I knew what he was. I saw him."

"A . . . a homosexual."

"No chile, not just that! He was a kind and loving man who had been through hell in his lifetime and still chose to love people and give them his best. That's what I saw."

We heard Righteous' car pull up in the driveway, and everybody piled out. They were singing the Oscar Meyer Wiener jingle and laughing real loud. I could hear Dennis' baritone, rich and strong, and it made me feel warm inside. Dora rose from the low lounger, surprisingly without incident. She grabbed the nearly empty bottle by the neck and headed back into the house. I stopped her.

"Dora, why did you tell me these things? Why did you tell me about Amos?"

She looked at me grinning through sad red eyes. "Because you need to look at that man in there and see who he really is, girl. What is really there. *Use your sight!* And then decide if you can accept it."

Use my sight! Hah! I had been blind for months, and now I didn't know who or what to trust. If I had seen any of this coming, I would have turned tail running the other way. It would have been so easy just to follow my heart, but even that was torn.

Today, I had been given a glimpse of what life could be with the man I thought I should have. Tonight, Dennis would be waiting in my bed to give me what I thought I wanted. I prayed that I would be satisfied.

Use your sight, she said. Use your sight. God, please let him be the one. I knew I was attracted to Dennis. He looked like what I wanted. He moved me. Turned me on!

But Ray excited me. Just the thought of him—the sound of him—thrilled me in a way that I had never experienced before. Deep down inside, I knew there was a passion in me waiting to erupt. A craving that had been newly stirred and hardly satisfied all because of him!

I had a fever and a thirst that was only quenched by the ringing of the telephone. Every time I heard his voice, I wanted more. I was falling in love with a phantom and a voice that made my body, mind, and spirit want nothing more than to be with him and to be his.

CHAPTER 8

◆

Marilyn's Story
The Pros and Cons of Dating a Con

I had everything I wanted. Dennis wore me on his arm like a diamond studded platinum Rolex. We were seen everywhere together—charitable events, international exhibit openings, artist's receptions, university banquets. Not only was I escorted around with the rich and influential but my children were, too. Dennis opened all kind of doors for Rakim and Zeta. In the fall, they were both enrolled in the finest private schools in the district. Rakim was awarded a coveted post as a teen aid at the Pentagon, and Zeta was tapped into *The Mix*—an exclusive club for young preteen girls. Only the most popular girls were approached for membership, and Zeta was thrilled. Dennis had made all this possible.

My old friends mysteriously stopped coming around. Dennis got me new friends—the wives of pro athletes, bank presidents, and corporate executives.

"We are a power couple now," Dennis said. "We need to have powerful friends." I nodded my head to show I understood. But I had to admit, I missed hanging out after the PTA meetings, joking with the girls at the beauty shop, and the occasional Friday night fish fry in the old neighborhood. Most of all, I missed card night with Righteous and the old aunts. I missed my life!

And I missed Ray! Dennis watched me like a hawk day and night, always beating me to the phone and checking the caller ID. But there was no need! Rayboy hadn't called me since that terrible night. It was like he had dropped off the face of the earth, and his absence had left me empty.

Tonight, we were getting dressed for yet another of the seemingly endless stream of fundraisers. Dennis had chosen his classic black Pierre Cardin tuxedo and was standing in front of my full length mirror admiring the fit. We were living together now—a move made purely out of convenience for him. He maintained his penthouse apartment in the city and usually spent nights there. But he monitored all of my moves, like I was under some kind of surveillance or house arrest. I felt like a prisoner!

I was fumbling through the cosmetics on my vanity table, trying to pull myself together. Earlier, I had selected my gown and had draped it across the bed. Dennis noticed it and cast a disapproving eye at me.

"Wear the black gown tonight," he said flatly, assured that his statement did not warrant discussion. It was not a suggestion.

"I would prefer to wear the midnight blue one," I said, steadying my hand as I applied my eyeliner.

"Wear the black, off the shoulder, hair up," Dennis said again as he straightened his tie in the mirror. He didn't yell; Dennis was far too dignified for that. Yet, his voice held a measure of intimidation that was meant to degrade me. I decided to tread lightly.

"Dennis, the black one is more of a cocktail dress. It is a bit too revealing for a presidential campaign fundraiser. The dark blue gown is more elegant," I said, and held my breath.

"You forget that we are fundraising, too, Regina. We need to let our potential patrons see what they can have for the right price," he said cooly, reaching for his emerald cufflinks.

"Dennis . . ."

"I said wear the black one. I want you to sparkle tonight. This will help." Dennis tossed a square velvet box on the bed and returned to the task of fixing his bow tie. I remembered the time when he would present me with a gift—an exotic treasure from halfway across the world—and I would melt with excitement. He would present his gifts to me, recounting their history.

I thought my reaction was due to the uniqueness of the gift. How priceless and rare it was! Now I realized that the gift was actually the giving of it, knowing that Dennis thought of me while he was away and cared enough for me to select just the right thing.

There was a velvet jewelry box on my bed, probably containing something very expensive. Something beautiful! There was a velvet jewelry box on my bed, and I hated it. He might as well have spat in my face.

There were so many things we did not talk about. We walked through our days like automatons—saying the right things, smiling the right smiles, going to all the right places. But when the days were over, we were pulled to opposite sides of the bed and sleep came pitifully and mercifully. We were together but so far apart.

We were a power couple, but I was powerless.

I put on the black dress.

An hour later, a valet was handing me out of a limousine to Dennis who escorted me down the red carpeted entrance of the Ritz-Carlton Hotel. The lobby was littered with the members of DC's A list—senators and ambassadors, foreign officials and diplomats, members of some of the wealthiest families in the country who owned the most admired art collections in the world.

Everybody who was anybody was there. The ladies were radiant and opulent, wearing runway originals and classic designs. I felt like a whore. My dress fit like a latex glove, accentuating every one of my curves. My breast felt like casaba melons pushed into a stocking cap, and my behind seemed to wag like a poodle in heat. I felt like everyone was staring at me, and I told Dennis so.

"They are not looking at you," he said. "They are looking at that jaw-dropping anchor you are wearing around your neck." That was sure true enough.

It was a king's ransom worth of the world's purest diamonds surrounding over hundred carats of lavishly sculpted rubies, the largest ones in the free world. The center ruby, which was twenty-eight carats alone, had a ghostly blue tint that revealed its authenticity and uniqueness. The gems were encrusted in gold, expertly detailed with ancient markings. Suddenly, there were photographers everywhere, and security guards rallied around us.

"Dennis, what is happening?" My pulse jumped; at any moment, I expected to see a SWAT team and drug-sniffing canines!

"Calm down, Regina and smile! The press is just excited because you are wearing a masterpiece—the one and only Blood of the Moor Necklace," he said with a wink. My eyes widened, and he laughed. Dennis had found it! He had actually found it, and I was wearing it around my neck!

Dennis had had it flown in this afternoon—a perk from a grateful curator who owed him a favor. It was on loan, and I was the only American woman to ever wear it. It was valued at over $10 million, and all of the upper crust cronies in attendance knew it. It looked fabulous against my brown skin, and the plunging neckline of my dress only helped to set it off perfectly. It was a piece fit for a queen and the only one of its kind. Admittedly, there were other pieces that rivaled its beauty but no other that had such a fascinating and romantic history. That is what made it so valuable to curators around the globe, and tonight, it was ours. Because of that, I threw my shoulders back and let the photographers do their thing. I was not wearing the dead Egyptian queen's necklace; it was wearing me.

All night, Dennis enjoyed nudging me forward and seeing the expression on the faces of his peers. Cameras were flashing everywhere! I had to admit it was a great publicity stunt for the museum . . . and for Dennis. It was his way of saying *"Yeah that's right! I have made it! I am the man! Can you get your hands on something this fine? Hell no! I can and I didn't need you or your money to do it! You can suck my big black dick!*

Halfway through the evening, and after three martinis, Dennis relaxed a little, trusting the hired security to do their job. Two Burmese collectors, who respected Dennis' work in Mediterranean lore, asked him to join them for a moment at their table. He hated leaving me behind. Like an overprotective parent, he barked a warning to the security agents before he walked away.

"Okay fellas, that's my entire life's work around her neck. Lose it and you're all fired," then he cast tender eyes on me and smiled. "The woman wearing the necklace is my life. Lose *her* and you're all dead."

I melted.

Dennis wasn't gone long and when he returned, he kissed me on the cheek and put his arm around me. He even told a newly appointed Supreme Court judge that I was the best thing that ever happened to him, and asked if he would marry us right then on the spot! My eyes got big as saucers, and the judge laughed. Dennis was joking of course. But our eyes met and we giggled, and it reminded me of the Dennis I use to know.

As the campaign speeches were being made, I laughed and clapped at the appropriate times while I counted the number of light bulbs in the gigantic glistening chandelier hanging over my head. Afterward, I continued to repeat the legend of the necklace for anybody that asked—and everybody did ask. My initial nervousness was gone. Now I was bored out of my gourd and self-conscious—a terrifying combination when you are surrounded by hundred-year-old white people with too much money and an open bar. I weaved and bobbed through mindless conversations about rising taxes and disappearing Social Security, when suddenly the band began to play. When the presidential favorite lead his wife onto the dance floor, the multitude followed, and I used it as an opportunity to escape. I wiggled across the floor to one of the more secluded bars, hoping to have a glass of wine and retreat into blissful anonymity.

I ordered the house wine, and the bartender looked offended. I was slightly embarrassed, realizing that by ordering the cheap wine, I was proving the point Dennis had been driving into my skull over and over again. I was use to not having the best, use to skimping and saving and very accustomed to being middle class. That is all going to change, he said.

I watched him working the floor, rubbing elbows with all the government officials and art world big wigs. He craned his neck to see over the crowd and found me. Dennis waved like a little boy being allowed to ride the roller coaster by himself for the first time. I smiled back. Granted, there was a boat load of tension between us, but I still understood him and appreciated his achievements. He had worked hard and tonight, Dennis was in his element! The sacrifices had been great. I just hoped his success would not cost him his freedom. I prayed he wouldn't loose his soul.

The bartender laid down a cocktail napkin and a stemmed glass in front of me. Just as I reached for it, the white woman sitting on the padded leather barstool beside me glanced at my hand, smirked and looked away.

"No ring," she mumbled making sure her comment was loud enough for me to hear.

"Excuse me?" I said, rather loudly myself.

"Oh, I'm sorry. I just couldn't help but notice. I mean, you've been flitting around here all night with that good-looking slice of chocolate pie over there, wearing enough rocks around your neck to feed a third world nation—and you're not wearing a ring." She laughed to herself, "Go figure."

Who the hell . . .

"Don't get me wrong. *Girlfriend, I ain't mad at you*—like you people say," she said in a Texas drawl. She waved her finger in the air in front of her like a "sistah" and popped a roasted peanut in her mouth, then said, "In fact, I am more than a little bit envious. You have got to tell me your secret. Or are you sitting on it?"

What the fuck . . .

"I gotta admit, I would have never figured you for the type. Don't get me wrong, you're cute and all that. But let's face it. He can do better," she said gesturing toward Dennis. "I mean, there are plenty of white girls here tonight who could steal him away from you with no problem."

There was a time, back in the day, when I was growing up on Clifton Terrace, I would have had my foot all the way up this bitch's ass and then asked her what her problem was. The heifer looked sane. She wasn't drooling from the mouth, and there were no crack marks on her arms. In fact, she was stunningly beautiful. Her strawberry blonde hair was pulled up in a classic roman chignon revealing the aristocratic lines in her face. She was older than me, at least by twenty years but was well preserved, most likely by a life of ease. Her make up was flawless, obviously done by a professional, and her gown looked as though it could have been designed for her. A deep eggplant, almost black, with a sheer bodice showing off her delicate bone structure—a Bob Mackie classic. It was tailored to perfection, accentuating her petite form.

Still, she was a bigot—a died-in-the-wool, grand old party redneck bigot—that for some strange reason, had sought me out to give her an ass kicking! And she couldn't stop talking! She looked at Dennis again, this time licking her lips.

"Man, oh, man, There ain't nothing better than a big black buck with a big fat wallet and a big fat juicy black . . ."

"Be careful, bitch," I snarled. I looked around for Dennis. God knows, the last thing I wanted to do was embarrass him tonight. But I was wind tight, stretched thin under the stress of the last few days. I was looking to unwind. Kicking my shoes off and beating down Miss Daisy might be just what I needed.

She laughed at me and took a sip from the champagne flute she was holding. "Look, girlie, don't pay me no mind. I'm just bored to tears and looking for something to do. *Or someone to do.*" She pointed to the waiter carrying a tray of hors d'ouvres across the room. "Look at that pretty piece, will ya now. Buttocks as tight as a Chesapeake Bay clamshell! Myyy . . my, my, my."

All I could do was stare at this point. I casually looked around, trying to remember who I had seen this loony tune with earlier in the evening. Perhaps I should alert someone. Maybe it was time for her medication or something.

"Look, ma'm, I'm not at all interested in your personal politics or your personal tastes. To each his own, you know. But I would certainly prefer if you kept your Southern-belle-plantation-gal-wish-I-were-in-the-land-o'cotton-singing-dixie-backwards opinions to yourself, okay? Because I don't give a damn." She had ruined any buzz I had worked to get tonight, and I clumsily slid down off the high leather seat, readjusted the black sausage I was squeezed into and headed for the dance floor. I could hear her laughing behind me.

"My, my, my. Ray sure didn't tell me you were such a firecracker. But he did tell me you were one in a million."

I froze in my tracks and swung around to look at her. Ray? Did she say 'Ray'? Maybe I had heard her wrong. Maybe I had been thinking about him so much that my head was swimming with his name. The white woman sat smugly in her chair, tapping her foot on the bar, waiting for me to turn around and take the bait. And I did! She pretended not to notice.

"Yeah, he described you as being some little meek and mild flower child. All gravy and biscuits." She turned her head slightly to look at me through thick black lashes, her eyes sharp with knowing. "But we women, well, we know better, don't we? We know how to give a man just what he needs—up close and personal," She nodded her head at Dennis who was still drowning in conversation, then added, "or over the phone."

"Who are you?" I demanded.

"Oh, just a friend," she sang. This bitch was hardly my friend, but obviously she knew Ray well enough to know about me.

"Tell me who you are or I'll . . ."

"Slow down, sugar. My name is Marilyn. Marilyn Marshall."

Marshall! Marshall! That name seemed to ring a bell. Then I remembered that sex scandal involving Big Daddy Beau Marshall at the women's correctional center down in Virginia.

"Are you Beau Marshall's wife?"

"That's right, sugar. The one and only."

The prison scandal unfolded in the newspapers during the summer of 1995. There were some allegations of gross impropriety and hefty fines levied. I had seen Marilyn entering and exiting the courthouse everyday, faithfully by her husband's side. After a full investigation, all charges were dropped, but Big Daddy was relieved of his duties at the women's facility. By midsummer, O.J. Simpson and his white Bronco were the new media fodder, and everybody forgot about Beau.

"What do you want?" I demanded again, and then Marilyn eyed the priceless necklace hoisted around my neck. I swear I stopped breathing. She laughed again. She thought we were telling jokes.

"Relax, honey, I don't need your little crackerjack box prize. I can get whatever I want whenever I want. But you know something about that, don't you?" She was toying with me, and I was getting pissed. But I had to stay cool. Let her do the talking.

"So you know Rayboy?" I asked somewhat casually like we were trading cheese dip recipes.

"Yes, I know him. Real well," she downed the rest of her champagne. "But I don't want to talk about him right now. I want to talk about you."

"Me?"

"Oh yes, honey. I think you are *vvverry* interesting. You see, I am on the horns of a terrible dilemma and I think you can help me."

"Help you how?"

"Let's be honest. You see, like you, I have a problem. I got two men—one on the inside and one on the outside—and I am going to have to make a choice between them soon."

"I think you have me confused with someone else. I don't . . ."

"I said, let's be honest!" she snapped.

"Okay. So what do you want from me?" I asked again.

"Maybe just a listening ear. I mean, there's not a lot of people I can discuss this with, now is there?" Marilyn was right about that. My world was getting smaller everyday. Everybody doesn't want to hear about your locked down relationship, and there are plenty of people you find yourself hiding it from.

"You know, there are no support groups for women like us. Not really! I know, I know. There are social workers, project chicks, and single mothers who can give you a little bit of advice. I've met them all, waiting in line outside the prison. So many prisons, and so many women!" Marilyn gestured to the bartender who scurried toward her, a bottle of Dom Perion in his hand. "A refill for me and a fresh glass for my friend." The bartender nodded and poured the expensive beverage into two glasses.

"You see, sugar, women like us . . . well . . . the stakes are much higher. We really have to weigh our options carefully."

"What do you mean?" I asked.

"I mean we have to be clear about what we want."

"Ms. Marshall, don't misunderstand me. I am not having a relationship with Ray. Dennis and I are solid. We are even considering marriage."

Marilyn face turned stern. "Who are you trying to fool, sugar? Me or yourself? If Mr. Wonderful over there was ringing all your bells, you wouldn't be sniffin' around cell block C."

"Ms. Marshall . . ."

"Please, call me Marilyn."

"Thank you. Marilyn . . ."

"Don't get me wrong, sugar. I understand. My husband is a good man—successful, dependable, and a good provider. Everything our mother's told us we should look for in a man. I'm sure your man is a carbon copy. But there is something missing! Something you can't quite name! Something that gets you hot in the middle of the night! Something that thrills you! Something dangerous!"

Dangerous. Yes!

"You daydream about him being locked away like an animal, with other animals with rolling muscles and piercing eyes. Held up in a cage because he's too vicious to walk around outside. Too masculine, too virile. Too much of a man."

Marilyn was painting a picture I had already sketched a thousand times in my head. Those late night conversations were wonderful. But underneath all the beautiful poetry and philosophical discussions, there was a carnal undercurrent full of sex and desire.

"And you wonder what it would be like to be with a man like that. Under him. Having him inside you. You're his prisoner."

Locked Down.

"And you're wondering how did it happen. One minute you have all the emotional freedom in the world. The next minute, you have given it all away."

"Oh, for sure, most women come into their locked down love affairs legitimately. They marry a man or have children by him, and then he goes to jail. That's different. Those women are already invested. Their hearts are already committed along with their lives. They are locked down in their own way. But that's not you, sugar. I'm not talking about your *jail house thrill.*"

"No, yours is the answer to all your romantic fantasies. He lives mostly in your head anyway. As handsome as you want him to be, as strong as you need him to be. As devoted as they come. Let's face it; what else does he have to do but think about you all day. Yearn to be with you! Want you! We imagine that he suffers the sweet agony of love that women have wallowed in since the beginning of time. We believe that we are free to love and we have chosen them, and they should be grateful. We have the power, and they have none. That's the story most women would tell if they were honest with themselves."

"Yes siree, one well-written letter from him—one hot erotic phone call in the middle of the night—can make a woman walk right past every Tom, Dick and Harry she meets on the street. A man behind bars can be a real silver-tongued devil! But then, you know that, don't you, sugar?"

The band transitioned from a long secession of Gershwin tunes to a top forty favorite, and more people headed for the dance floor. The house lights were dimmed, and the sparkle of glittering sequence and fabulous jewels cast tiny shimmering specks on the walls of the grand ballroom. Marilyn and I sat unmoved at the bar, like specters. I felt very apart from the other guests, not because of my dress, or because I was one of the few black women in the room; I was even use to that by now. But there were other reasons. In more ways than one, I was now in league with this white nigga-hatin' Daughter of the Confederacy, and the association was disturbing. She seemed to read my thoughts and coyly patted my hand.

"And then there are the rest of us, sugar. Girls like you and me who were raised to sit meekly by the side of the right man and smile the right smile and say all the right things and attend the right functions and join the right country clubs and support the right charities. And you scheme and strategize hard to get to that position just to find out that you have neglected to feed an important part of who you are."

"Astonishingly enough, you come to realize that part of you is really a bad little girl who is looking for a really bad boy."

Her face turned hard. Marilyn peered into her glass as if she were staring into a mirror.

"Or worse. You're a woman who yearns to be emotionally controlled, overpowered, tragically entangled or even victimized . . . because that is what love looks like to you. You've never even seen a good relationship at work. Don't even know what one looks like. You can't even make yourself *cum* without him making you feel subordinate, used, jeopardized . . . and maybe just a little nasty. That you, sugar? You want to feel nasty?"

Now this was getting way too personal. Her questions sounded less hypothetical and more like an intrusion into my already too-complicated life.

"You don't have to answer that," she said. "I think I know. I have met your Dr. Dickerson . . . and your jail house squeeze. They are both delicious chocolate dreams. You got a tough decision to make. Like I said, there are options to weigh. But, first you have to know the pros and cons of dating a con.

A woman came up to me, asking about my necklace—*again*—and I practically shooed her away. I wasn't sure I wanted to hear this, but Marilyn obviously needed to say it. So I listened as she gave me the inside story—the truth about Big Daddy Beau Marshall and the 1995 Beck's Creek Prison Scandal.

★★★★★

Big Daddy Beau Marshall had been an infamous character in the Del-Mar-Va area since he was a child. He was part of an illustrious family of men who all served as warden of the women's prison in Beck's Creek, Virginia. He was a card-playing, whiskey-drinking, straight-shooting son of the south that lived to uphold and defend the purity of southern womanhood and the grand ole flag. He also had an eye for the ladies. That only served to add to his charm.

Beau did not deviate from his predecessors or their proud family traditions. He figured what had worked for them would work for him.

Pity it was a new century!

Beau married the state beauty queen, as did all the Marshall men. Her name was Marilyn Wentworth, heir to the canned vegetable fortune, and they settled into the Marshall's sprawling plantation home just shy of the Tennessee state line.

Beau lived up to the family reputation of wealth and high-spending until one day it was brought to his attention that his ends were not quite meeting.

"We need more inmates and a bigger prison, boys. More inmates translate into more federal dollars. That's good business." So Beau went out in search of more money to accommodate his girls. Well, unfortunately, the wrong party was in office, and funds for prison reform and expansion were nonexistent. He would have to look elsewhere. Luckily, there was private enterprise—well-meaning corporations that were well invested in the future of this great nation. One such company gave Beau the money for his expansion. They only wanted a little something in return—a few simple, minimal tasks—screwing nuts on bolts. That sort of thing! Perhaps the little ladies could work a few hours and of course, the corporate boys would slip Beau a little something on the side.

Beau thought it was a great idea. The community working together! Beau considered the possibilities while he was tickling the nipples of a pretty young thing that had gotten his attention a few weeks earlier. She was nineteen and a first time offender willing to do just about anything to get out of laundry detail. Later that night, he was hoping to see just how much this little filly was willing to do. Not that it mattered; she would do whatever he wanted. Beau believed that all of the inmates were *his gals*, but some were part of a hand-picked tribe that saw to his *special needs*.

Now mind you, he loved Marilyn! This was just something he did to pass the time. It was part of the Marshall tradition, one of the perks and privileges of the job.

Well, in no time at all, Beck's Creek had a new wing and a new industry. Business was booming, and the corporate boys who wrote the checks became

Beau's new best friends. They played poker together and drank smooth Kentucky hooch in the middle of the afternoon.

Sometimes, Beau would be in conference with his special gals. Not to be inhospitable or less than the southern gentleman he was, Beau would always ask if his new buddies would like to partake of a little female companionship. Of course, not to be rude and to ensure community relations, they felt obligated to participate.

By the end of that year, Beau's corporate benefactors had their own suite in the prison's new wing where they could be entertained by the inmate of their choice. Beau Marshall was seeing to his own sexual pleasure and that of his peers, and Marilyn was none the wiser. A new Mercedes here and a Greek Island cruise there kept her as content as a tic in an old shag rug.

The recent addition to the women's prison started to take on a whole new look—wall-to-wall carpeting, Lazy Boy loungers, three new pool tables and sixteen top-of-the-line Oceanic Dream Machine king-size waterbeds—with the six-year double durability warranty. The newly formed enterprise made up of Beau and his friends, was open for business 24/7 with a stable of female inmates that were spending more time on their backs than they were on their feet. There was no end to the sucking and grinding, howling and growling, licking and whipping that went on at the new improved Beck's Creek. Beau thought he had died and gone to Good Ole Boy Heaven!

Things seemed to be getting along just fine until the undercover investigative reporter from that popular nighttime news show seemed to pop up from out of nowhere. Big Daddy Beau Marshall was literally caught with his pants down, along with about a half-dozen city icons, sampling the charms of a wayward few.

The shit had hit the fan. The corporate heads claimed inculpability, covering their tracks all the way, leaving Beau Marshall holding the bag. After all, they were *his girls* in *his prison*. They got a slap on the wrist for being bad boys, while Big Daddy Beau was left hung out to dry. The night before the hearing, Beau Marshall went home and told his wife the whole ugly truth. He hid a single bullet in his breast pocket, expecting the worse.

Death before dishonor!

Much to his surprise, Marilyn took it well. She got busy calling in a few favors, transferring Beau's massive wealth and by the following morning, Beau had stopped cleaning his hand gun and had a new lease on life. He also had a new appreciation for his wife, who he realized was not only beautiful but kind, forgiving, and more than a little savvy.

Together, Marilyn and Beau made it through the crucifying media frenzy. Everyday, she played the dutiful wife, the model of southern virtue, supportive to the end. When it was all over, she only asked her husband for two things. The first was that he accept the state attorney's plea bargain and serve as assistant warden in an all male prison. The second request was a little more bizarre.

★★★★★

The bartender noticed our glasses were empty and tried to refill them, but Marilyn refused. "No more for me," she said, holding her hand over the glass. "I've got to stay lucid for tonight." She began to rattle on about the band and the endless speeches until I could take no more.

"Marilyn, what was your second request?"

"Pardon me?"

"From Beau, your husband. What did you ask for?"

Marilyn popped another peanut into her mouth then pulled her compact from out of her tiny jeweled purse. She made a big deal about checking her lipstick, then I noticed she was using the mirror to check out the perimeters of the room. She was looking for someone. Suddenly, she clapped the compact shut and looked directly at me.

"Oh! What did you say, sugar?"

"I asked you what was the other thing you wanted from your husband." Just then, a very handsome young black man came up behind Marilyn. He suggestively rubbed her shoulders as he pretended to help her with her coat, and Marilyn arched like a cat leaning back into his arms.

"Not what, but *whom*, sugar," she grinned allowing the young stud to work his magic, copping a feel on the side on her breast.

"You see, now *I* have *privileges* at the prison," she giggled. And he was truly a fine privilege to have—tall and well built, his generous display of muscles barely masked by his tuxedo. He was cute with a boyish face and probably not even half Marilyn's age. But he was obviously into her and very devoted.

"Surprised?" She delighted in asking.

"Quite," I said but then realized that no one could justify having a sex slave better than Marilyn Wentworth Marshall. I was sure that had been part of the Wentworth legacy from way back. Just another southern tradition!

"I just couldn't resist him," she said. "And I wanted to see what all the fuss was about. You know, find out if all the rumors were true."

"Rumors?"

"You know. 'Once you go black, you never go back.' 'Nothing hangs bigger than a nigger.' 'The blacker the berry, the sweeter the . . .'"

"I think I got it," I said quite disgusted by now. Marilyn looked sincerely hurt by my comment, and she waved her young man on, telling him she would meet him at the car.

"His name is Thomas. He's a good boy, but not the one that has me tied up in knots. I couldn't bring that one. He's too hunky. *Too dangerous*! They can hardly let him up to see me without putting him in shackles." I could see her excitement just thinking about him. Her face reddened.

"He is so black and soooo big . . . and he hurts me just enough to make me beg. He is a really bad boy, and I can have him anytime I want. He's rough enough to make it fun and exciting, but he's gentle enough to make me feel safe. And he has to be good to me, or I'll walk away and choose another. At least, that was the way it started out. That's my problem. I've become addicted. That's the downside of dating a con. He gave me exactly what I wanted, and now I need it all the time."

"You're having sex with cons."

"Oh, believe me, sugar. They are on a mighty short leash. One false move, and it won't be pretty. They know the deal," Marilyn assured.

We both saw Dennis approaching, and Marilyn extended her hand to him. He cleared his throat immediately recognizing Marilyn then tried to play it off.

"Good evening, Mrs. Marshall," Dennis said. "I see you have met Regina." He helped her down, anxious for her to leave.

"Why, Dr. Dickerson, don't you look handsome tonight. *So odd to see you outside of the prison!* You are there so often, I thought you were an inmate," Marilyn crooned.

"Well, you know what they say—*we all look alike.*" I had to say it. It was probably the only racist remark she had missed saying tonight. Dennis' eyes rolled to the back of his head.

"I'll walk you to your car," He said to Marilyn, then looked at me and added, "Get your coat. We are leaving. Security will follow you and I'll meet you outside."

I slid down from the stool, blotched my lipstick with a cocktail napkin and noticed an envelope with my name on it beside my glass. "*G.i.n.a.*" I looked at each letter of my name; this was Ray's handwriting. It had to be! There was only one person in the world that called me that. I stared at the small envelope for at least two minutes. The letters were all capital, each constructed with care. Not like calligraphy, but with precision and purpose.

He had taken his time with them, like a man getting dressed to meet a woman for the first time. He wanted to make a good impression.

I held my breath as I ran my finger along the corners of the envelope. Ray had sent me a message by way of the warden's crazy redneck wife. Tears welled in my eyes. I was flooded with relief. So many times in the past few days, I had pictured him dead, stabbed to death in some prison mess hall fight. Or bleeding profusely, stuffed in a forgotten corner of that hellhole. But he was alive! He was being careful not to call me with Dennis around. In his way, he was trying to take care of me.

I clumsily stuck a fingernail into the fold, trying to open the note. I was excited and nervous, like a new bride. I had gotten it open, pulling out the notebook paper inside. Then, a hand grabbed my arm, pulling me away from the bar.

"Are you coming?" Dennis asked rather forcefully.

I quickly stuffed the #10 envelope and pages down into my tiny cocktail purse and jammed it closed. I struggled to fasten it, and Dennis pulled the purse out of my hand, flinging it open.

"You're forcing it. Let me help you," he said. The envelope was so big, it damn near popped out of the purse like a jack-in-the-box, falling into Dennis' hand. Without giving it a second thought, he folded it twice then stuffed it back in. "There," he said, handing the purse back to me. "We have to go now."

"What's the rush . . . and where is your *friend*?" I asked boldly, realizing I had just dodged a bullet. If Dennis had known I had a letter from Rayboy, I'm not sure what he would have done.

"Marilyn is in the limo with Thomas and her husband," I noticed how the names rolled so easily off his tongue. He knew these people well and made no excuses for it.

"We are going home?" I asked.

"No, you are going home," he said with that same forcefulness I was supposed to get accustomed to. "I have some business to conduct with Marilyn and Beau. It shouldn't take long . . . but don't wait up for me."

"Dennis, you promised me . . ."

"There are just a few loose ends I have to tie up. It's nothing," he insisted.

"But you don't want me there with you!" I spoke the question a little too loudly. There was a break in the music, and people turned around to stare at us, and the security goons got jumpy. Dennis smiled for the little audience and then cavalierly brought me into his arms.

"Regina, don't ruin this night for me. It's been like a dream. And I'd like to think the best part is yet to come." Dennis leaned into me, kissing me soundly on my lips. He eyed the necklace again, smiling. He was truly proud of himself. Then his hands dropped a few inches lower, and he caressed me seductively.

"Do you know what I want?" he asked, whispering hotly into my ear.

"You want to make love to me," I answered, very conscious of the few people still staring. Dennis' hands began to roam a little too freely along my body. My thin form fitting dress had begun to feel like a second skin, and I could almost feel Dennis' fingerprints on my back. I tried to pull away. He wasn't having it.

"No, I don't want to just make love to you," he breathed, his lips rubbing softly against my lobes. "I want to *worship* you in bed, treat you like the goddess that you are. I want my lips to know every inch of your skin. I want our bodies to fuse together in a fiery blaze of passion that is so hot that it melts our two souls into one. And after I have loved you, touched the deepest inner core of you, I want you to rest in my arms knowing that I am your king and that you belong to me. That's what I want."

Wow! Dennis was turned on, charged by the many elements of the night—the dress, the multimillion dollar necklace, the high dollar players, and the deals to be made. And maybe a little bit by me! He was stoked and on fire! He felt powerful and in control. Now, he was ready to burn!

Unbelievably, we had not made love once. Sure we had done everything else—bumping and grinding, kissing and cuddling, but it usually ended in nothing. Most nights, he didn't stay with me at all. Those were the nights, I worried the most. Not about another woman; that would have been easy to overcome. Our "other woman" was "the deal." I had nightmares of him walking the dark streets of DC—art dealer by day, drug dealer by night. 5Dennis, you're embarrassing me," I said, pulling out of his embrace.

"Just be ready for me when I get home," He gave me a light peck on the forehead—a show for the onlookers—but his eyes pierced me with intent.

The two of us walked out into the hotel lobby amidst a feathering of handshakes and polite hugs. Our limo was waiting, and Dennis handed me in. After I was seated, he ran his hand along the exquisite diamond and ruby necklace.

"I know you didn't want to wear this," he said. "Didn't even want to wear that damn dress. But you did it anyway . . . for me." He picked up my hand and kissed it. "You were beautiful tonight, everything I ever dreamed. Thank you. See you at home." He gently closed the door, and the driver began to slowly pull away.

Home, he had called it. Funny, it hadn't felt like home in weeks! We were saying all the right things, doing what was expected of an up and coming social climbing black family, yet there was something missing. The children seemed happy, but we were fakes, stand-ins in a bad Brady Brunch sequel. We were both trying so hard to be normal, avoiding the issues that might tear us apart.

In the rearview mirror, I watched Dennis get into the warden's limo. I wondered for a moment if Beau Marshall was a player in this game. Could he be running drugs in his own prison? I wanted to ask, but I was afraid to know the answer. When I was sure Dennis was gone, and my limo had picked up speed, I took the letter out and began to read.

Hey, Sweet baby girl,

I miss talking to you so much. I wonder all the time if you are ok or if dickerson has hurt you. But I dont what to waste no ink on dickerson. This is abt me and you, Gina. It always has been.

You are in my soul. like music. I wake up with you in me moving me thru the day. You are the rhythm in my blues. This place is like a house of zombies. All gray and cold with no where for the light to come in. And if the light does find its way in, we dont know it because we so use to not seeing it that it dont seem real.

You say sometime "how can we be so close when we aint never seen each other." Well I can answer that. It is because what we have is real. More real than anything I can touch in here. You are the sun, Gina. You got in.

I like reading poetry with you and listening to music with you and just knowing you on the other end of the phone. You dont have to say nothing. Nothing at all. Cause when that happens, I imagine that I am touching you. When you get quiet I tell myself thats ok cause thats when you be really feeling me the way I am feeling you.

Then we hang up and you go back to whatever you were doing. You go back to your life. But its different for me. I hang up and I take your last words with me. Painting pictures in my head. When I am going back to my cell, you are walking beside me, all soft and beautiful like I imagine you to be. The way I no you are. And at lights out, you come alive for me. Your last words run around in my head like children on a playground. keeping me awake and I cant do nothing until I imagine you touching me, waking up the parts of me that have been dead for so long. You Gina. Your words touch me like the sun keeping me alive.

I aint trying to get all heavy on you. Like I no you into dickerson. I aint going to play you tho. That shit hurts me. When I first called you, I thought he was just your boss. He is such a asshole I figured he must have people on his job that had it out for him. But I was wrong. Anyway, it aint nothing but a thing. He got every reason to want you. And so do I.

Its all fucked up. But hey Gina, you can no this. I am a man and I want what I want. Me being locked up aint change none of that. In fact, it made it worse. Dont think for a minute I cant be your man cause I can. I can give you what you need. All of it. I want to so bad.

You already got my mind. You already own my spirit. My body is locked down. Everything else belongs to you.

I aint worryed abt that punk dickerson eether. He gonna slip up. and he cant bulldog the phone 24/7. And I dont want you trying to visit me in no goddamn prison. Dont worry about getting to me. I will get to you.

Just do 1 thing for me. 2nite when you taking a bath, think abt me. pretend that my hands are on you sliding on the soap. Let the water soothe you like I no I can. Pretend that I am caressing you underneath your breast and between your legs, soaking you with my love. Know its me, baby and before long, it will be.

Ray

You already own my spirit, Ray said. It had barely been a month since that first phone call, and I was sure he owned mine. On the way home, I read the letter three more times. When I got into the house, it was late and both

Zeta and Rakim were asleep. I tiptoed upstairs and put the letter down. Then I took off all of my clothes, walked into the shower and grabbed the soap.

It was the longest shower of my life.

Afterward, I picked the letter back up and climbed into bed with it. I clutched my pillow as if it were the man in cell block C and with my other hand, I aroused myself in the way he aroused me with his words. My legs began to move rhythmically, hugging the sheets until the friction created enough heat for me to feel his presence. I heard myself moan aloud as my own moist juices drowned my fingertips and the pleasure it brought rocked me safely to sleep. But even in sleep, I found Ray again, waiting for me to come into his arms.

During the night, I was nudged gently. Arms encircled my waist as I felt a slight chill. Gone now, and warmth surrounded me again, luring me into consciousness. But I would not awaken. Sleep was too peacefully delicious, too sexy, too welcomed to let it go. There was a man waiting for me in my dreams. There were lips on my spine and the smell of Ralph Lauren teased my nostrils as a pair of determined hands roamed my body. So real! Were they seeking satisfaction? I smiled with my eyes still shut tight. I could give it to them. I was beautiful! I was desirable! I was sunlight in darkness, and a man had given me his mind and spirit. A man who had never once even seen my face!

I must be the shit and don't know it.

Hot wet lips moved up my neck and around my head. A tongue laved me with succulent kisses, handling my breast, then sliding down to my stomach. The tongue entered my navel as strong arms wrapped around my legs like snakes, and I was exposed. The cool air shocks my nipples, and my own hands rushed to comfort them. The cold disappointed me but the heat returns, hotter now, nestled between my thighs. My legs spread to accommodate my joy as I was sucked and massaged below. I am separated, pulled apart like freshly peeled fruit and sweetly devoured by one who is hungry for my love. I reached down and ran my fingers through his soft hair as he eats me, and I am filled as he is filled. But our bodies' are greedy, still thirsty for the spring of heaven that runs slow and deep inside me. I feel his weight on top of me, and I crave more. I want him everywhere, and he knows it. He brings his mouth to my ear and I hear my name spoken through a dream.

"Reggginaaa."

Something crashed inside my head, and I opened my eyes just as Dennis entered me. He was hot and throbbing, sweat glistening off of him. He raised my knees to my chest and thrust deeper inside me until I thought I would burst. His stroke got longer and harder until the bed began to move, and I braced myself against the headboard. Dennis was keeping his promise. I held on to him, and he called my name again, spouting more promises to love me forever and cherish me always. Then he shuddered and collapsed into my arms.

I laid there in the dark holding on to him, tears forming puddles in the corners of my eyes. Dennis had come home to me tonight just as he had promised. And Ray had been there, too, just as he had said he would be. I had felt them both, had been touched by them both, and now I felt a little insane. I stroked the sleeping muscles that held me in the dark. Shrouded by the night, they could belong to any man; all I had to do was close my eyes. There were two men in my life. There were two men living in my head, and now there were two men in my bed.

CHAPTER 9

◆

Aunt Betty's Story

The True Born Believers Church Prison Ministry

"For real, you look terrible, Mamma," Rakim was standing over me with a fresh cup of coffee, trying to get my attention before he put it down on the breakfast table in front of me. I had come downstairs early this morning. Might as well since I had been awake most of the night! Dennis was sleeping soundly, and unless I woke her for church, Zeta would sleep until the early afternoon.

I had crept downstairs still in my robe to get the morning paper. Not to read it but to hide it from Dennis. That man loved reading *The Post* and would get up at the crack of dawn on Sundays, thumb through the Arts and Leisure section and plan our entire day.

I wasn't moving today. Not one damn inch!

"Why are you up so early this morning?" I asked him.

"Project due at school. I want to finish it now so I can go to the movies later. That cool with you?"

"That's cool," I answered as I watched my son move around the kitchen slicing bagels and spreading jam. He selected a golden chunk of ripe mango, tossed it on the plate and laid it down beside my coffee. Where did I get this child, I thought to myself.

"For me?" I asked.

"For you," he smiled as he turned his back to me, reaching into the frig. "You gotto keep up your strength if you going to *be carrying on all loud* like you were last night!"

Oh my God!

"Man, you and Dr. D were *all the way live*! I thought the roof was gonna cave in on this . . ."

"Rakim!" He was laughing hysterically and doing some kind of crazy touchdown dance around the table.

"Pleeaassse make sure your door is closed all the way next time! I thought ya'll were some wild animals up in there . . ."

He continued to laugh, sticking his tongue out like a lizard. I kept swatting at him, but he kept dodging my hand. I was so embarrassed, and he was happy, truly happy—not the serious-minded young man he had become the last few years. Since Dennis had been in the house, Rakim seemed to relax. In his mind, everything was as it should be. We had a provider and protector, and his mother didn't have to work so hard. And for a little while, he had time to be a boy. I had seen the change in Zeta, too. She was calmer, more settled, and much more respectful to me. If for no other reason than that, it was good having a man in the house.

Rakim grabbed a cinnamon bun and came to sit down beside me. "For real, mom. It's nice to be a normal family again." Then his demeanor changed. He absent-mindedly played with my fingers just as he used to do when he was a little boy. "But on the real, just know I always got your back, alright! No matter what!"

So that was it. Rakim was telling me that Dennis moving in was cool. He would give Dennis his proper respect, but *he* was still the man of the house and would be there for me no matter what. I smiled gently and played the stupid finger game with him. I decided not to elaborate on Rakim's statement. That would have been too many words for a fourteen-year-old and only make him uncomfortable. I just nodded and took a last good look at my boy. He was turning into a man right before my eyes.

We ate breakfast together, Rakim telling me all about his geography project. Dennis had helped him create a holographic map. Rakim loved geography, studying about distant lands and people. I told myself that it was a trait he had inherited from me. My love for other cultures led me into my museum career. But I knew it wasn't that! Rakim had wanderlust just like his father and stepfather. I seemed to be attracted to men that were destined to love me and leave me, and now I had birthed one. Even with Dennis, I had to reconcile his need to be with me with his equally aggressive need to be away from me.

Maybe the warden's redneck wife was right. Maybe part of my magnetic attraction to Ray was that I always knew where he was, and there was always a good chance that he was thinking about me. I was his world, and I liked that. That was a fantasy I could live with.

Fantasies! Last night had been one. I had made myself come twice just thinking about Rayboy, yet I didn't have an orgasm at all with Dennis, the real thing. I arched my back thinking about the acrobatics of the night before. Dennis was a good lover, tender when I needed him to be. Aggressive when I wanted him to be. This is going to work, I thought. Dennis is what I need! I just need to get that *third person* out of my bed!

I was about to round the stairs back up to my bedroom when the doorbell rang. I looked a mess but since I was closer than Rakim, I answered it.

"Good mornin', baby," my Aunt Betty stood in front of me at the door wearing one of her original outfits. She had an outrageously hideous creation on her head—a milliner's nightmare, plumed with yellow roses and pink, green and white striped ribbon. She wore a pink and black satin suit with silver buttons and a green velvet lapel. She completed the ensemble with pea green orthopedic pumps and a matching flowered pocketbook big enough to be a picnic basket. She carried one of everything in it including a large print Bible thick enough to be mistaken for a telephone directory.

Soaring through the flowers on her hat was a giant dove with beady glass eyes that seemed to be staring directly at me. I took two steps backwards, giving her plenty of room just in case it came in for a landing.

"Hi, Aunt Betty! I am surprised to see you here so early this morning." Her eyes got real big, and then I remembered.

"Regina Darlene Lambert Jackson, please don't tell me that you forgot what today is! I just took two buses and walked further than my bad leg can tolerate just so you can drive me to the church quarterly meeting!" Betty reached down and touched her knee with a white-gloved hand. "You know how bad I suffer with the gout. Lord! It 'bout killed me!"

I winced. Betty had asked me weeks ago to drive her down to the old home church. Every few months, the small congregations of several storefront churches came together for worship. All of them had stemmed from a tiny church lodged deep in the woods. Every time folks got to feuding, they would branch off taking a loyal few with them. This happened at least once every three years until the parent church was too small to conduct certain rituals. One important ritual was the annual foot washing at the pond. I had volunteered to drive Betty this morning because she was too old to safely make the trip by herself. She looked at my robe and fluffy slippers and screeched.

"Regina, you have got to hurry and get dressed. I cannot be late today. I am giving the scripture reading this mornin'." She spun me around and pointed me upstairs. "Now go up there and get ready!"

I entered the bedroom quickly, yet quietly, not wanting to wake Dennis. To my surprise, he was sitting up in bed, his back against the headboard and arms folded behind his head. His biceps were singing love songs to me, and the shadow of a beard played on his face. God, he was so sexy, laying there smiling at me like a man who *knew* he had put it down real good on his woman. I came near the bed, and Dennis pulled me into it, circling me in strong arms.

"Good morning, Regina," he purred.

"Good morning, Dennis," I echoed, hypnotized by the sultry expression in his eyes. It was hard to pull away. "Dennis, Aunt Betty's downstairs. I have to . . ."

"I heard. Better you than me! Remember, I made that run last time," he reminded me as he settled back down into the sheets. It occurred to me that Dennis had made that pilgrimage to the old church with Betty, when I was too sick one Sunday to do it. I looked at him and smiled. Dennis Dickerson was truly a nice man—who *was turning into a drug dealer*. My smile disappeared, and the unspoken questions of last night rushed back into my head.

Dennis, where did you go last night with the Marshalls? What did you do? Did you go do a drug run at the prison? Did you go see that Shaka Blu character? Tell me what happened!

But I didn't ask any of them. Dennis had plied me with sex, and I let him. All I wanted was to be happy! All I wanted was not to be alone!

"Betty's waiting downstairs," I said again, turning away from him. "I better hurry."

Moments later, the three of us—me, Betty, and the giant condor-like thing in Betty's hat—were climbing into my new gun-metal green Chrysler 300. Dennis had surprised me with it last week—the morning after *the first time* he had stayed out all night. It was fully loaded and stocked with all my favorite CDs. It did help to lessen my bite. Betty oohed and aahed over it for at least ten minutes.

"Regina, this car is beautiful! Girl, you are so lucky to have a man like that." She was quiet for about half a minute, then she started. "Regina, honey, you ain't still got no crazy notions about that jailbird, do you?"

I didn't say a word. I did not want to get into a long drawn-out conversation about my morality or my spiritual well-being. This road trip was too long for me to get stupid in the car with a woman who still thought thongs were a Chinese appetizer.

"I cannot tell you how dangerous these jail people are. How hurtful and insensitive. How cruel and . . ."

"Betty, how would you know!?" I snapped taking my eyes off the road just long enough to get scared straight by that damn bird staring down at me. It looked like it was about to attack!

Aunt Betty got quiet, and I started to apologize for yelling at her. Then she began to talk about a problem in the church that caused this last split in the congregation. It set mother against daughter and ended with a sordid scandal involving the pastor's wife. She was quick to say that it had nothing to do with their devotion to doing the Lord's work but had everything to do with the newly formed, short-lived and recently disbanded church prison ministry.

★★★★★

Aunt Betty had been a respected mother of the church for over twenty years. She had helped build the tiny church from the ground up, established the building fund and seen it dwindle away to nothing more than once. Betty and the church elders were starting to doubt the commitment of their flock and decided to redirect their ministry.

"God said to spread His word among all the people," crowed the head elder, and so they did. A massive community outreach was started to save lost souls and increase the church rolls. It has suggested by Brother Leroy that a prison ministry be established. It was just the good Christian thing to do.

Betty and the other church mothers got busy making arrangements to visit the incarcerate heathen at the minimum security prison as soon as possible. The church put money aside for Bibles, prayer cloths, and little crosses on chains to leave with the men after their visit. Mother Hester, the pastor's wife, was put in charge, and four women were assigned the task of visitation. Betty was one of them.

The women entered the Wattsville Correctional Center for Men hand in hand, softly spouting scriptures as the inmates were ushered in. Clad in black dresses that covered their knees and prim little hats, they stood in a tight straight line—a barrier between good and evil. As the inmates entered, the ladies were shocked at what a big burly presentable group they were. The picture of health and vigor! Have mercy!

"My, my, their bodies are certainly *temples to the Lord*," said Betty.

"Some of God's finest work," said Mother Hester.

"Must be that celibate lifestyle they lead in here," Nora Jean said.

"We should all look that . . . *robust,*" Gladys May said, thinking that her own celibacy hadn't treated her that well.

"Good afternoon, Ladies," greeted one convict. He had a deep gash in his chin and very masculine sideburns that reminded Betty of Elvis Presley. And strangely enough, that gash made his face more appealing, like he was smiling all the time. The little bible-toting crew all looked surprise as if they didn't think the men would even speak English. None of them had ever even been in a prison in their whole God-fearing lives. The men smiled, offered the church ladies seats and acted like proper gentleman.

"We have good news. Jesus died so your sins would be forgiven," the church ladies told them.

"Well now, that is good news. Does that mean we get to go home with you pretty things tonight?" the biggest and burliest one said. The ladies all blushed and laughed nervously. Nora Jean batted her eyes, while Gladys May actually crossed her legs! Mother Hester gave her a stern look, as she readjusted her hat, revealing a lock of her good hair.

They were allowed an hour of Bible study, prayer, and devotion. When their time was up, the ladies left, vowing to return next week to deliver the good word. They were all aflutter, feeling strangely rejuvenated after their hour together. Betty tried to give the inmates the tiny crosses, but the guards said no, saying it was against prison rules. One particularly handsome convict assured Betty that was alright.

"You hold on to that for me, ma'am. Nothing would give me more pleasure than to think about it hanging around your pearly sweet neck." His eyes burned her. "You got skin like fresh churned buttermilk."

"Praise the Lord," said Betty, breathlessly.

A week later, the little band of Christian soldiers was back, with a few changes in protocol. They wore brighter colors and more fashionable hairstyles and *sleeveless* blouses. Mother Hester thought it would make a better impression on the heathens if they shined like the Light of The Word. The others agreed. Gladys May even wore open-toed shoes!

"We can save them, sisters," declared Nora Jean.

"It is going to take dedication. We will have to spend a lot of time with them," said Betty.

"Oh yes, sister. They will need all our attention," agreed Mother Hester.

"I am willing to give whatever it takes," proclaimed Gladys May.

"Have you ever seen so many muscles? God can use men like that."

"We have got to bring these men home . . . to the Lord, that is."

"Poor things, all shut up like that. We have got to give them some comfort and love."

"Oh yes! Its our duty to give them comfort . . . and lots and lots of good loving . . . I mean, love."

When the men arrived, they started devotions by singing "Onward Christian Soldiers" because Nora Jean thought it was one of the more masculine selections in the hymnal. Their deep baritones made her massive bosoms swell to the delight of the inmates. Afterward, they decided to break up into smaller groups for individual Bible study. The men were permitted to sit closer to the ladies and suddenly, the little cotton prayer cloths that were supposed to go to the men, were used to fan and dapple the bosoms of the dedicated missionaries. The temperature in the visitation room seemed to rise twenty degrees! Betty's heart was racing; none of them had realized how *exciting* it would be to do the Lord's work. The ladies began to read the scripture and over the weeks, boy, did their new flock respond!

"Jesus wept."

"I wept when you left last week, wondering if I would ever see you again."

"The Lord is my Shepherd."

"Thank God he has lead you to me . . . *with your fine self."*

"Everything is possible for him who believes."

"I sure as hell hope so because I believe I am falling in love with you, hun."

"God wants us to love one another."

"I think about *lovin'* you all the time. Slide a little closer to me, sugar! I feel closer to heaven when I am with you."

After a while, there seemed to be less praying and more straying. The prison ministry ladies were heard all over the block giggling like school girls. This went on for months, until one day, Gladys May, in a moment of great zeal, decided to make an unscheduled visit to the prison to have a private prayer session with one of the inmates, who said he was particularly in need. It was the big burly one with the scar on his chin and sideburns like Elvis. She took extra care with her appearance that day, wanting to make a good impression since she was representing her Holy Father.

Gladys May ascended the prison steps with an extra bounce in her walk. She had been truly uplifted and blessed by her ministry. She felt like a new woman, especially blessed by the passionate, loving letters that she had received from this particular inmate. Ignoring Mother Hester's warnings, Gladys May had entered into a pen pal relationship with one of them. He had written beautiful letters to her expressing his gratitude and joy since she had entered his life. She had slipped him her address when he suggested that he needed to bare his soul and confess some things to her. She was special, he had said. She was the key to his redemption, he had said. Yes indeed, Gladys May had come prepared to show her true dedication to this inmate today.

Imagine her surprise when she got there and saw Mother Hester's name written in the visitation log book just above the space she was now writing hers. The guard thought nothing of it since the ladies usually came together and allowed Gladys May in to visit the same prisoner. Gladys entered just in time to see Mother Hester—*pastor's wife*—sliding her bare leg over Elvis' knee and him rubbing his hand along her big fat ham hock thighs! Holy Jesus!

Well, quite literally, all hell broke loose. Gladys May dived into Hester, knocking her off of Elvis' lap, and they were embroiled in the worst catfight ever recorded in the history of the men's prison. The Pastor himself had to come down and get his wife out of the county lockup along with his rambunctious parishioner. However, all was not lost! Pastor did have an opportunity to pass out tracts to the poor misguided females that shared the county cell with his wife.

Understandably, the church's prison ministry is still currently under review giving Mother Hester's black eye a chance to fade and Gladys May's nose an opportunity to reset. The entire church family is in prayer for them knowing God heals all wounds. They pledged to continue to pray for the heathen horde that populates the prison. Surely this incident was Satan's folly at its worse, and they would never speak of it again.

"We will forgive our sisters," the pastor said. "We will not send our pure vessels to that den of iniquity again. If those lawless devils could possess the mind of our pious first lady, then it surely must be the simmering fires of hell itself!" That was Pastor's final word.

★★★★★

Betty and that beady-eyed bird in her hat both looked at me sadly. "This will be our first service together since that terrible incident," she lamented. "I am praying that everything has calmed down. We need to restore peace in the church."

We pulled into the small graveled parking lot at the church just in time to see the congregation making the trek down to the pond. The foot washing would start soon, and Betty was asked to read the scripture to begin worship. She checked her hat in the rearview mirror and smoothed the lapels on her suit. I touched her arm, wanting to ask a question about the story she had told me.

"Aunt Betty, did you ever get any letters from that convict?"

Betty gave me a sweet smile and took a deep reflective breath. "God only knows, child. God only knows."

Aunt Betty went to join the assembly of women standing at the edge of the water. They were hugging and kissing, happy to be brought together again in the Spirit of the Lord. They helped each other cover their heads in white muslin in the tradition of their mothers and grandmothers. Then they sat by the pond, took off their shoes and dangled their feet in the flow. The men sang "Wade In The Water" as the women took turns washing each other's feet. This was the ultimate sign of forgiveness and humility. Everyone in the church was expected to participate, and everyone did. All but two finely dressed women standing in the corner under a tall oak tree. The two women seemed to be arguing, their faces balled up in anger. Suddenly, the shorter of the two (the one with the bandage over her nose) took a step forward and pushed the taller one (the one wearing the dark sunglasses) into the pond! A round of curses like you wouldn't believe followed! Aunt Betty tried to calm them by reading the scriptures as loud as she could.

> *The way of PEACE they know not*
> *and there is no judgment in their goings*
> *they have made them crooked paths;*
> *whosoever goeth therein shall not know PEACE.*
> "We want to know PEACE!!!!!"

Betty was yelling at the top of her lungs, but it did no good at all. The two women continued to battle it out in the middle of the baptismal pond as a handful of elderly men tried to pull them apart. Arms and legs were thrashing around like an explosion in a mannequin factory. Soon, Betty just gave up, slamming her Bible shut. She picked up her green orthopedics and walked back to the car.

She was silent all the way home but looked surprisingly tranquil. As we pulled in front of her apartment, she slid on her shoes and giggled.

"What are you thinking about, Auntie," I asked.

"Oh, nuthin'. I'm fine, child," she said. "I'm just laughin' 'bout them two old dried-up prunes out there splashing around like jellyfish." Betty laughed in earnest now, holding her side with one hand and slapping her knee with the other.

"Aunt Betty, what is so funny?"

"Well, them old goat rags think that fine man wants either one of them? You should have read the letters he sent *me*!" Betty calmed her laughter long enough to get out of the car and say, "That man is in love with me, Regina! He told me so!"

Betty was corresponding with a convict? I looked at her in horror.

"Oh, don't be so shocked. I'm not a hypocrite. I meant what I said before. Regina, you are young with a family. Your needs are different than mine. His letters kinda keep me company, that's all."

"Does Righteous know?"

"No, she don't. Nobody does, and I would appreciate them *not* finding out, you hear?"

"Yes ma'am," I said. The bird in her hat gave me the evil eye.

I watched Betty hobble to the entrance, turn and wave, then disappear behind the big glass doors of her unit. There was no need to stop her and point out how she was making a fool of herself. That inmate's letters were giving her the thrill of her life. She was excited and felt beautiful for the first time in a long time. Who was I to take that away from her? And besides, Betty probably felt safe within her locked-down love affair. She knew exactly where he was—unlike Vincent, the love of her life. Her Elvis look-a-like couldn't leave or disappoint her.

I understood how Betty felt. I kept reminding myself that I had never even met Rayboy in person—at least Betty had that—but it didn't matter. The sound of his voice, and the call of his words were enough. I was hooked, locked down to a phantom lover that moved me like no other man had ever done before. And something inside me did not want to give it up. I got a charge out of the secrecy of it, the hidden, underground sweetness of it, and I didn't want to let it go. In my mind, Ray was becoming something bigger than life. Like Zoro, who hid behind a mask, Ray was kept from me by cement walls. The perfect combination of fantasy and reality, and he was all mine.

Or was he? Betty's story had proven how one inmate could easily manipulate several relationships at one time. He could make many women feel special. Tell each one that she is the only one, and who would know different? This guy had Betty convinced that she was the one he loved even though he was seeing two of her friends!

Was I being used like that? And worse, was I about to flush a perfectly good relationship with Dennis down the toilet on the say-so of a two-timing convict?

I took the long way home as I examined my options. One thing for sure, Dennis was into some deep shit, and I might need Rayboy's help to get him out of it. But would he help? Ray obviously hated Dennis and for good reason. And what about Dennis? Ray had not brought drugs into my house or put my family at risk—Dennis had! How could I ever trust him?

I had to pull the Chrysler over because my head was beginning to hurt. Righteous is right; I do think too much. I slammed my forehead against the steering wheel in frustration. I didn't know what to do, but I was sure of one thing—I was not going to let some jail dick two-time or three-time me from no damn prison cell! Ray wants to be Zoro? I can be Wonder Woman! Tomorrow, I would leave the museum early and go meet Ray Boden in person at the Montgomery County Prison. I would put a stop to both Ray and Dennis playing me like some puppet.

Tomorrow, this would all come to an end!

CHAPTER 10

◆

Carmela's Story
Jail House Rock

The signs of progress were everywhere at Mirathi. The museum was flourishing, and the foundation was growing in prestige. So many new projects had been set in motion through Dennis' hard work and diligence. The board was so pleased with all of his efforts. Dennis could do no wrong. He was their golden boy, and with his leadership, Mirathi would soon be recognized as one of the largest exhibitors of Africa antiquities in the nation.

The construction of the new wing started last Thursday and promised to be an architectural masterpiece. Patti was busy directing workman through the facility as well as performing her regular duties of answering the phones and shuffling paperwork. She met me at the door with a grimace.

"The installers are here with the new vault, Ms. Jackson," she said, already looking worn thin, and it was only 9 a.m. At Dennis' insistence, the builders reported in at 7 o'clock, so Patti had to come in early.

"A new vault? Who ordered that?" I asked.

"Who do you think?" Patti laid the acquisition paperwork on my desk and gave me a wink.

"Why did Dennis order a new vault?"

"Because we needed a bigger one. And now since the pieces are more valuable, we need better security. We are still responsible for "The Blood of the Moor" necklace, you know. Dr. Dickerson is guarding it with his life. This new vault he ordered is state of the art. Impenetrable! Nobody's getting into it without the code." Patti handed me a brochure concerning the new security system.

"It's really happening, Ms. J. It is really happening. This place is turning into a real state of the art museum. Dr. Dickerson has ordered nothing but the best materials from all over the world! Hebron glass! Italian marble! There is even a buttress outside they say was a piece of the Parthenon! Can you believe that? How does he do it?"

Patti continued to carefully check the acquisition's list when she stopped in her tracks recognizing the name on the next crate. She looked at me then back at the box in total joy.

"They . . . they are Thornhills. We actually have Thornhills. He got Thornhills."

"Yes, Thornhills especially with you in mind," I chirped. Patti leaned over the crate as it was opened and the workers pulled out three stunning portraits from James Thornhill's Journey to the Motherland Collection. Gripping images of Ghanian women and cihildren wrapped in brlliant hues with the ocean lying before them. Tears welled in Patti's eyes.

"They are beautiful," she said. Then, she looked up at me, "It's really happening."

She was right; the place was buzzing with growth and activity—new pieces, an expansion, more employees, and higher security. She had asked, how does he do it? Well Patti, it takes the right connections, a million frequent flyer miles, a cooperative girlfriend and . . . oh yes, more than a few kilos of cocaine and a murderous convict to fence it! That should do it!

Just then, a familiar lizard slithered past me making her way down the freshly carpeted hallway. Her blood red pumps left little indentures in the pile like killer ant holes in the jungle floor. It was that bitch Tina. She ambled close enough to me so that I would know it was her, covetously eyeing the Thornhills then slithering down the hall. She was obviously on her way to Dennis' office.

"What is Tina Benchford doing here?" I asked Patti.

"Oh, Ms. Benchford has an appointment to see Foster this morning," Patti said.

"Not Dennis?" I asked.

"No, not Dr. Dickerson this time. He is not even in yet. He phoned in a while ago. Said he would be late. I thought maybe you were the cause of that," she winked again.

"Not this time," I smiled, although the shrew inside me was itching for Tina to know that Dennis had moved in with me. Impulsively, I followed her down the hall to the senior accountant's office. Just as I was about to call her name, Foster came out of his office to greet her. He ushered Tina in quickly and closed the door behind them. Obviously, they didn't want to be disturbed. What were they talking about in there? Tina had been dismissed weeks ago. She told her staff that she had grown bored with the project and quit, but everybody knew the truth. She had been put out on her ass, but I didn't quite understand why. I'd missed the opportunity to find out and to rub my relationship with Dennis in her face today. I was sure there would be others. I knew I would see Tina Benchford again. I even hoped so. I had to admit that I missed having Tina around. We had our personal problems, but she was a good employee and an admirable opponent. Part of me wanted to salute as she walked pass. What a crazy thought; I started down the maze of hallways with a smile on my face.

I closed the door to my office, which by the way, had been newly furnished as of Friday. Dennis had actually hired an interior designer to redo all of the executive and administrative offices. I reminded him that he had just rewarded me with the corner office a month ago. Everything in it was new! But he insisted, saying that the space needed to reflect the "up-and-coming" me. My design was Mediterranean with bold colors and hanging fabrics. Very romantic and original, like the woman in it, he said and I was flattered.

There was only one concession—*Flowers at Sunset* had to stay. The designer grimaced, saying that it didn't flow with the total scheme. Didn't fit! Was out of place! I had to agree but knew that was exactly why I loved it so. The Hayes piece spoke to me like no other—glistening lilies waving in an ordinary sky. It was the "everyday" clashing with the spectacular. I pondered the artist's vision and wondered if her life was anything like mine. Did she ever feel alone or misunderstood by those who professed to know her well? Did she ever second guess herself or stumble over simple things that surely she should have mastered by now—like lovin' a man, finding her peace or keeping herself safe from her own fantasies? Every now and then, I'd just stand there and look at those audacious flowers—*watch them* as if they were actually moving on the canvas—waving as if to say "hey, I am here! I am here! Can you see me?!" Inspired, I pulled out my cell phone.

"Patti!"

"Yes?"

"Draft a memo to Diane Hayes."

"The artist?"

"Yes."

"Alright," I imagined her pulling out her pad. "What's it saying?"

"Tell her . . . Tell her I see her! That I hear her! And I am here, too."

"Ooookkkaaaay. You sure about that, boss?"

"Positive," and I flipped the phone shut, feeling like a giant.

I rifled through the few task remaining in my daybook. Today, I was getting out of here early. Nothing was going to keep me from seeing Rayboy. On my way into work, I poked my head into the museum cafe. Trisha was busy, so I told CeCe about my plans. She looked puzzled and just nodded at me. Then she asked if I had mentioned my plans to Trisha. Of course I hadn't and saw no need to. Then, CeCe just walked away. I looked up at the wall clock—9:30—I really had to hurry. I didn't know what time visitation started, but I knew it had to be early, and I still had a long drive ahead of me.

"Hey, Mssss. Jackson," Trisha said with a smile. She was wearing her uniform which fit a little more snugly now. The pregnancy was beginning to show, and it also showed on her face. Already young and beautiful, Trisha was radiant. She stepped into my office, closing the door behind her and set a small white paper bag on my desk.

"Hello, Trisha, how are you? Its good to see you," I said knowing that I see her almost every day. Even though we worked on the same job and sincerely liked each other, we were from different worlds. But truth be told, we both knew why we didn't talk more often. It was because the ties between us were wrought with pain and just a little bit of shame. At least for me, and Trisha respected that.

"Oh, its all good. Its all good," she said as she opened the bag, took out two lemon tarts and one cup of coffee. Trisha sash-shayed around my new office, much like the day she first walked into the old one, as if she expected a tour. And just like before, I looked at the clock wondering how I could get her to leave. Her timing was not the best, and I had to go.

"Trisha, this was so sweet of you, but I . . ."

"I brought you two tarts, your favorite, and the coffee is for you, too. The doctor said that women having babies should not drink caffeine, but that's okay because I don't even drink coffee no way, but I do like Pepsi, and I couldn't believe he took me off of that because . . ."

"Trisha . . ."

"I like what you did to this place," she continued. "You got real style and them colors really . . ."

"Trisha, sweetie, I am kind of in a hurry." Trisha continued to mule around the room until she selected a chair to sit in. Then she looked up at me like she was *my* BOSS.

"Mssss. Jackson, let me explain something to you. Sit down, please," she said coyly as if she were pretending to be me. Trisha pointed to the nearest chair, and I did as she asked.

"CeCe told me what you were plannin' to do, and I don't think you know what you doin'."

"Excuse me? I thought you were happy I had a *real man* in my life."

"That was before I knew it was Ray Boden! I hear he is a cold-blooded killer."

"I know what I am doing."

"Ms . . . Regina, have you been to see this man before?"

"Well, no but I . . ."

"Did he tell you to come see him?"

"Well, not at all but . . ."

"Are you even on the list? Have you had a background check or anything?"

"Background check? Well, no, I . . ."

"See, Ms. J, it's like this. You out here free. You been free all your life. You useta telling people what to do and they do it. You useta asking for things and gettin' it. Well, it ain't like that in the joint. It ain't even like that for folks going to visit people up in the joint."

I looked at Trisha dumbfounded. She threw her arms out wide in frustration.

"Now Ms. J, you can do a lot of things, but you cannot go to a prison to see a prisoner who don't want to be seen. That is one of the few rights they got."

I must have looked defeated, so Trisha tried to soften the blow. "And it might not be he don't want to see you. He don't have but so many opportunities to have visitors. He might have to use them to see his lawyer or his PO or anybody he gotta see even if he wanna see you."

Actually, I had seen enough cop shows on TV to know that. None of it mattered. Besides, Ray had a way of making things happen. If he wanted to see me, he would. "Trisha, I appreciate your concern, but I am determined to go see Ray today," I said reaching for my purse again.

"Okay, Miss Thing, have it your way. I do think you in luck though. If I remember right, Monday is visitation day at Montgomery."

"You mean, you can't visit everyday?"

Trisha rolled her eyes to the back of her head. "No, it ain't like a hospital. You can't just go up in there everyday. If it weren't so late, I would hook you up with a transpo."

"What's a transpo?"

"Oh, usually just some enterprising dudes that rent a bus or some vans and pick up people at different stops and take them to the prisons. They post flyers in the projects, and you just sign up. Women pay big bucks—sometimes as much as $100 for a seat. And if you got kids going, well, they just be getting your whole check."

"What time do they leave?"

"Early in the morning, around 5 or 6 a.m., because they be making so many stops."

A sweaty bus ride did not sound very appealing. I would just take my car. I headed for the door.

"So you really going?"

"Yes, I am."

"Then be careful! Montgomery is a rough place, and you will meet some rough types up in there. They been in the news a lot, too, Ms. J. A lot of trouble! Gangs bangin' big up in there over dope, you know what I'm saying?"

"I know what you're saying," I answered, *better than you think.*

Trisha stood up and gave me a hug, a look of worry plastered over her face.

"Please call me when you get back, okay?"

She was sweet, and I appreciated her concern. For one so young Trisha was a tower of kindness and strength. Cowboy was indeed a lucky man! I hugged Trisha back and left her standing in my office. I was on my way to Montgomery.

The sun was shining, yet the day seemed dark. A climate of foreboding seemed to hang in the air. The road to Montgomery was paved with trepidation, and I considered turning back many times. I took Ray's letter out and laid it on the seat beside me. I didn't have to look at it. I had memorized every word.

And I dont want you trying to visit me in no goddamn prison. Dont worry about getting to me. I will get to you.

I folded the letter and replaced it in the envelope. He had claimed to love me. Said I was the sun and the keeper of his soul. Ray knew I was coming. He knew me well enough to know that if he demanded me to stay away from him, I would run to him. I laughed to myself. Rayboy! This man had little to do but study my moves. He was a strategist; probably a high-ranking general in a very powerful gang. What other reason would this Shaka Blu—another general—be after him?

My mind raced through the many phone conversations we had. Between all the romantic poetry, all my candlelight and his music, Ray had been plotting his moves. I realized then that I was going to have to wise up. Men like Dennis and Ray played at love just like they did everything else—to win. I was either going to be a player in the game or a pawn to be played with. I would have to get smart because the stakes were high. If Dennis got caught, I would surely be implicated in his crime. The paper trail would lead straight to my office; not to mention the countless calls from the prison to my home and cell phone. If Dennis didn't stop bringing the drugs in, Ray had made it clear he would kill him. There would surely be an investigation. I laughed to myself, too bad I couldn't get the cell beside Ray's. That would solve everything.

Suddenly I clutched the steering wheel so tight that my knuckles turned white. I really could go to prison, and Dennis really could die at the hands of these convicts. If this was the game, I could not afford to lose. I had to keep going.

Trisha told me about, but I was not prepared for, the scores of buses lining the perimeter of the prison fence. One of the smaller buses parked near me, and I couldn't help but peer up into its high windows. It was filled with women and children crammed three to a seat. Some were standing near the back looking as though they had stood the whole trip. The children looked weary; theirs were the faces of those who had been wakened early for a wonderful adventure then forced to sit through endless torture. The luster of the morning had passed, and now they would have to rekindle their enthusiasm at seeing big brother or daddy again.

And the women! Their faces looked worn yet relieved to be finally at the prison. They adjusted their clothing, pressing out the wrinkles with their palms, and wiped the sandwich crumbs from the children's faces. They swiped at hair, repairing the damage from napping on the bus, leaning against the stranger sitting next to them.

I imagined how this journey may have started for these women. They rose early with the sun, while their children still slept, in order to choose the right dress or outfit to wear. Then, they took their time applying their makeup. After all, they are the face of the outside world to those they visit. While standing in front of the bathroom mirror, they enact what they will say, and what they will do when they first arrive. They always want to make the best impression. Then they will chat about family and friends and news from the outside. They may share a meal, or be allowed to leave a gift. Finally, they prepare to leave, wanting their last words to be meaningful or haunting or just memorable, enough to sustain both of them until the next time.

I watched as they slowly alighted and was surprised to see the diversity of ages and races of the passengers. Mostly Black and Hispanic but some were White, holding the hand of a mixed race child. There were young fly diva project chicks wearing the latest fashions with expertly done nails and hair. There were silver-haired grandmothers who had taken the trip in stride because they had made it so many times before. And there were women with young children that obviously didn't speak any English at all. They stayed to themselves, watching the moves of the others very carefully.

There was one particular Hispanic woman, who got my attention. She was very short, less than five feet, and I almost mistook her for a child. She had on a bright orange and yellow ruffled skirt with a matching blouse and earrings that dangled all the way down to her shoulders. She caught me staring at her, and I tried to look away. Before I knew it, she was standing in my face.

"Hola," she said smiling, obviously glad she had gotten my attention.

"Good morning," I said. "How are you?"

"Fine, and better than chu will be by the end of the day," she laughed, pointing at my feet.

"What do you mean?"

"Chour shoes! Dey are a dead give-a-way. Dis is chour first time visiting a maximum security prison," her English was good, but her accent was thick.

"Oh, I hadn't thought of that," I said. I made the trip rather impulsively." The woman had stopped listening to me and was rummaging around in a big bag she had slung over her shoulder.

"Here," she said, producing a pair of turquoise and fuchsia flip flops with giant rhinestones plastered on them. 5Chu got a lot of walking and standing to do today, chica. Not to mention the searches. Do chu know how many times chu gonna have to take those things off and put dem back on?"

My shoes were rather intricate—Bruno Maglio's with buckles and straps galore! But they matched my silk suit impeccably!

"Thank you, but no! My arches are too high to wear those," I lied, wrinkling my nose at the hideous footwear. Suddenly, another woman standing a few feet away said something in Spanish, and a handful of women laughed in response.

"What's so funny?" I asked the little woman.

"Oh, nothing! She say chour nose is too far up chour ass to know anything about how chour feet gonna feel." The little woman spit several harsh words over her shoulder at them in Spanish then looked back at me.

"Dem hoochies. Don't chu pay any attention to dem. I'm Carmela, chica. Nice to meet chu."

"I'm . . . Gina," I said, never introducing myself to anyone by that shortened name before. I suppose in some way, I did not want to be Regina Jackson today. I wanted to be Gina, Ray Boden's woman. I thought back to the look on Trisha's face when she mentioned his name. Ray's notoriety gave him an odd kind of respect, and for a brief moment, that respect spilled over to me. I was the paramour of a dangerous man.

"You just stick with me, Gina. I will show chu the ropes. Chu be okay."

About that time, thick metal double doors flew open, and about two dozen heavily armed guards came out. The guards spread all over the parking lot conducting random searches of buses and vehicles. Apparently, anything that is not fastened to the vehicle is not allowed inside the prison compound. I had not considered any of this. I prayed they would pass over my car. If not, I would have a long walk in and out of the facility.

After the vehicle searches, we were escorted onto a little tram that took us into the compound. Carmela explained that the visitor's entrance wasn't far, but no one is allowed to just walk up. We were gathered and herded like cattle, then pointed toward the tram. Once inside, everyone had to register and present proper identification. Then, we passed through the metal detector. Some of the younger children looked petrified, clinging to their mothers and burying their faces down in the folds of their skirts. I could only imagine how they felt, and wondered how my own children would have reacted. But then, regretfully, this kind of thing was becoming commonplace for our children. Still, this was a lot more intense for me, more than my trip to Bakersfield with Trisha and CeCe.

Next, we were stuffed into a little glass room that was about six feet by eight feet. We were pushed from room to room in a series of different searches, doors closing behind us as others opened before us. The muffled clanging of the doors was making me a little crazy. They closed with such finality as if they would never reopen. My only solace was that I was a visitor, soon to be getting out of here. I hoped.

After the guards established which prisoner the visitors were there to see, they had to find out where he was housed. This was a long process for some because prisoners are often moved for many different reasons. One older white woman was pulled all the way out of our group and lead into another room without windows. I had visions of the Nazis interrogating innocent people, and then locking them away in concentration camps. I shook the images from my head; his whole experience already felt like something out of *roots*—people being herded and stuffed and labeled and separated and isolated. Even with all the technology, this was like stepping back in time.

Later, we found out that the woman's son had been killed in a brawl in the mess hall the night before. He had only been at Montgomery three weeks. This was her first visit. I looked down at Carmela who was looking up at me with sad eyes and a faint smile.

"It's okay, chica," she whispered, patting my hand.

We were packed onto the mini bus that would take us to the right incarceration unit. To my shock, the bus was surrounded by very aggressive drug-sniffing canines. At first, I wondered how Dennis ever made it in, and then it occurred to me that he would never be subjected to this process. Big Daddy Beau Marshall probably met him at the gates with tea and crumb cakes . . . and maybe a "little honey" on the side! The gates of the prison and the full scope of southern hospitality were wide open for him.

The desk officer asked for my ID and visitors slip. He read my name as if it were written in code, then pulled me out of line from the others and asked me to have a seat. I got scared but since he was wearing a gun, and I wasn't, I did as he asked.

"I am here to see Ray Boden," I said like a madwoman, terrified of being left in a tiny room. My eyes shot to Carmela, who in the space of thirty minutes had become my best girlfriend and tower of strength. She walked up to the guard like she was Andre the Giant and started to spit out demands at him in Spanish. The frustrated guard led her to me and asked her to have a seat.

"Why did they take me out of line?" I asked Carmela.

"I don't know. Are chu a felon of the law?"

"*No!*" I answered emphatically. *Not yet*!

"Den we will just be patient and see, okay, chica?" She squeezed my hand again. "While we wait, you will tell me about chour man, okay?"

I said nothing. As kind as this woman had been to me, no words would come out. I felt them rise up in my throat then stop midway, choking me. But the tears were there, ready to flow. Like a mother, Carmela patted my lap and laughed sympathetically.

"Chu no have to say nothing. We just sit here. I will wait with chu and tell chu about my Milagro. He was just transferred here."

I wanted to ask who Milagro was, but I was afraid that if I opened my mouth all I would do was scream. I was expecting a firing squad to come through the door at any moment. Carmela began to talk. Her voice was like the soothing notes of a familiar song. And she comforted both of us with the telling of her story.

★★★★★

Carmela Maria Fedorna Rodriguez was always the last girl to do everything. She was the last to get hired at the town bakery, and she worked the last shift. At the age of thirty-nine, she was the only one of her friends who was still single, and the last girl to get knocked up by the town gigolo. He told her she was the first girl he had ever loved. Sadly, that was the last time she saw him.

So at the age of forty, Carmela had her first—and last—baby, a boy that she named Milagro. Already an embarrassment to her family, Carmela moved far away from home to raise her baby. She got a job as the confectioner's assistant, making exotic Spanish treats for local restaurants. Carmela dreamed of being a great chef. She worked hard and spent many nights alone, just her and the baby, but she did not care. For the first time, she was first in somebody's life, and that was a great feeling.

Like all good mothers, Carmela sacrificed a lot to give little Milagro everything a child could want. He was first to get a bike and later, first to get his own car. In due time, he was first to drop out of high school, first among his crowd to get arrested and first to go to jail. He was charged with breaking and entering and grand theft. Miraculously, he beat both of those charges but was sentenced to four years for possession. He would serve his time in the State's premiere correctional institution—Melicahess Prison, better known by its occupants as *Hell-of-a-Mess* Prison. It was famous for spontaneous rioting and a convict-organized boxing league.

Carmela was devastated. Her little Milli, as he was affectionately called, was barely eighteen, serving time with men who had committed terrible crimes and loved to fight. Short in stature and small framed like his mother, Milli was destined to suffer the worse kind of treatment imaginable. Carmela was consumed with worry.

As soon as possible, she went to visit her Milli. She paled when she saw him. He looked terrible, as if he had been in a fight with the prison heavyweight champion! He had a black eye, his leg had a huge gash in it and a plug of hair was missing from his temple.

Carmela went home and called everyone from the governor to the town dog catcher, trying to obtain Milli's release. Nothing helped!. Drowning in despair, she went into her kitchen and baked a huge batch of her arroz con leche—rice pudding—as she cried out her anguish over her one and only child.

The next week, Carmela returned, and Milli looked worse than before. She almost fainted. However, the boy swore he was fine and told Carmela not to worry. She gave him a kiss and left him with a little bowl of her famous con leche, flavored with lemon and cinnamon. Carmela sadly returned home and threw herself into the kitchen which was her only comfort. As she cried, she made more con leche for her dear little boy.

The next time Carmela came to see Milli, he looked much better, and he was sitting with a man. He was much older, honed and solid. When Carmela came in, he bowed like a gentleman, offering her a seat in the modest visitation room. He said his name was Hernando, and he was a new friend of Milli's.

Carmela brightened, happy her son had made a friend. She told Hernando what a sweet boy Milli had always been. Hernando's face darkened, however, as he described Milli as a spoiled brat that needed to grow up. Senor Hernando said he could help Milli. Prison is where boys learn to be men or die, he told her. Seeing her shock, he smiled, telling Carmela she was a beautiful and intelligent woman that just needed a little help with her son. He would work with Milli. In return, all he wanted was her company and more of her con leche.

Milli patiently sat as Hernando and his mother talked. Carmela observed this and realized patience was a virtue new to Milli. He must be learning something.

Carmela went home slightly more content than usual. Her son had seemed different. Calmer! Disciplined! She smiled. And what of Senor Hernando? Carmela smiled again; he had called her beautiful and intelligent. Now, that was a first. Carmela began to cry tears of joy and raced to the kitchen to prepare a con leche fit for a king!

Months went by, and Carmela continued to see the positive changes in her son. Milagro was maturing, becoming more respectful and even looked happier. Each time Carmela entered the visitation room, Hernando and Milli would stand, bow courteously, and offer her a seat. Milagro was certainly getting his manhood lessons from a real Spanish gentleman. Carmela found that she and Hernando had many things in common, and after a while, her visits were to see him as much as they were to see Milli.

Hernando began to write Carmela letters telling her about his life back in Madrid. He told her about his career as a matador back in his youth and his boxing training at a gentleman's academy in Seville. Carmela told him about her desire to be a cook and of her love for dancing. They vowed to travel together one day to Spain and dance on the moonlit beaches of Barcelona.

After two years, Carmela's son had grown into someone she could be proud of. It truly was a miracle! Shortly, Milli would be up for parole. Carmela continued her relationship with Hernando and also brought more and more of her con leche to the prison. On her birthday, Carmela, Milli and Hernando celebrated in the visitation room as a family, and quite to her surprise, Hernando asked for her hand in marriage.

This was a first for Carmela, and the last thing she would do was say "no!" The couple toasted with apple juice, and Carmela presented a flowing bowl of con leche to her intended with pride, waving it under his nose.

Hernando scowled. "Ma Dios! What are you going to do with *that*?" he asked, staring wide-eyed at the dessert.

"I am going to feed my husband-to-be his favorite food," Carmela declared.

Hernando looked at Carmela painfully and smiled. "Bella, we do not *eat* the con leche in here. It is *truly awful* for eating! We use it for a very special salve in the training rooms for the boxers! We put it on aching muscles; let it get hard as a rock and voila! The pain is gone! "

Carmela was crushed. Her dreams of being a great cook were dashed, but Hernando's next words were all she ever needed to hear.

"Bella, the love in your con leche healed us. It lead me to you."

Carmela smiled joyfully, tossing the dessert aside. She gazed into the loving eyes of Hernando, the man who had given her a real family. She was happy at last!

Carmela finished her story by inviting me to her upcoming wedding. I was about to accept when suddenly, there was an explosion of bells and alarms echoed throughout the prison compound. The clanging sound of heavy doors surrounded us on all sides. The alarms got louder and louder and lights were flashing, and people in heavy boots were running down the many passage ways. Something was terribly wrong. Guards were shouting, and in the distance we heard the unmistakable sound of gunfire. Panic seized me. I looked at Carmela in confusion.

"Prison riot," she croaked. Her eyes said the rest.

"Carmela, we have got to get out of here!" I screamed. The alarms were deafening now, and gunfire was raging all around us.

"How? We are locked in," she screamed back at me.

I rushed to the door and gave it a simple push, and it swung open like the gate on a picket fence. It had been left open. It had never been locked. I began to shake with terror. Prison doors were not just left unlocked by mistake. I had been sent to this room for a reason. Someone had wanted to get me alone and unprotected.

As the door flew open, smoke poured in. Flames danced in the distance; it was utter chaos. There were men running and yelling, and guards shouting orders. An ominous voice of authority boomed over the address system, bellowing out warnings and procedures as the smoke filled the tiny little room.

I called for Carmela, but she did not answer. I walked backward and bent over into the room with my arms wide thinking that she may have passed out from the smoke. She was nowhere to be found. Had she left me? I walked slowly back to the entrance, my eyes stinging hot. My breathing was sporadic as I fought for air, trying to think what to do. I had to get out! Gasping, I fell to my knees just in time to see the hollow outline of a uniformed figure a few feet in front of me. A guard, I thought, and I reached out to him as a new blanket of smoke fell down over me. But as the figure came closer, I saw that it was not the blue and gray uniform of the guards. It was a bright orange uniform worn by a prisoner.

"Yeah. this is her! This is the one!" he shouted over his shoulder. He was not alone. As he came in closer, another orange clad image, much bigger, darker, came into the room and stood behind him.

"Well, pick her ass up and bring her to me. What the fuck you waiting for, nigga!" the big orange one shouted. "I'm gonna get my fuck on first."

"Do her here. She ain't fightin'. Look at her," said the closer, familiar voice.

"Too much smoke in here, shithead. Do what I said!" ordered the bigger man.

The first inmate came closer and into view, reaching for my elbow to hoist me up. I peered at him through watery eyes and recognized him immediately. It was the same baby face I had seen at the presidential fundraiser. This was Marilyn's jailbird boy toy, Thomas. His face looked harder now, like a criminal who was use to doing criminal acts. I was flat on my backside, scooting childishly away as he locked his fist around my wrist.

"Stop playing games with me, bitch!" he growled as he yanked me up effortlessly from the floor. I was crying earnestly now, swinging at him with my free hand. Quite by accident, I kicked him in the groin, and Thomas let me fall with a howl. I started to crawl around on the floor, trying to find the door when my hand landed in something warm and wet. Water? I brought my hand up to my face and saw it was dripping red! Was I bleeding? I placed my hand back down, landing on a prostrate shoulder and an earring. It was Carmela. I began to scream hysterically, calling her name and shaking her, hoping she would answer.

In the middle of my fit, I vaguely heard a scuffle above my head. Men were cursing at each other, throwing blows. The few chairs in the room went crashing against the walls, and arms and legs were flailing within inches of my face. There were three men in the tiny room now. One, which I could identify as Thomas, was lying unconscious on the floor near my feet. The other two fought like gladiators, each taunting the other to throw the next blow.

"That all you got, muthafucka? That all you got?"

"I shoulda killed you when I had the chance!"

"Your chance now, Shaka . . . or you too busy beatin' women?"

"Boden, you already dead and don't know it."

"Then let's finish this, bitch!"

Still blinded by the smoke, I could hear bodies clashing together. And I recognized a voice that sounded like music to my ears.

"Ray? Ray!" I screamed, struggling to get on my feet.

"Gina, baby stay down!" he yelled as a fist cut through the black air.

Suddenly, there was a thud and total silence. For a full minute, I was unable to speak, sure that Rayboy lay somewhere in the fog, either dead or unconscious. I had to find him. Then realization hit; if Rayboy was dead, the inmate who killed him was still in the room looking for me.

My strength was waning, and I could not see at all. Soon, there would be no air to breath. I would have to get on my feet and make a run for it if I were going to get out alive. Maybe I could find help. Maybe Ray wasn't dead! I had to try to escape. With the aid of the metal bench in the corner, I pulled myself up and flung my legs toward the door. I took three steps before I felt myself losing consciousness, and a pair of strong tender arms folded around me.

"Gina, sweet baby, I told you not to come. I told you not to come," Ray moaned.

"I had to come . . . for you." I struggled to speak, the smoke burning my throat and nose. I tried to open my eyes but couldn't. Ray threw my arms around his neck and lifted me gently into his arms. I laid my hand on his face and touched him. The man I never thought I would touch. Tears of joy singed my hot cheeks. I felt his lips against my skin, lips I thought I would never kiss. My last conscious memory was of being nestled safe against his chest and hearing him whisper my name over and over again. Like music.

"Gina, my sweet Gina."

Hours later, I woke up lying comfortably in my own bed in the sanctuary of my own home. I had been bathed, and my hair had been washed. I wore a clean cotton nightgown, and there were flowers in a vase on my night stand. Had it all been a dream? Had I not gone to the prison at all? Then my soar eyes focused on the images in the room. From left to right—my silk suit laid in a sooty pile in the corner of the room, ruined, along with my shoes. Next, there was my daughter, Zeta, looking very worried and holding a glass of water in her favorite SpongeBob glass. Then, there was my Aunt Hazel who was undoubtedly called in especially for me. And then there was Righteous, standing at the foot of the bed scowling with her Bible in her hand. She had probably prayed me back to the land of the living just so she could kill me.

"Praise God, she lives," Righteous growled, beating her Bible against the bed post. My mother and aunt were both big women and had probably wrestled through the task of cleaning me up. Now, they looked ready to beat me black and blue. I knew they only held their tongues because Zeta was in the room, close to tears.

"Mamma, what happened?" she asked softly, pressing the glass of water into my hand.

Gingerly, I tried to sit up as I eyed the women. I didn't know exactly how much they knew about what had happened, and I didn't want to say too much.

"Where . . . where is Dennis?" I asked, trying to change the subject.

"Mamma, why are your clothes all smokey? Why did those men carry you into the house? And . . . there was blood on your hands! What . . ." Zeta's voice had risen an octave which meant she was about to lose it.

"Zeta, baby, I . . ." I tried to explain.

"Your mother was with me," a sultry southern drawl came from the far corner of the room, and the women parted so that I could see who it came from. Marilyn Marshall sat on the over stuffed chaise, legs crossed and poised, as she absent-mindedly poked at the items on my vanity. She looked at Zeta and smiled.

"Your mother, being the sweet darling that she is, tried to help me get ready for my garden party tonight. Well, I got too close to one of the tiki torches and damn near burnt my fool house down. Your mamma saved the day. I had my Mexican yard boys bring her home. All wetbacks, you know. Those *jumpin' beans* sure do know what to do with a hoe and a bag of dirt. Had that fire out in no time." Marilyn shook out her long blonde hair and checked her nails as my family looked at her stupefied.

"And . . . and how is Carmela?" I asked shyly.

"Oh, she is just fine. Nothing a little tequila and a taco can't fix. You know how *those people* are. Don't get me wrong, I love those little *border-jumpers* but after they take a drink, you gotta count the silver, you know what I mean?" Marilyn winked at me slyly, and I smiled painfully. She was covering for me like my best girlfriend, but she was still a redneck bigoted slut.

"So you weren't at de prison?" Righteous asked.

"Prison? Why do you ask?" I looked away from my mother. She could always tell when I was lying.

"'Cause you were rambling on 'bout a prison while you were sleepin'," Righteous said, hands on both hips.

"No, she said 'prism'," Marilyn said. It's the name of my ladies' garden club. Like it?"

Mamma and Aunt Hazel had that look they get when they think the cashier shortchanged them at the corner store. Marilyn smiled her sweetest smile and came to sit beside me on the bed.

"I think this gal needs some rest now, don't you?" Marilyn said. Righteous and Zeta both nodded.

"We'll go downstairs and start dinner," Aunt Hazel said, pushing my mother toward the door. "Ms. Marshall, are you staying for dinner?" she asked, as they were leaving.

"Oh, no deep fried chitlins and watermelon for me tonight, ladies. Although I bet two *Aunt Jemimas* like you can cook up a storm!"

"What did you say!??" I imagined horns popping out of Aunt Hazel's head!

"Nothing!" I shouted a little too loudly. "You two go on downstairs. We'll be alright." My voice was still very raspy. Righteous and Hazel looked at the little white woman from the corners of their eyes, wondering if they should leave me alone in my depleted state with such a wacko. Very slowly, they headed down the stairs with Zeta in tow. Marilyn laughed gaily, a sound that reminded me of Tinkerbell.

"You enjoy doing that, don't you?" I asked.

"Immensely," she said.

"Thank you for helping me today," I said.

"You're welcome," she said.

Slowly my eyes began to fill with tears. Marilyn rose to close the bedroom door then returned to my bedside.

"Marilyn, I was so close to him. I was with him. What happened?"

Marilyn closed my hand inside of hers to comfort me. "Baby, they are in the middle of a war. The gangs are feuding in there just like they're feuding out here. They are fighting over their turf. Some are fighting over drugs and money. But mostly, they're just fighting. That's what they do." She took out her cell phone and flipped it open.

"I didn't know it would be like that. I didn't know they would be like caged up animals. I . . . I didn't know that . . . that I . . ."

"That you loved him," she said the words for me.

"Here," she said, handing me her cell phone. "It's for you."

"But I didn't hear it ring."

"I dialed. *Here*," she said again pushing the phone into my hand.

"Ray?" I asked excitedly.

"Who else, silly," she laughed and again rose from the bed. She walked over to the window, raising it a bit to let in the cool evening air.

"Gina, babygirl, I was so worried about you! Are you okay?" The sound of Ray's voice illuminated the room, filling it with joy.

"Yes! Yes!" I exclaimed. "Oh, Ray, I love you so much."

"Gina, you should not have come here. This is the last place you need to be. Shaka is dope crazy, you hear me? You gotta be careful. He got soldiers everywhere, and you can't trust nobody. Got that? He knows something is up. Shaka knows Dickerson is trying to pull out, and he ain't havin' that shit! Baby, you gotta listen to me! Dickerson don't know who he messin' with. Shaka is stone cold crazy. He will do anything to win. Anything."

Ray seemed to be rattling on, and I was only half listening. I was just glad to hear his voice and know that he was fine. I swung my legs off the side of the bed, instantly feeling better. I had been with Ray today, and suddenly that was all that mattered.

"Ray, baby, you held me in your arms." All kinds of romantic images were running through my head. Ray, the fireman carrying me to safety. Ray, the dragonslayer! Ray, the martyred hero!

Rayboy sighed! "Yeah, baby, I did and you as phat and fine as I knew you would be. But listen to me . . ."

"And you kissed me. You saved me."

"Baby, I need you to pay attention . . ."

Ray lectured on about me being careful and talking sense into Dennis, telling me to get him to leave town for a while. I was willing to do anything he said as long as he would just say that he loved me.

"Ray, I need to hear you say it."

"Baby . . . say what?"

"You know, say that you love me," I mooed, gliding over to stand beside Marilyn at the window. We looked out together as we saw Rakim getting out of a car. He had gone with friends after school to see that new marital arts movie that he had missed on Sunday. His friends drove off, and he gazed up at the window. He waved at me, and I waved back, trying to figure out why Rayboy was still talking so excitedly.

"Ray, honey, calm down. It's over! We're okay! You beat that guy up today, didn't you? Everything is fine."

"Gina, are you listening to me? It ain't fine! We did not end anything today. We started it! It's on! Gina, you gotta listen to me!"

But I had stopped listening. As Ray spoke, a champagne-colored Electra 225 swerved around the corner barreling down toward my house. Rakim turned to face it and in seconds, a shot rang out, something was thrown from the car, and Rakim, my beautiful son, lay bloody and motionless on the ground.

CHAPTER 11

◆

Rosetta's Story
The $1.5 Million Con

It had been a drive-by shooting. A drive-by shooting in my nice suburban Maryland upper middle-class neighborhood! It all seemed hard to believe but here we were, on the third floor of Holy Cross Hospital watching my son fight for his life. Rakim had been critically injured, shot in the chest just above his heart. He had lost a lot of blood. But he was strong, the doctor had said, and would recover with plenty of care and rest.

Last night had been touch and go! Rakim had wandered in and out of consciousness, fighting a fever. His vital signs had been erratic. This morning, the doctors said he was stabilizing, and I should go home and get some rest. I couldn't. I was glued to that chair and had no intention of leaving that hospital without my baby.

I watched the nurses tiptoeing in and out of the private room. When they were in the hallway and thought I could not hear, I listened to them talking about my boy.

Just another one of those street thugs, they said.

When will they ever learn? they said.

All they think about is drugs, sex and gangs.

Parents don't half raise these kids. What do they expect?

But Rakim wasn't "just another street thug." He wasn't half raised. He came from a good caring family. I had given every ounce of my life's blood to give him the best that life had to offer. I had taught him right from wrong. I had shown him a world of endless possibilities and taught him to do good and treat people well. Rakim was a good boy destined to be a fine young man. This should have never happened.

Righteous had called Anna to come take care of the house and stay with Zeta while she and the aunts took turns sitting with me at the hospital. I knew they were trying not to leave me alone. In case the worse happened! Righteous asked if we should call Rakim's father. Jabari should be here, she said, and I suppose he should. I don't know why I didn't pick up the phone and call him. There were just too many issues still between us, I guess. I didn't even think about calling Stephen.

Of course, Dennis had come, too! He was more a mess than any of us. Racked with guilt, all he did was pace the floor, wringing his hands and mumbling to himself. He was making me a nervous wreck. I knew he felt responsible for what had happened, and I knew there was something he was not telling me. When Marilyn and I gave our statements to the police, we both reported seeing something fly out of the car window. It should have landed in the front yard, but the police found nothing. I kept looking at Dennis, and he could hardly make decent eye contact with me. He was hiding something. But then, he was good at that.

Night turned into day and then turned back into night again as I sat, keeping vigil in Rakim's room. And then, at about midnight, there was a timid knock on the door. Righteous peeked her head in quietly and gave me a gentle smile.

"How you holdin' up, girl?"

"Fine. Fine" I lied. All I could think about were the events of the last few weeks, and how I had let this poison into my life. Surely, God was punishing me for the choices I had made. Silently, in the dark, I begged

God not to make my son a sacrifice for my wanton selfish deeds. And did He hear me? I didn't know. I hadn't prayed in so long. I wept tears from my heart that no one else could see. Was there forgiveness for a mother who had invited destruction into the lives of her own children? Was there redemption or enough love to make this right? I just didn't know.

"There is someone here to see you," Righteous said, and a tall slender figure, looking just like my mother, slid through the door. It was my sister, Rosetta.

"Oh my God!" I whispered, finally rising from the chair and sailing into her arms. Rosetta and I hadn't seen each other in years, and I hadn't realized how much I had missed her until just then. We held on to one another, rocking back and forth, and in her arms, I allowed myself to cry. I wept huge alligator tears—buckets of them—until my chest ached. All the while, Rosetta whispered loving things into my ear, reassuring me that everything would be just fine. And I felt that it would be, now that she was here.

"You just fly in?" I asked, reaching for a kleenex.

"Yes, about an hour ago. Mamma and your Dr. Dickerson picked me up from BWI," she tilted her head a bit and looked at me from the corner of her eye. "Reggie, I like him. What you waiting on, girl?"

"Roz, It's so complicated." We had slipped back into our childhood pet names so easily. "Dennis is great. He . . . I . . ." I stopped, shaking my head. There was so much to say yet with my sister, words were hardly needed.

Rosetta and I walked over to the hospital bed. Rakim, was nearly six feet tall, but now he seemed so small and vulnerable, much like the baby I had brought home fourteen years earlier wrapped in a blanket my sister had made.

"Roz?"

"Yeah?" she answered as she ran her fingers through Rakim's hair, pressing light kisses on his forehead.

"Do you remember that baby blanket you made Rakim way back then?"

She laughed to herself. "Jesus, I remember that thing!"

"It was soooo big. Righteous wanted to hang it from the ceiling and use it as a room divider!" I laughed for the first time in days. "We put Rakim in it that first time and *lost him*! Remember?"

"I had been knitting that thing for months and didn't know when to stop!"

"And it was bright Big Bird yellow with little pink flowers on it! What were you thinking? You knew I was having a boy!" We were both laughing pretty hysterically for a moment until I looked into my sister's eyes and saw she had stopped. She brought her attention back down to her nephew.

"Actually, Reggie, the truth is, it wasn't for Rakim. I was knitting that thing for you," she said softly.

"For me!?"

"Yeah, we were so young, practically teenagers. When you and Jabari told me you were having a baby . . . well . . . I just began to picture you sitting there holding him with a beautiful shawl around your shoulders. Just like that picture of the Madonna Big Mamma use to keep over her bed." Roz looked up at me. "I knew you would be the perfect mother."

Rosetta's face turned stern as she remembered.

"And I knew Jabari wasn't going to stick with you. No sir, he just didn't have it in him. I made you the shawl so that you would know that you were always covered—just like the Madonna. Raising a baby by yourself but never alone."

I was clutching the bed rails as tight as I could, not wanting to cry anymore. I looked across the bed at my sister and wondered how I had made it all these years without her. But like she'd said, she had me covered. And if my sister's love had never left me, maybe God was still there, too.

The nurse came in to take Rakim's temperature. Rosetta and I sat in the corner and waited for her to give us an update on his condition. It was good just to sit there with her, just to be in her presence again. It seemed that my sister was always pulling up roots, moving from place to place and never getting settled. She went from one great job to the next and for a long time, I envied her mobility. She had never married nor had any children. More importantly, Rosetta never came home.

My sister and I stayed with Rakim all night, talking about the past and making up for lost time. Before we knew it, the sun was coming up again, and there was another knock at the door. This time, it was Righteous and Anna. Rosetta looked at me slyly.

"Reggie, we thought it might be a good idea for you to go home and get some rest. Mamma brought your housekeeper here. She can watch Rakim for a while."

Go home? My housekeeper? Righteous was sure good at getting things her way. It was obvious I was being ambushed, and I couldn't fight them all.

"Who is home with Zeta?" I asked.

"Its Wednesday, chile. She be at school. Against my betta judgment, I let dat crazy white woman friend of yours help out in your time of need. She sent her limo to take Zeta to school dis morning, and that grandchile of mine 'bout had a fit jumpin' up and down when it pull up!"

"Besides," Rosetta continued, "You sure as hell need a good bath! And it wouldn't hurt to brush your teeth and comb that mop head of yours either," she teased.

"Okay, okay. I get it."

Anna came in, with the Bible in hand and purposely took a seat at Rakim's bedside.

Righteous whispered to me smiling, "She gonna call forth *de Word*. Don't you worry 'bout a ting. Ya'll run along now." Righteous practically pushed us out of the room. Clad in black from head to toe, Anna looked like a bible-thumping-fire-and-brimstone-spitting arch angel that would beat you to death with the Cross of Jesus! Death was not coming anywhere near my son on her watch!

Rosetta and I took a thirty-mile detour leaving the hospital and going home. We drove through the old neighborhood and had breakfast at the Florida Avenue Grill. We stopped at one of the black-owned shops near Howard University, and Rosetta bought some oils and a retro poster of Angela Davis from the movement, complete with giant afro and leather jacket. We walked pass Clifton Terrace and our old high school and talked about how much the Northwest had changed. Of course, we got around to talking about Dennis. I told Roz about our work together at Mirathi and about the art foundation. I gave vivid descriptions of his gifts to me and the children and all the beauty he had brought into my life. I listened to my own words and realized all of it was true. I did have a beautiful life, and Dennis was a big part of it.

I didn't talk about the ugly part. She asked about old friends and family. I didn't mention my "new friend" or the botched prison visit. Then we got around to what was on both of our minds.

"You ever hear from daddy?" Roz asked.

"No," I said flatly. "*And don't care if I ever do*," was the rest of that sentence.

"Nothing?" she asked again.

"*Nothing*!" I snapped back at her.

"Okay, okay," she said, not wanting to upset me, knowing that my nerves were already shot. The rest of the drive home was pretty quiet. I knew she wanted to talk about Daddy, but I still wasn't ready. I had read enough self-help books to know that a lot of my issues with men stemmed from my abandonment issues with my father. But I had a life and a mortgage and a career and a family and two men making me crazy, and no time to dwell on the past. Little did I realize that the past was dwelling in me.

When we pulled into my driveway, there was a big silver limousine parked in front of my house. Marilyn Marshall sat on a lawn chair, neck extended and legs stretched out, sunning herself for all the neighbors to see. We were both tired and had eaten too much, and Rosetta rudely rushed past Marilyn, heading into the house.

"How's your boy?" she drawled.

"Doing better, thank you! And thanks for all your help today. Where is Zeta?" I asked.

"Oh, she had a meeting with The Mix this afternoon. Zeta is in The Mix," Marilyn said, obviously very impressed. "What a social-climbing little minx she is. You know, I remember the day they never would have let a colored girl on their membership rolls. My, how things have changed! Anyway, I had my driver drop her off in my car. Hah! You should have seen those girls heads turn!"

I never knew how to respond to Marilyn Marshall half of the time. She was the kind of woman I had every reason to hate. But I had to admit that she was kind and thoughtful and had already pulled my chestnuts out of the fire more than once. I simply nodded and invited her in.

"Marilyn, this is my sister, Rosetta. Rosetta, this is Marilyn Marshall."

"Nice to meet you, Mar . . ." Roz took one good look at Marilyn and stopped in mid sentence. She backed away as if she had seen a ghost. She almost tripped over my ottoman and lost a shoe trying to get away from us. Marilyn just stood there, smiling coyly in that little irritating way she had while Roz made a fool of herself.

"Roz, what is the matter with you?"

"I think your sister and I have met," Marilyn said.

"Oh, I doubt that. Roz hasn't lived here in years," I said, still stunned at my sister's behavior. "Roz, you may recognize Marilyn though. She is a genuine title-holding beauty queen," I said trying to lighten the mood.

Roz looked as if she were about to faint. Impulsively, she almost ran to the other side of the room, pretending to get a closer look at my Moroccan tapestry.

"Oh, I don't think Roz and I met here in the DC area at all. Let me think . . . it was quite a long while ago . . . I think the first time was actually in Carolina down in the tobacco belt." I could tell Marilyn was painfully drawing this out at my sister's expense.

"What's going on here?" I demanded.

"Nothing, Reggie," Rosetta said. My sister stood with her back to me, taking inventory of the room. She saw the things I had described—the photographs, the Muzi, murals, and the works of art that Dennis had brought back from all over the world. They seemed to make her sad. Why would pictures of my life make her so sad?

"Bullshit!" I said. "Roz, tell me what's going on."

"*Rozzy,* are you going to tell her or shall I?" Marilyn seemed to slither across the room to where Rosetta was standing. She got close enough behind her to pluck a piece of lint from off of her sweater, and I could see Roz flinch under her touch.

"Okay, stop this," I yelled. "Somebody better start talking."

"Alright then! I guess I'll tell the story. I like telling stories. It's a rather entertaining tale about a very married up-and-coming tobacco executive, a torrid love affair, and $1.5 million worth of stolen merchandise. That about cover it, sugar?" Marilyn slung at Roz's back. Roz was really starting to squirm, and Marilyn was enjoying this too much. Roz finally turned to look at me, defeat and shame in her eyes.

"That's enough out of you!" she snapped at Marilyn, then to me she said, "I'll tell you what happened. I'll tell you all about it. Then you will understand why I never came back home, why I never married or had a family of my own."

"Roz, I don't understand."

"Linnnwwwood PPPPride," Marilyn sang, spindly arms folded in front of her.

"Lin . . . Linwood Pride?" I had heard that name before. "Not that guy we went to high school with. I thought he was dead!"

Roz left Marilyn standing by the wall and lead me to the sofa to have a seat. Then, as if I were her priest, she slowly confessed all, casting off a burden she had carried for much too long.

★★★★★

Linwood Pride was the pride of Cardoza High School in Northwest D.C. He was tall and handsome, captain of the basketball team and star long-distance runner on the track team. He was an Olympic hopeful until he got hurt. In an inspiring act of heroism, Linwood shattered his kneecap while rescuing an old man from a burning building. Already an academic standout and now a local hero, Linwood was awarded a full scholarship to the college of his choice.

Rosetta Lambert had a huge crush on Linwood, and everybody at Cardoza knew it. Every decision she made in high school was somehow based on the comings and goings of Linwood Pride. Rosetta tried to take the same classes or at least be on the same hall with him every day. She would plan her wardrobe based on how many times she would see Linwood in a day. She even chose her college major based on his interest and after much hard work and sacrifice, Roz followed him to the same university, North Carolina A & T. Go, Aggies!

Linwood was on straight scholarship—a free ride for four years—while Roz had to take every job that came her way just to make ends meet. Linwood's popularity also followed him to Carolina. Roz had to work equally as hard to keep up with his social schedule—showing up at the right parties, joining the right clubs—so that he would hopefully one day do more than just notice her. And one day, he did! Their senior year, Linwood stopped by her dorm on regular bases. Roz couldn't believe her luck and couldn't explain what had happened to make Linwood take such an interest in her. He even walked Roz to her room on several occasions just to be invited in. They studied together. He was courteous to her friends. And three months after graduation, Linwood Pride married Roz's roommate, Lynette Henderson.

Roz spiraled downward after that. She took a mediocre job in her field, making much less than she was worth, just to keep a low profile. In the meantime, Linwood went on to graduate school, soared in his profession and set records in production for his company, a leading tobacco producer down south. Lynette, his beautiful wife, became a newscaster, and her picture was plastered on billboards up and down the beltway. Roz read news article after news article about their success. She even clipped the birth announcement when Linwood and Lynette had twin girls and then again when Lynette gave birth to the first baby born in the new year. A darling little boy that Linwood named after himself! Roz was drowning in heartache and jealousy.

Then one day, the perfect little Pride Family seemed to hit a brick wall. Lynette's job got more demanding, and she had to move back to DC full time, taking the children with her. A year later, Linwood was charged with trading insider secrets and extortion. He was sentenced to three years in prison.

Roz was devastated. It's Lynette's fault, she told herself. She should have never left Linwood alone. He is the kind of man who always needs a woman by his side. I would have never left him, she told herself. Impulsively, she packed her bags and headed for North Carolina.

Linwood was genuinely glad to see her. Now in prison, his friends had all but turned away from him. He thanked Roz for being a true friend. He said he didn't know why he had never realized it before. Roz took a leave of absence to be by Linwood's side. They got better acquainted, and Roz was there the painful day that the divorce papers came. "What would

I do without you?" he confessed. "I love you, Roz." That was all she ever wanted to hear.

Roz flew back to work and spoke to her supervisors in her department. Although less than aggressive, she was naturally talented and had received several promotions within the company. She told the vice presidents all about Linwood. Of course, they had heard of him and had tracked his success over the years. Roz boldly suggested that Linwood be entered into the state work release program that the company had taken part in as a service to the community. The board was skeptical, noting that the program was mainly for blue collar workers in the factories, certainly not executives. But Roz was insistent, pressing the point that a man like Linwood would be highly sought after when he was released. So, on her recommendation, the well-known international Fortune 500 tobacco conglomerate had Linwood extradited to Virginia and immediately employed.

But there were conditions. For the first year, Linwood had to remain behind bars at night. That was inconvenient for the two of them, but Roz did everything she could to make Linwood more comfortable. Linwood didn't ask for much—except cigarettes and *lots* of them. Roz didn't understand how one man could smoke so many. She hadn't noticed that Linwood smoked at all. But then, he was such a gentleman; he would never smoke around her.

After that year, Linwood had proved himself to the tobacco executives, and Roz was given another promotion for demonstrating superior savvy and a good business acumen. Roz became Linwood's supervisor; they were working side by side just as she had dreamed.

Being the civic-minded man he was, Linwood spent many hours at the prison "giving back" to his community. He donated his time and other "miscellaneous items" to the inmates hoping to help rehabilitate those less fortunate than himself. He had gotten back on his feet, and prosperity was blooming everywhere in his life—a Rolls Royce here, a Spanish villa there.

Linwood Pride was back in the game. Roz was so proud of him and herself. She had proven that true love conquers all.

Everything was going just great until one day the corporate VPs called Roz into the office to give her some startling news—and an ultimatum. Linwood had been caught smuggling cigarettes into the prison. *Lots* of them! Roz just laughed. Is that all, she asked. If it's a problem, I will pay for them. Fine, they said and handed her a bill for $1.5 million. Apparently, Linwood had been selling the cigarettes on the side in the prison. Cigarettes are like currency on the inside. Pity Roz had no idea! She made a deal to pay every penny back if the company would not press charges. The company agreed, and then summarily fired both of them. Roz watched all her hard work of climbing the corporate ladder go down the drain.

Linwood apologized to Roz, stating he didn't know what had come over him. Perhaps he just needed a good woman by his side. Two days later, he went back to his wife.

★★★★★

My sister told that whole story with her head hanging down in her lap. All I could do was look at her with my mouth hanging open. *$1.5 million?!* My sister was responsible for paying that back so *somebody else's man* wouldn't have to go back to jail?—where he belonged?? I wanted to beat her silly!

"You know, he set that fire," Marilyn was busy standing in front of the mirrored wall I had in my living room, playing with her hair.

"What fire?" I asked incredulously.

"When he was a teenager. Yeah, he saved the man alright, but he also started the fire. He was 'tutoring' the man's granddaughter, and things got out of control. While they were screwing, they knocked over a candle they had used to light his bong. They set the house on fire."

"How do you know so much, Marilyn?" I asked.

"Honey, I know everything about everybody who commits a white collar crime on this coast. And I know everything about everybody who pulls down any real money in this town. Yeah, your sister was in real high cotton for a while. So was her boyfriend! I saw them at a few cocktail parties on The Hill. Don't get me wrong, they looked real cute together, but it would take a fool not to see Linwood Pride for what he really was."

"That's right. A real fool," Roz said finally raising her head. She looked at me and sighed. "I am well employed. My record did not follow me. I have paid back almost half of it. I cashed in my 401K and . . ."

"Rosetta! It would be easier to kill him and let his wife pay the balance with his life insurance!" I screamed.

Roz looked at me horrified, her bottom lip trembling as the words formed in her mouth. "But . . . Reggie . . . you don't understand. *I love him.*"

In an instant, I understood why my sister had not come home. There was no way me or my mother would have tolerated any of this madness! Ever! Roz had sacrificed her entire life for a man that was not worthy of her at all.

Roz jumped off the sofa in frustration, running her hands through her hair and completely ruining her hairdo. She stared wide-eyed at me and Marilyn.

"You don't know what it's like to love a man beyond reason," she lamented as she paced the floor. "To love a man so desperately that nothing else matters."

Both Marilyn and I were silent, knowing we were guilty of the same thing.

"I knew it was wrong. I knew it didn't make any sense. But loneliness sometimes leads to desperation and a woman will do anything . . ."

"Anything," Marilyn said sadly, tucking a wayward curl back in place.

"Anything to be with a man," Roz continued. "Even a sensible, rational woman. I cannot tell you how many times I thought about what I was getting into. How many times I sat down to weigh . . . the pros and cons . . ."

"Yes, the pros and cons," Marilyn seemed to be looking through herself in the mirror, and I understood why. As unbelievable as Roz's story was, we were all living out the same drama. The same pain! Roz's words echoed through both of us.

"In my heart, I knew he was making a fool of me. I prayed that I was wrong. I wanted to believe the best about him. I only wanted to see the best."

"You saw what you wanted to see," I said.

"She saw what she needed to see," Marilyn said turning toward us and away from her own image. "When you are with him, you feel complete, whole and nothing else matters."

"And even when you are not with him, the thought of him being locked away from you—locked away by marriage, distance or prison walls—makes you want him more."

"And you know it's wrong."

"And you know it's wrong."

"And you know it's wrong," we all said.

"But you can't help it." Roz looked more tired than I had ever seen her, yet there was an aura of peace that emanated from her. She was glad she had let this go. Glad for the release! Now, she could finally start to heal. But I was still very worried about her.

"Roz . . ."

"Reggie, I am exhausted. I don't want to talk about this anymore. All I want to do is sleep."

"You can't live your life like this, locked down to this man. Mamma would die if she . . ."

"Oh pleeeaassse don't tell Mamma!" she pleaded. "It would break her heart."

"*Our* mother would cut Linwood Pride into teeny weeny little pieces and serve him up over curried rice," I said. We both tried to smile.

"I'm going upstairs now," she said quietly. Then to Marilyn she said, "Ms. Marshall, it was good to see you again. I mean that sincerely."

"Good luck to you, babydoll." Roz headed upstairs to the guest room.

Marilyn picked up her purse and headed for the door. "I'm leaving, Regina. My driver will pick your little girl up and bring her home. Don't you worry about that." She checked her make up one more time before she opened the door. Now it was my turn to give some advice.

"You really have to end this thing with Thomas. I know you think this is just a game to get back at your husband, but he is dangerous. Thomas is like some crazy little Chucky doll who . . ."

"Thomas is nothing," Marilyn said, her hand trembling as she attempted to correct her lipstick. "It's the other one I can't let go of . . . I . . . ," and she walked away without finishing her sentence, too ashamed to say more.

Suddenly, I felt very tired. The events of the last few days were coming down on me hard. My legs felt like lead weights as I climbed the stairs to my room. I need to call the hospital, I thought, and check on Rakim. If he was okay, I'd take my family's advice by taking a shower and going to bed. I grabbed the rail and pulled myself up, one step at a time. The family photographs on the wall seemed to pass slowly by me like an old home movie. Zeta had done such a great job with this little project. I had to make sure I told her so; she was growing up so fast. I had been so busy; those photos would have stayed in the box another ten years if it had been left up to me.

There were pictures of all of us at the last reunion and at the state fair. And in a small bamboo frame I had not noticed before, there was an old baby picture of me. I laughed at first, thinking that the toddler in the picture was Zeta, but it was definitely me, and I was sitting on my father's knee. My father! A ghost of a presence in my life! Another example of men abandoning me! I turned my head away and moved on.

I opened the door to my room and was amazed at how dark it was for the middle of the day. The curtains were drawn, and the shades were pulled, and little strips of light peeked through the sides. It was dreary, even for sleeping, so I stepped over to the window to lift the shade.

"Please don't," said a voice from behind me. Dennis sat in the corner of the room beside the bed. He was unshaven, and his clothes looked as if he had slept in them. He looked terrible. I knelt beside him and reached for his hand,

"Baby, what's the matter?" I asked, knowing but needing to hear it from him, and I knew he needed to say it.

"Rakim," he said softly. I went into an instant panic.

"Oh God, did the hospital call!! Is he alright!!"

"Yes, he's fine. Doing much better! I just got off the phone with his doctor. He is doing just fine." Dennis squeezed my hand in his to reassure me. "I spoke with Anna, too. She said his color is back and he is sleeping peacefully."

I could have danced if I had not been so tired. Instead, I leaned back on Dennis with a slump and let him hold me. He was full of tension, but I did not ask why. I gave him time to tell me.

"Regina, baby, this is all my fault. The drive-by was no random shooting. Those men meant to come here. They meant to hurt us."

"I know, tell me. Why did they come?" I asked.

"They were not trying to kill Rakim. It was a warning."

"How do you know?"

"Because they left something behind," Dennis reached under the bed and pulled out a rolled up newspaper.

"*The Post?*" I asked, amazed.

"No, not just *The Post*," Dennis unrolled the newspaper and out came a knife covered with blood.

"Oh my God! *Oh my God!*" I wailed. "The blood . . . whose blood is it? Is it Rakim's?"

Dennis shook his head. "No, I know whose blood it is. It belongs to Shaka Blu."

"Shaka? That lunatic in prison?! What is his blood doing on a knife in my house??"

"On one of my visits to the prison, I told the inmates about the *Legend of the Blood of the Moor*. I told them about the princess and the war that has fought to claim her. We talked about the Moors—how they were great warriors—and how they would cut themselves before a battle as a show of strength. Then send the knife with their own blood to their enemies."

I was confused. "What does a moldy old legend have to do with us!" I yelled. Dennis' chin fell.

"Shaka is calling me out. He knows I want to stop being his mule, and he doesn't like it. He sees it as a betrayal and in his army, there is only one way out."

Dennis stared straight ahead at the wall as he spoke to me. I could tell that he had been thinking about his next move all day. He knew he had made a terrible mistake; he was in league with dangerous men who now wanted to kill him. He knew that staying in or getting out, he could wind up dead.

"What are you going to do?"

Dennis forced a smile and kissed me on the forehead. "The only thing I can do. Protect my family."

I had no idea what that meant. I started to shake all over. Dennis stood and helped me up. We held each other tight and kissed like it could be for the last time. Then, he pulled away dragging me over to my bathroom door.

"You need a bath, woman," he tried to grin. He hated seeing the worry on my face. It hurt him even more knowing he had put it there.

"So everybody keeps telling me," I grinned back. I laid my palm against his cheek and looked into his eyes. "Are you alright?"

"I am more than alright," he answered. "Take that shower, and I will prove it to you," Dennis said winking and nodding toward the bed.

I grimaced a bit, knowing I did not feel up to having sex, but it would be nice to just sleep in a man's arms.

"I'll be waiting for you," he said, diving onto the bed. I laughed to myself. He would probably be asleep himself within ten minutes. I knew he was emotionally and spiritually worn out. For months, Dennis had been wrestling with the choices he had made. Now things were coming to a head! He was trying to be strong.

I showered and washed my hair, glad to feel the warm water against my skin. When I came out, I appreciated the dark room and slipped underneath the covers beside Dennis. He was drawn to my warmth and rolled toward me. His arms automatically sought me out, and I purred like a kitten between them. His hands moved across my body as if he dreamed of me in his sleep, and I welcomed his touch. It was the comfort I needed, and I wanted him to know that. I also wanted him to know that I didn't blame him for what had happened to Rakim. Not any of it! I thought I was as much to blame.

We settled in together, a ménage of arms and legs entwined. Eyes closed, I felt him smile, just happy to be lying like this with me.

And then the phone rang!

My heart stopped. Somehow, I knew who it was. We both knew, and the magic of that moment was over. It rang again and again, and I prayed it would stop. When it rang the fifth time, it rolled over to the answering machine and soon Ray's voice would be in the room sliding in between us. I tried to get up to answer it, but Dennis held me to him.

"No," he said.

"Dennis, let me . . ."

"No."

A second later, Ray's voice was everywhere, as real as if he were standing in the middle of the room.

"Gina, baby, I been doing nothing but thinking about you. What is happening . . . One minute I was trying to talk to you, and the next you were screaming . . . Is your boy alright? I been trying to call you and Marilyn, but you guys are not picking up . . . Baby, please don't lock me out . . . I need to know you alright . . . Baby I know you are there . . . please pick up the phone."

It was killing me to hear him pleading like that. The concern in his voice was genuine. He was worried. In fact, he was trying to warn me of the danger the last time he called. If I had listened, if I had been paying attention, maybe known of this would have happened.

"Gina . . . Gina!"

Dennis' body grew tenser by the moment. I felt like I was coiled up in an Anaconda. I couldn't take it anymore! I broke free from his hold and bolted for the phone.

"Ray, Rayboy, it's me. I'm here," I said.

"Oh baby . . . Gina, I been so worried about you! This shit is making me crazy. I ain't use to caring about nobody like this, girl. You can't shut me out. Turn your celly back on. It cost me a lot to make that kind of call in here. Find a guard on the take that's willing to deal. But you are worth it to me. Please don't shut me out."

"I was in the hospital ICU. I had to turn it off," I whispered, not trying to make Dennis a part of my conversation. "I . . . I wasn't trying to shut you out, Ray."

Rayboy continued to talk to me, asking me questions that I couldn't answer. All I could do was see the hurt, angry, then defeated look on Dennis' face. We stared at each other eye to eye, having a whole different conversation.

"You cannot have both of us".

"He cares so much. I care for him, too."

"You can't have it both ways."

"He is hurting and scared just like we are."

"This cannot go on."

"I know. It can't go on like this."

All of a sudden, Dennis bolted off the bed, grabbed his shoes and his jacket, and he headed for the door.

"Wait! Where are you going?" I asked.

He looked at me apologetically as is he didn't know what to say. Or maybe he was afraid to say that he was just giving up.

"Dennis! Wait," I screamed, but he was out the door. Seconds later, I heard his car pulling out of the garage and the tires of the Mercedes screeching down the street.

"Gina? Gina? You still there?"

"Yes, Ray, I'm still here." I droned, feeling as though I was in a trance.

We both held the phone in silence. So many painful things to say, but they had to be said just the same.

"Gina, you know it can't go on like this."

"No, it can't go on like this."

"He can't protect you, baby. Not like I can."

"You can't *be* with me Ray, not like *he* can."

"Dickerson can't *be* with you either, because Shaka is going to kill him!"

"Dennis is smart, and he is strong, and he has the law on his side."

"Do you hear yourself, Gina? If Dickerson talks, he won't walk. He will wind up locked inside here with the rest of us . . . *and Shaka will kill him*! Shaka will have him killed, inside or out."

How had we gotten into this impossible situation? Tears streamed down my face, and Ray listened to me cry. As always, he was in control, and he wanted to make sure I understood a few things. I fell to my knees with the phone still in my hand.

"Ray," I pleaded. "You've got to help me. You've got to help Dennis."

"It's way too late for that, baby. They have drawn first blood. The blood of the Moor! And Gina, don't get it twisted. If Shaka doesn't kill Dickerson, I will."

CHAPTER 12

◆

Inside and Out

Ray Boden stared out over the prison yard at the scattering of men below. Trouble was brewing, tension was thick in the air, and the slightest offense was provocation for the worst kind of retaliation. Someone was about to get shanked! He could feel it. Ray cursed and looked away. This situation didn't happen overnight. It had been building over the past few months, ever sense he had found out that Shaka Blu was being transferred to Montgomery.

And he had been a busy boy ever since he had arrived. Shaka was spending a small fortune buying allegiances among the prison staff, promising anything that would get their attention. And Shaka could deliver; he had managed to build a sizable empire on the outside. He had the means to make a working man's dreams come true. Rayboy did not have that kind of bank, but he did possess an uncanny knowledge of human nature that Shaka lacked.

A good hustler always knew his mark, and Ray was a hustler from way back. No doubt!

Ray knew that the guards were men, just like other men, who rarely traded their ethics out of greed. A man's principles were usually laid aside out of necessity—when the mortgage is way past due, or a child is sick, or a mistress threatens to go to the wife. An unauthorized phone call was not too difficult to make. A grilled steak smothered with onions and some female companionship was far more costly but not impossible to obtain. All men have needs, and like the prisoners, the guards were always looking for a way out of something.

Ray put out his cigarette, squashing it against the gray cement. Smoking was just another bad habit he had picked up in the joint. Bribery, extortion, and blackmail had been others. He had found himself in the impossible position of trying to stop a war, using any means necessary. Ironically, it was the same war he had helped to start over two decades ago. As a teenager, Ray Boden had grown up on the streets of Southwest DC—a stone's throw from the nation's capitol where he viewed opulence everyday while living in overt poverty. He was drafted into drug culture early, being a child of the sixties. But unlike so many others, Ray chose not to be a user but a seller of the commodity. He was a businessman.

Ray was good-looking with charm to spare. The hustle came natural to him, and he was good at it. With a face that seemed to be ageless and the wisdom of his years, Ray was unstoppable, making deal after deal, building his empire. Rayboy, the playboy, the women called him. And he never had a shortage of them either. But to his credit, he was a gentleman (as pimps and drug dealers go), and he never left a woman unsatisfied.

He was an original member of The WildDogs—one of the most notorious gangs on the East coast. Gang! Ray hated that word. He thought it sounded trivial and small because what he had created was an international corporation—a conglomerate—with the best of the best in its ranks. It was more than his business and to him, like the mafia, it was a way of life.

But as Ray matured, so did his passions and the urge to "make the deal" began to wane. And one day, a woman from his past (with Ray, it was always a woman) made him take inventory of his life. He had had enough! All of his friends were either dead or dying—rotting away in some prison. It was time for a change.

Old Man had helped him see that, too. Old Man was Ray's cell mate. He had been an inmate at Montgomery for twenty-eight years—a lifer—and had seen more of his share of everything in the joint. Ray was grateful to have him as a cell mate. Old Man was smart, had a good sense of humor and knew when to stop talking—all valuable traits to possess when you are sharing housing with a shit load of perverts and killers. Old Man turned over slowly in the bottom bunk, waking up from his afternoon nap. He carefully placed his feet on the floor, one at a time, his arthritis bothering him today.

"Where you going, Old Man?" Ray asked, turning the dial on the tiny radio to the Big Band station the older man liked.

He stretched his arms out, scratched the stubble on his chin, and focused his failing eyes on Ray. "Well, I'm gonna start by having tea with Queen Elizabeth and Madonna. Later, I might check in with my stockbroker and if I can fit it in my schedule, I'll play a few rounds of golf with Bill Gates."

Ray smiled. "Sorry, he's booked today. Threesome with Rosey and Martha, I think."

He pretended disappointment as he stretched with caution. "Well then, I guess I'll settle for a little walk out in the yard. Crack these old bones. Look like a nice day." he said.

Ray frowned. "Not today, old man! Shit is on the horizon. Think you better stay put."

Old Man nodded and accepted that in his easygoing way. Ray smiled. It was hard for him to believe that this man had ever killed anybody. But then, it only takes a moment to change the direction of a man's life. Ray knew that all too well.

Prison had definitely not been in Ray's plan. Sure, he had been living his life by the law of the street for as long as he could remember. But Ray loved his freedom and had considered himself to be a player, always running the smart hustle. Too sophisticated to get caught! In the gangs, doing time was like a man's badge of honor. A prison sentence was like getting awarded the Purple Heart, and Ray was not afraid of that.

The thing he hated was being without a woman!

The idea was totally foreign to him. Ray Boden loved women and for the life of him, could not understand how men pulled long stretches without them. He knew there were men who had no shame or sense of common decency that would jack off in any corner in the middle of the day. To each, his own, he thought. Then there were those who "bitched out" other men. These men were not necessarily gay. It was just understood that playing the bitch was part of prison life. Ray just could not get with that. In his mind, there was absolutely no replacement for pussy. Then there were those who only needed a little female stimulation to take matters into there own hand, sort of speak. Men who randomly dialed numbers were called "fishermen". If a woman answered and a con could keep her talking for 30 seconds, she was "hooked". Some inmates actually wrote letters to dozens of women at a time, telling them anything they thought they wanted to hear—

I was framed. I'm really innocent.

I am very shy and from a broken home.

Nobody ever loved me. I grew up alone.

They would get the addresses from other convicts or other women who visited the prison. Then after they get the woman's attention, they would close in for the kill.

You are the first woman I could ever talk to like this.

I wish I had met you sooner. My life would have been totally different.

I love you.

In due time, these women were not only sending hot letters and pictures for the inmates to beat off to, they would also send money and clothes. Ray learned in the joint, these prolific writers were called "milkmen" because they would milk a woman for everything they could get before they moved on.

Ray had watched Old Man write letters like that, mostly to pass the time. He never accepted gifts from the women, though. He just liked writing the letters. Ray asked him once why he just didn't write his wife—he guessed he must have had one somewhere. And a family, too! That was the only time Ray ever saw Old Man get mad. Ray never brought the subject up again.

Ray took inventory of how narrow his own world had gotten. He had to be honest with himself. Since he had met Gina, the days had gotten shorter, and the time had gotten easier to pull. In one month, she had opened his eyes to life again. She was his reason to care again, and he didn't want to let her go.

He looked back over the yard. There were some men playing basketball, faking a steal, trying to win the game. He admitted he had played Gina like that. Faked her out from the very beginning, but that was just who he was. He always approached women like they were a game, like a kitten with a ball of string. Not because he didn't respect them, but because they were the excitement of his life. He loved the hunt, the adventure of romance.

But this was no game! Nothing had happened the way he planned. He had only meant to find an ally on the outside. Someone to help him stop Dickerson! He hadn't meant to get so caught up. And he certainly hadn't meant to fall in love with a woman over the phone.

Ray watched Old Man pull his pad and blunt pencil from under his mattress. With a twinkle in his eye, he dabbed the lead point on his tongue as if he were William Shakespeare himself and began to compose a love letter destined to knock some woman's socks off. Ray wanted to do something for Gina. Something that she would never forget! He decided to consult with an expert.

"Hey, Old Man, I got a question for you. How do you show a woman that you love her?"

"You serious?"

"Yeah," Ray said, directing his gaze through the barred window, pass the courts and beyond the prison walls.

The old convict looked away from his pad for a moment and spent a few seconds in sincere reflection. Then his eyes widened in revelation as if the answer were crystal clear.

"Hell, that's easy, Ray. You give her whatever she wants."

Ray had considered asking Old Man if that was what he had done for his wife, then he thought better of it. Although he never talked about them, Ray knew there were photos under the old man's bed that he never shared with anyone. He would probably kill Ray if he had known he'd already rifled through them.

"Why not come down to the book room with me," Ray suggested.

"That museum guy coming back today?"

"Yeah, he's coming. I'm sure of that." The muscles in Ray's face tensed as he thought of Dickerson. That stupid punk bitch! He's really stinking it up for me in here, he thought. All Ray had wanted to do was serve his time and get out. Stay clean while he was locked up, but his past would not let him. He and Shaka had a bone to pick—some shit about some drugs, money and of course, a woman—and Shaka was never going to let it go.

Old Man could tell where Ray's mind had drifted. "Shaka is buying up C block fast. There ain't hardly a guard over there that ain't in his pocket. And he got plenty of muscle, too."

"Don't mean shit, Old Man," Ray said. "I know all about punks like Shaka. I wrote the gangster manual before he was born. I was probably fuckin' his mamma when I wrote it! Shaka can buy all the niggas he wants. In the end, it's going to come down to just me and him. It's got to. No other way."

"Don't much like that either, Ray," he said laying back down on the bunk. "Not much at all."

Ray looked over at the man in the bottom bunk. He was tired and worn and had probably been through more cellmates than he cared to remember. He didn't want to lose another halfway decent one.

"It's all gonna be cool," Ray said in an attempt to erase the worry from Old Man's face. "The guard should be coming soon. Sure you don't wanna hang out with me? What if I run into Lola Falana or Pam Grier on the way? I can't handle both of those pussies by myself!"

"Boy, you couldn't handle one of them pussies by yourself!"

A moment later, uniformed guards lined the halls, the doors clanked open, and a handful of prisoners were escorted out. Ray walked the line to the book room. He sighed! Because of a woman, he would delay his plans. Today, he would give Dickerson his last chance to get it right.

Dennis Dickerson was a proud man with a lot to lose. And he never got use to this—miles and miles of electrified fences, tons upon tons of impenetrable stone, hundreds of armed guards at the watch, ready to shoot anything that moved, millions of dollars worth of surveillance cameras, thousands of electronic locks and barricades—enough handcuffs, shackles and chains to reach from Compton to Brooklyn. And one unscrupulous demoted warden with an ax to grind!

As he sat in his Mercedes in the prison parking lot, he reviewed his options for the thousandth time. All of them looked grim. Of course, there was the one option that he had considered after leaving Regina on the phone with that convict last night. Run! Just get in his car and drive to the ends of the earth and start again! But he was tired of running. Tired of the tough guys beating him out! It was time to take a stand.

As Dennis flipped through his presentation notes, his mind flipped through the pages of his life. His mother had been one of his greatest influences. She had been well educated, an art teacher in the public school system, and had sought to bring beauty into the lives of her students. She taught him eloquence and culture and an appreciation for finer things. She played the piano, and on days when the other boys in the neighborhood were jacking cars and knocking over convenient stores, Dennis sat at home by her side. Until she finally died, her spirit (and her liver) crushed by an abusive husband.

Dennis and his father never got along. He thought his son wasn't tough enough. *Dennis, you should have been a girl*, he would say. But I got ways to make a man out of you. The beatings started early and persisted throughout his childhood. Dennis hardly had a memory of his father that didn't include him holding a belt. He had made his life, and that of his mother, utterly miserable. When he died, Dennis had him cremated just to make sure he was dead. Then he tossed his ashes into the dumpster behind the old house where they'd lived.

He met Regina Lambert Jackson that same year. Regina—a smart, beautiful, caring single mother that shared his passion for art! It had been easy to fall in love with her. Now, Dennis was hoping that it wasn't all falling apart.

Dennis wondered what Regina saw when she looked at him. Did she see beyond the expensive suits and fancy degrees? The women he met seemed to swing like pendulums, preferring a "thug" one minute and a "metrosexual" the next. It was hard to know what they wanted. Most women sliced him up, assigned a dollar value to each piece, then added him up again. Dennis hoped Regina knew he was worth far more than the sum of his parts.

There was no doubt that he loved her. He tried to show her everyday by giving her what he thought she wanted—beauty, romance, and a happy family life. Dennis could not understand why women were so damned insecure. What had made Regina turn to a ruthless convict to fulfill her needs?

In truth, Dennis knew that Ray Boden was far from ruthless. In fact, as far as men go, he was quite a gentleman with a real sense of honor. Even in prison, he lived by a code, a system of checks and balances that ensured that the weak were protected, and everyone got what they deserved. Dennis had upset that balance by aligning with Shaka Blu. Ray was just trying to set things straight.

Dennis cursed to himself. Why had he done it anyway? Dennis knew he never had any intention of being a *drug dealer!!* He had just seen his involvement as good business, an opportunity to get ahead. He was peddling drugs in a controlled environment. Who could possibly get hurt? But he had been so wrong! Dennis cringed every time he thought of Rakim lying in that hospital bed. Even though he was not his natural son, Dennis looked at Rakim and saw himself. He watched him with Regina, and Dennis saw himself and his own mother. A new determination seized him; he was going to make this family picture right. If Rakim getting shot was not bad enough, the pain in Regina's eyes was more than enough to make him quit. This madness had to stop.

It was a strange coincidence that drew Dennis to volunteer at the prison. He didn't quite understand it himself. He was fascinated by the violent nature of men, how they seemed to thrive on destruction and cruelly. In some way, he thought he was trying to relive his relationship with his father. He prayed not but the alternative was worse. Deep down, he wondered if he was trying to define his own masculinity.

He smirked to himself. He was definitely *not* gay—that being a question that had popped up several times from his peers since puberty. Dennis loved women and loved sex, and like most men, he liked to think he was good at it. But people, even those closest to him, often misunderstand his passion for beauty as if that made him less of a man. His father had been that way. Luckily, his mother had taken the time to teach him about men who were strong and valued artistry—black men who were talented and knew how to fight. The Moors! The Moorish warriors, predecessors to the

Roman gladiators, fought to preserve the finer aspects of their culture. It was common for these soldiers to be artists and fine craftsmen. Dennis wondered when things got to be so twisted.

Dennis closed the notebook with a snap. Yes, he was tired of running; tired of taking the sensible, rational, polite-boy route of doing things. Especially now! Even Regina, the woman he had always seen as his soul mate, was having a fling with a con! Dennis crumpled the papers in his fist. He tried to ignore it for what it was—a fling. He tried to rationalize it as her need to be kind and generous to someone less fortunate than herself. But deep down, Dennis knew that Regina, and women like her, harbored some ridiculous romantic fantasy about jailhouse dick! It rankled him! So much so that he wanted to strangle her!

And that was his point—Dennis knew he was a civilized man with uncivilized tendencies and that was the only thing that separated him from the men in the joint.

Would Regina find him more attractive if he kicked her around a little bit? Would she lose the need to play phone tag with criminals if he slapped her from time to time? Dennis had played with snorting the cocaine that night just to see if it would turn her on. Did the tiny bruises he had given Regina on her wrist thrill her more than the priceless bracelet he had given her just a few weeks earlier? Dennis wasn't sure, but he knew he had been disgusted with himself.

There had to be a better way to love her!

Dennis entered Montgomery Prison as if it were Montgomery Mall. From one formidable portal to the next, the guards waved him on, giving him *carte blanc* through the locked down facility. He liked to think it was because he was a person of great importance, or because he was friends with Big Daddy Beau Marshall, but Dennis was no fool. He knew his safe passage had been bought and paid for by his star pupil—inmate #519-84, Emmanuel Sutherland. *Aka* Shaka Blu!

Dennis took his place in the book room. One of the guards that escorted him laid down a box containing a few "non-offensive" pieces that he would be discussing today. Non-offensive because they could not be made into a weapon by this captive audience.

Within minutes, Ray Boden and his "tribe" came in and sat on one side of the small classroom. Many were handcuffed and shackled. Dennis still had not gotten use to that. In a moment, the room would be littered with men in orange uniforms who always sat with the same "tribe" for protection or out of loyalty. Tribes were gangs, and Dennis had learned that gang affiliation among men on the inside was as important as those of men on the outside.

The room was almost full, with about twenty-five inmates, when Shaka made his entrance. He was not a big man and only about twenty-seven or twenty-eight years old. But he was formidable and full of bravado with rippling muscles across his blue/black chest. He was the darkest man Dennis had ever seen, and he wondered if that was why he had given himself the Zulu name. Surprisingly, he smiled a lot, revealing a display of gold teeth that reminded Dennis of piano keys. Although he appeared to be jovial enough, Dennis knew there was no humor in that smile. He imagined that often it was a prelude to a despicable, if not deadly, act.

On his heels as always, was Thomas or Little T as they called him on the inside. He followed Shaka around like a lap dog, always walking two steps in his shadow. Dennis figured Thomas was Shaka's right hand or second in command. Maybe he was still in training, and Shaka was teaching him the ropes. Regardless, the image of baby-faced Thomas following Marilyn Marshall around on a leash made him grin. He pictured them taking turns wearing leather, lace, and high heels shoes.

Dennis started the lecture as soon as the men were seated, never giving them an opportunity to socialize. That might lead to chaos. Instead, he hopped right in, beginning with a question.

"What makes a man?"

The inmates looked around at each other. A man never spoke out of turn in the joint. He would let his "superiors" in his tribe answer first. If given permission, he would knock once on his desk or on his seat to let the teacher know he wanted to respond. This also kept the men's hands in plain view which was mandatory. Rayboy knocked on the desk in front of him almost as a joke. He had no superiors. Dennis completely ignored him. He knew it was immature, but it was hard to be polite to a piece of slime that he knew wanted to fuck his girlfriend.

"What the fuck kind of question is that?" asked Thomas.

"One you can't answer, bitch," replied Ray from the other side of the room, and the other inmates laughed hysterically.

"That earned you both four demerits a piece for inappropriate language. Now, shut-up!" shouted one of the guards who actually laughed himself under his breath.

"Let me rephrase that," Dennis said. "We have been talking about the Moors of ancient Mauritania. They were fighting men. Why? What were they fighting for?"

A knock from the front of the room! "Same shit all men fight for," said Shaka.

"Four demerits, Sutherland," the guard shouted.

"Fuck you! I am tryin' to answer the man's goddamn muthafucking question." Surprisingly, the guard said no more, and Shaka continued. "Nigga's fight for the same thing all the time."

"And what is that?" Dennis asked.

"To be on top," Shaka said smoothly.

"You ever get to be on top, Thomas?" An unidentified voice rang out from the back, and the class broke out in laughter again. Thomas made a move to rise and was quickly restrained by the nearest guard.

"And what puts a man 'on top' as you put it, Shaka?" Dennis asked pointedly.

Shaka did not answer but looked at Dennis like he thought he was being baited. Shaka shifted his weight in the chair and stared Dennis down. Ray saw the tension building between the two men and attempted to answer the question. He knocked on the desk.

"Ugly Boy up there is right. Men have always wanted the same things—territory and wealth."

Shaka growled but kept his eyes on Dennis. Dennis looked shocked to hear the right answer. Boden had obviously done some reading, and the teacher in him was proud. However, the man in him was pissed off. Dennis had to suppress the urge to say *"I didn't know you read anything other than love poetry, you sick bastard."*

"Exactly, Boden." A pimply faced inmate sitting in the back caught Dennis' attention. "You have to remember that these soldiers who made up the Moorish armies were not much older than this young man," Dennis immediately felt sorry for him. "Men killed people over territory and agricultural wealth. Back in those days, agricultural wealth was considered gold and precious metals. Sometimes it was food and water."

Another knock from the corner of the room, "Now it's drugs," Ray said the words softly, but his voice rang like a cannon through the small room.

"Yes, drugs. So we fight over drug territory," Dennis said. "The only other resource that comes close is oil."

A knock from the center aisle! "I guess them boys back then had a lot in common with these boys now."

"Right again. The Moors came from small tribes . . . cities in Europe, Africa and India . . . all fighting for the same thing . . . like gangs," Dennis said, and their was an uncomfortable pause in the academic conversation. The inmates eyed each other as if they were calling each other out. A throat cleared here! An indiscriminate mumble there! Then suddenly, some of the men started to hoop and howl the war calls of their "tribes." The guards tried to shut them up but it was no use. The sounds got cacophonous, until both

Rayboy and Shaka stood up and squared off from their opposite corners of the room. Like giant chess pieces, they just stood there, and everyone else settled down. Two of the more nervous guards pulled out their tasers and stood at the ready. Shaka only smiled and turned back toward Dennis.

"I guess niggas will do anything to be the man," he said mockingly. Shaka was well aware of Rayboy's reputation in and out of prison. He had earned the respect of the men on the block, and that was more reason for Shaka to hate him. With all he had done to buy and build up his army, Shaka Blu was still second. Shaka did not like being second!

"You are right. They would do anything," Dennis said.

"Even draw their own blood in an invitation to battle. You wanna dance with me, Shaka?" Ray asked a little too politely. "You feelin' like one of them Moors today?"

"I'll dance with you, nigga. Anytime, anyplace," he answered with that trademark acidic smile plastered on his face.

It was a call to war. They had done everything but beat on their chests. The two convicts looked like gladiators, each ready to annihilate the other. If this had been ancient Mauritania—if this had been the Yaksas and the Nagas—they would be wielding deadly knifes, smooth on one side, jagged on the other. They would first cut themselves then fight to bury the blade in the heart of the other. In this kind of gruesome battle, usually both warriors died. The object was to not die first. Dennis shook his head; centuries of evolution had come down to this.

Dennis smiled to himself. He had to admit his plan was working. It had occurred to Dennis in the middle of the night, that he had one thing in his favor—two murderous convicts who hated each other as much as they hated him—wanted him dead. If Dennis could insight enough anger between them, his problem might take care of itself. If he could goad them enough—give them enough cause, make it hot enough—Ray and Shaka could both be dead by the end of the day.

The guards were jerking prisoners back into a line. Everyone could see that class was definitely over. Half the men had earned so many demerits for yelling or cursing that they had to be taken out of the room. The rest, the bitches, simply waited for their men or just to be taken back to their cells. Ray took this opportunity to approach the man at the head of the class. When the guards were not looking, Ray ran his finger lightly over the fabric of Dennis' Armani suit directly over his heart.

"You know you're no good for her, Dickerson. You are the cause of all of her problems," Ray whispered as if he were asking a question about the items coming out of the box.

Dennis grinned back. "No, Boden, you are, and I'll be glad when Shaka sticks a shank in you."

"The only reason you are standing here now, breathing my air, is because a woman I care about pleaded for your life. Your life ain't worth dog shit to me."

"Call Regina again, and I will kill you myself," Dennis was surprise to hear himself issue the threat.

Rayboy smiled as he noticed guards walking toward him. "I'll be ready for the test, Dr. Dickerson. Looking forward to it." And Ray was ushered away, leaving Dennis alone in the room with Shaka and Little T. There were two guards posted at the door, but they were more to keep anyone from going in and interrupting Shaka's business. When he was sure everyone was gone, Shaka approached the box in great expectation.

"I been waiting for this all week, Dickerson." He signaled to Thomas to empty the contents of the box. Thomas rifled through it clumsily, pictures, cloths and paper models littered the floor. When the box was empty, Thomas turned it upside down and unfolded the flaps in the bottom. There should have been two envelopes, each containing enough coke to satisfy his customers in C and D block. Thomas looked up at Shaka. The box was empty.

"What game you playin', Dickerson?" Shaka asked, grinding the gold in his mouth.

"No game. I just quit, that's all." Dennis made a show of packing his notes in a manila folder.

"You quit?!" Thomas asked wide-eyed. "Nigga, you must be crazy! Do you know who you messin' with? Don't nobody 'quit' on Shaka Blu 'less he going to the grave. That where you going, muthafucka?"

The sound of Thomas' voice was beginning to irritate Shaka, and he looked over at the door. He wanted to make sure he had the privacy he needed for whatever was about to happen. Shaka tried to keep his composure—a decidedly new approach for the drug dealer/murderer/pimp.

"Dickerson, I am in a good mood today, so I am going to give you another chance. Now, you and me been doing just fine up until now. My men on the outside set up the deals, you go get the stuff and bring it back. I get my shit and you get paid. Right?"

Dennis did not answer. He was sure the question was completely rhetorical.

"You get some good business contacts and get to buy some of them pretty pictures—or whatever the fuck it is you want." Shaka was losing some of that composure now, and the empty box went flying across the room. Dennis flinched but stood his ground.

"*Where is my shit*?!" Shaka asked more directly.

Still Dennis didn't say a word. He wasn't sure what his next move would be. Ray had played it cooler than he had anticipated. Now Dennis had to deal with Shaka on his own. His only hope was that Marshall knew he was still in the building and would be expecting him to stop in before he checked out.

"I'm not working for you. Not anymore . . . I . . ."

Before Dennis could complete his sentence, Shaka gave him an upper cut to the chin, quickly followed by a pummeling right hook. Dennis was unconscious before he hit the floor.

Thomas whooped like a school boy, and danced around Dennis' still body, lying in a heap at Shaka's feet.

"Damn, Shaka! Damn, Shaka!" Thomas sang giddily.

Shaka was in no mood for stupidity. He had to think what to do. Dickerson had showed more balls than he had given him credit for. This was not going to be good for his rep. When Boden found out, Shaka would be the laughing stock of the prison and everybody's joke. Shaka had to figure out how to make this work in his favor.

"Dammnnn Shaka! Dammnn!" Thomas continued, now flapping his arms like he was some kind of bird. Shaka was growing tired of him with every passing day. He only had one real use for him anyway.

Shaka continued to pick apart the elements of his dilemma. He had no coke to sell or with which to buy his alliances. He had a rival gang leader ready to go to war with him. And now, he had assaulted a prominent doctor in Beau Marshall's pen. Not even Beau would let this roll, even if he increased his cut.

"Damn, Shaka, Shaka . . ." Thomas was having his own party in the middle of the floor.

"Shut up and let me think a minute, goddammit!" he yelled.

Thomas calmed down immediately, suppressing the second chorus of his song. In a rare moment of reflection, Shaka Blu tilted his head to one side, and narrowed his eyes. He scanned the younger man's face—fine delicate features, soft wavy hair, and a face too pretty to be a man's. Thomas lowered his head under the gang lord's scrutiny. He swallowed hard. He knew what was about to come next. He watched Shaka ready his hammer-like fists.

"Little T, you tryin' to mess me up? You going WildDog on me?"

"Nah . . . nah, Shaka," Thomas yelped as that trademark venomous grin took shape.

"Hmm, I can see why Old Beauty Queen likes you so much. You are simply gorgeous, baby. Simply gorgeous!" Shaka stroked the curls on the side of the young man's head, entangling his fingers in the fine hairs. "I'll bet you're really good to her. You love her, T?"

"*No!*" he said quickly.

"Like Beauty Queen better than you like me?"

"No, Shaka, it ain't like that!"

"Good. Then show me." Shaka's right fist flew to Thomas' midsection and the left connected with his side. Thomas doubled over in pain. "Show me how much you like me," he whispered into Thomas' ear, pushing his head down just below his waist, forcing him down on his knees.

Thomas hesitated again, not wanting to submit to the humiliation. Shaka rammed his knee into Thomas's jaw. Blood spattered everywhere! "That's for making me wait!" he said.

The baby-faced inmate slowly obeyed, reaching into Shaka's pants and lowering his head to take him full in his mouth. Shaka smiled! "Don't make you less than a man, T. Just make you more my man, that's all."

Thomas started slowly and shyly, wrapping his tongue around Shaka's member—the way he knew Shaka liked it—then became more aggressive. Shaka moved in and out of the pretty boy's mouth, holding Thomas' head so tight that hairs snapped in his fist.

"That's good. That's good," he moaned. "I . . . I think I figured this shit out. Just let me come . . . ooohh . . . yeeah . . . let me co . . . Ahhh . . . . !

With a jerk, Shaka let his head go, and Thomas dropped to all fours, blood and semen dripping from his mouth. Finished with him, Shaka turned his attention to the prostrate figure still lying unconscious on the floor. *I should have had my boys stick that bloody knife in his back, he thought.* Giving him a warning was a waste of my time. Shaka took a good hard look at the well-dressed man at his feet, and a plan formulated in his head. Thomas began to crawl away but was halted by the sound of Shaka's voice.

"Now, this is what you're gonna do, T. Do whatever you got to do to get our beauty queen down here. But first, take that suit off of that fool . . . and don't wrinkle it. I like Armani."

CHAPTER 13

◆

Blood Of The Moor

Today was Zeta's birthday, and she had decided to spend it in the hospital with Rakim. I let her skip school since her mind would be someplace else anyway.

"I'm twelve today. You should let me skip school for twelve days," she said.

"No way," I said.

Dennis had not come home last night and had not answered his cell phone. There had been no word from him, and it was unusual for him to miss a family event. I needed Dennis with me. My sister looked at me suspiciously.

"Is everything alright with you two?"

"Everything's fine," I lied. "He probably had to be at the museum early this morning. We have a lot of construction going on. The test for the new vault and security system is today. He would want to oversee that."

She seemed to buy that lame explanation. Roz and I took Zeta to the new mall. We told her she could have anything she wanted. Dennis usually took the kids shopping, and now I was remembering how valuable that was. After two hours of looking, I was exhausted. We settled on a black globe that lit up with tiny lights. She was very proud of her purchase.

"It's beautiful," I said. "But I didn't know you were so interested in geography, Zeta."

"I'm not. It's for Rakim."

"But Zeta, this was suppose to be your birthday present," Roz noted.

"I know. All I want is to see Rakim happy! This will make him happy."

Wow! I thought. My daughter is growing up!

Moments later, the three of us piled out of the third floor hospital elevator to hear laughter coming from Rakim's room. Righteous ushered us in, and to my joy, there were balloons everywhere! My son was sitting up in bed, looking weak but smiling his ass off. There were women standing all around him—Righteous, Sister Dora, Anna, Aunt Betty—and one skinny little teenage girl to Rakim's right. She was leaning over the bed rail and *holding his hand*!

"Mamma, this is Sierra. She goes to my school," he said, beaming like he had won the lottery.

"Hi Sierra," I said trying to mask my irrational tinge of jealousy. "Shouldn't you be at school, young lady?" Rakim winced at me.

"Sierra's dad is a doctor in this hospital. He told her I was here. It was nice of her to come see me, wasn't it, mother?"

"It's good to meet you, Ms. Jackson," the girl said politely. I wanted to kill her! My face wrinkled up, wanting so badly to stage some kind of protest. My sister came to my rescue.

"Sierra, why don't you help Rakim's sister with her presents. Lay them out over there on that little table, okay?" Sierra walked away. Roz lead me away from the bed and out into the hall. She pinched my arm hard.

"Ouch!"

"What is the matter with you?" She whispered hotly.

"I don't know," I whispered back honestly. But I did know! There was a girl here to see my son. Rakim, the only male in my life that had never abandoned me! It occurred to me then that my relationship with my son had been the longest relationship that I had had with any male. I was pathetic!

"He has got to grow up, you know," Roz barked.

I just stood there wondering if growing up always meant growing away. I had visions of myself as Norman Bates' mother in the movie "Psycho!" Yes, the sign of a good mother is when children move on. I looked at my sister who was smiling assuredly at me. Yes, I was a good mother—who would one day be alone again.

Where the hell was Dennis?

Just then, Trisha and CeCe burst through the heavy wooden door carrying a huge sheet cake. Twelve candles were already lit, and Zeta's eyes' bulged as they came into the room.

"We heard somebody was having a birthday," Trisha sang as CeCe pushed her way into the crowded room. CeCe was trying to close the door before the nurses had a fit over the burning candles. There were two on the rampage coming down the hall, but Marilyn Marshall and Carmela Rodriguez cut them off as they exited the elevator and headed our way. They were quite a picture—sophisticated Marilyn and colorful Carmela—each carrying gifts for the birthday girl.

"Chica," Carmela greeted me warmly as Marilyn idled up behind the nurses.

"You gals busy?" she asked the women in white. "I hope not because there is some horny young man roaming the halls wearing his hospital gown backwards! That kid is hung like a horse! Said he wanted to put these beds to better use, if you know what I mean," Marilyn's voice got louder as she approached the horrified nurses. She winked at me as the nurses tore down the hall in the opposite direction.

"You really do enjoy that, don't you?" I asked.

"Mission accomplished," she grinned.

The ladies slid in pass me as I wondered where they had all come from, these women who were so new to my life yet so close. Sopranos and altos chimed the birthday song as Marilyn took a place at Rakim's bed side. Marilyn playfully hunched Zeta, and she beamed. She slid her little hand into Marilyn's, and they shared a smile. In such a short time, a friendship had been forged between them that I had not been aware of. I wasn't sure I approved.

Then I looked around the room at the carousel of women, laughing, talking, and getting ready to eat cake. They were all there to support me in my time of need. They were of different ages, from different backgrounds, and different walks of life. Still they embraced me and each other with a nurturing fortitude that I had never experienced before. It can only be called sisterhood—the special love that sustains women in a way that a man's love cannot.

Trisha and Righteous had gotten into a conversation about motherhood. As a new informed expectant mom, Trisha was trying to give my mother advice on today's youth. Righteous reared up like a thunder storm. "Girl, I know you ain't tryin' to tell me nothin 'bout raising no children. I got pocketbooks older than you!" she said. The room shook with laughter. A moment later, CeCe was pulling me aside.

"I didn't see Dr. D at the museum cafe' this morning, Ms. J. He always comes in for his morning coffee," she said.

"Is that right?" I asked, trying to play off my concern.

"That's right and at around 11:00, Patti came down looking for him. She had questions about the new vault. There was this real fine brother with her. Patti looked like she was showing him around."

CeCe kept looking at me in anticipation. I sighed! "I guess I should go in today. Just to make sure things go smoothly." CeCe nodded as if I had made the right decision, and we headed for the door. My mother and sister said they would play hostess and keep an eye on the kids. On our way out, Marilyn sprinted passed us, grabbing the last space in the crowded elevator.

"Leaving so soon?" I asked.

"Have to! Just came to delivery birthday goodies to our little lady." I hadn't seen what Marilyn had gotten Zeta, but I was sure it was spectacular and could be measured in carats. "Hate to rush off but I have a date. *He* is waiting for me . . . and *he* doesn't like to wait. Ta ta."

The elevator door closed on her blushing cheeks, and I imagined her languishing in the arms of her big black prison stud while she made Big Daddy Beau Marshall watch. Marilyn truly needed a good therapist.

When I entered Mirathi, it was abuzz with activity. Workman in uniforms were sharing the halls with well-dressed executives in a race to make this facility the showplace of the art world. Patti spotted me immediately and approached me as if she were on the attack.

"Ms. Jackson, where is Dr. Dickerson? Is he with you?" she asked with some concern.

"I am not sure where he is. What do you need? Can I help?"

Patti began to run through a veritable laundry list of piddly little details that had to be addressed. Although they were small, they had to be seen to by someone who could authorize them with a signature. Patti began to run through the more important ones first but as she spoke, an unfamiliar figure caught my attention. It was a man, brutally attractive, very dark with pronounced features that were possibly Nigerian. He looked rather menacing, and I guessed he thought he did too, because he grinned in an effort to appear friendly.

"Who is that?" I asked.

"Oh, that's somebody here to see Dr. Dickerson. Said it was important. His name sounded African. I can't pronounce it." Patti was embarrassed by that.

"Did you tell him he was not in?" I asked.

"Yes, but he said that he would wait. He's just been looking around admiring our progress."

"Where's he from?"

"I don't know. He doesn't talk much. Might be a language barrier! I didn't push. Besides, we have been so busy. Did you take a look at these estimates?" Patti brought my attention back to her list, but I continued to keep an eye on the man with the toothless grin. Something about him started to feel very familiar. I raised my head to take a second look. But in the hustle and bustle of the hallway, he had vanished.

The rest of the afternoon, I was busy getting a handle on the new security system. It was a monster of fail-safe devices that would alert the police if the slightest intrusion occurred. The installers ran a test for us that was more than impressive. If the locks or censors were disturbed in the tiniest bit, the entire museum would lock down tight as a clam's butt. At the touch of a button or a simple telephoned voice command, every lock in the building would activate. Since Dennis was not here, the chief installer gave me the honor of trying the system for the first time. I dialed the code, and instantly the clinking sound of metal hitting metal could be heard all around us. Everyone applauded! Everyone except for our mysterious visitor who seemed to have eyes only for me! I turned away, unable to meet his gaze, and urged the workman to show me the vault.

It was pretty impressive, too—four tons of galvanized metal and compressed air. It was twelve feet square with coded lock boxes welded to its walls. It was not only designed to protect the most valuable gems in the world but also to preserve written materials. Three ancient scrolls, the papyrus journals of an Egyptian king and a Bible that was handwritten during the Crusades were the first treasures to be stored there. And in the center, in its own storage container, was *The Blood of the Moor*—a priceless array of diamonds and rubies. The board had wanted to display it immediately, building an entire exhibit around it. But Dennis wanted to be cautious, not letting the public near it until we were properly protected and insured. I had hoped that was the real reason. I couldn't help but think that maybe we might have to take it back to wherever he had gotten it. I didn't know what kind of deal he had made to get it in the first place.

At about 3:30, Zeta and Roz came down to the museum. Zeta guided her aunt through the Cadillac tour like a professional, then down the hall to see the Muzi exhibition. "You'll like these, Aunt Roz. Muzi's stuff is kinda political. He is a social re . . . what is it, mamma?"

"Social realist, baby."

"Yeah, right. And he's a musician, too." Zeta was impressed by her own knowledge, and my sister beamed. It was Roz's first-time seeing what I do, and I could tell she was proud of me. That meant a lot! My sister and I stood in the middle of the exhibition, with works spanning thirty years of history, and we saw our lives playing out on the canvases. Like music, the images tapped out a rhythm of divine composition and memory, and for a moment, we were girls again, just like Zeta.

"I like this guy. Is he new?" Roz said, standing in front of an oil portrait of a woman dressed like an industrial worker of the forties with a toddler strapped to her back. It was haunting, reminding her of similar images of women in an African market or even the Madonna. She reached out to touch the acrylics—thick and heavy, multidimentional—but she knew better. It was worth a fortune.

"No. He's been around for a minute. Muzi's style has changed over the years, but his message is still the same."

"Yeah? What's that?"

"The importance of history . . . and family. You'll come back, Roz, won't you?"

"Oh, I'm comin' back . . . for the weddidng! Regina Lambert Jackson Dickerson. I kinda like that but it's a mouthful, girl," she teased, and even I laughed.

Not wanting to relive the DC rush hour experience, they headed home, urging me to come with them. I told them I had to work late and I wouldn't be home until after seven. I promised to finish the birthday celebration then, and Zeta actually hugged me goodbye. I walked them out just in time to see the Nigerian-looking man again, standing across the street watching us. He hadn't fooled me one bit! He had heard Roz mention Dennis' name only moments before. He didn't say a word, just stared at me then headed out the door. He was making me uncomfortable, and I just could not take it anymore. I walked up to the curb to talk to him, but a bus passed between us, and again, he was gone.

At about 6:30, I started to get weary, tiring from doing my work and Dennis', too. I was wondering why he hadn't at least called. I thought back to the dejected look on his face the night before. A shudder ran through me! No, he would not just up and leave me. But then, maybe he had seen that as his only way out. Yesterday, he had been weighing his options, and maybe the only option he had was to disappear.

A lump formed in my throat as my eyes filmed with tears. Could he be gone? Fear and sadness mingled with a feeling of desperation. I reached for the phone, not sure who I would call. I just had to do something. Suddenly, I was startled by the sound of the phone, ringing inches away from my hand.

"Dennis? Dennis?" I repeated into the receiver. Who else would call my office this late? But there was no one there, and I hung up. Must have been a wrong number, I thought. Moments later, the phone rang again, and I let it ring a second time for no real reason.

"Hello? Dennis? Is that you?" Again, there was only silence! I slammed the receiver back down in its cradle.

My nerves were a little shot now. It was nearly seven, and the building was completely empty. Maybe, I'm just a little jittery with all that talk today about security and break-ins. Or maybe I was losing my mind over my son getting shot and the man of my dreams dealing drugs on the side! Or could I be feeling a little crazy because two murderous convicts were trying to kill him? Or maybe because I thought I was in love with one of them. The phone rang again, and I nearly jumped out of my skin.

"Hello!?" I screamed at the phone. "Who is this? Who keeps calling?"

The sniveling muffled voice of a female was crying my name, and I strained to make out who it was.

"Marilyn . . . Marilyn, is that you?"

"Oh Regina . . . I did a terrible thing," she moaned. "I . . . I'm so sorry. I told him everything."

"Marilyn, calm down! What are you talking about?" She was crying so hard that I could barely understand her. "Marilyn, what's wrong?"

"I . . . just wanted to be with him, that's all . . . I just wanted to be what he wanted. I tried so hard . . . it was a game. We were just having a little fun."

"Fun with whom, Marilyn? Who are you talking about? Thomas?"

" No, no no! Not him! The other one! The bad one! He told me I was beautiful," she sniveled, crying woefully now. "He . . . he called me beautiful . . . his beauty queen."

"Who said you were beautiful? Who are you talking about?"

"And . . . and it was more than that. We are a lot alike, you know . . . me and him . . . we live hard . . . love hard . . . play by our own rules . . . We are predators . . . we don't take crap off of people."

I could tell she was drunk. I tried to remember who she said she was meeting with today. Marilyn had mentioned having a date. She mumbled on about her still being desirable even though her husband had been unfaithful. She swore, calling Beau Marshall everything but a child of God.

"That lousy son of a bitch! If he had just done right by me . . . if he hadn't gone around fucking cheap little jail cunt . . . Regina, I would not have done it. Any of it!" she wailed. "I'm a good girl, you know."

"I know, I know," I said trying to calm her down. She sounded so drunk and miserable; I started to get concerned for her safety. "Marilyn, where are you?"

"I'm . . . I'm at home. I went to see him . . . needed to see him . . . but he was gone! He was gone!"she cried, her suffering renewed.

"Who was gone? Beau?" I asked, trying to follow her rambling.

"No, no . . ." she moaned painfully. "Nooooooo . . . ," and then there was dead silence.

"Marilyn! Marilyn!" I yelled into the phone, knowing it was pointless. She had hung up.

I looked up at the clock again. 7:15! I grabbed my bag, fished out my car keys and headed for the door. I could stop by Marilyn's estate before going home. Make sure she was okay! She just needed to sleep this off, I said to myself. But in the back of my mind, her first words echoed over and over again.

I did a terrible thing. I'm sorry.

The building was deathly quiet. Not one security guard in sight. That was strange since we had just hired a fleet of them. I walked quickly through the maze-like hallways, very aware of how alone I was. Still, there seemed to be a presence there with me. I heard nothing and saw nothing, yet, something was there in the dark, and a feeling of dread pulsed through me. I moved faster, in then out of the elevator and swiftly into the executive parking lot, heading toward my car. I was less than twenty feet away from it when I noticed the flat tire. I cursed out loud, frozen in my tracks thinking what to do.

"It's flat," came a voice from behind me. I jumped ten feet in the air then swung around, losing my balance in the process. A strong arm wrapped around me, holding me up, righting me back on my feet. Piercing dark eyes gazed at me through skin as black as night, as the Nigerian-looking man held me in his arms.

"You okay?" he asked softly.

I didn't answer. The nearness of him startled me. After feeling strangely stalked by him all day, it felt bizarre to be this close to him. And then there was that other feeling—of knowing him and not knowing him—that caused me just to stare at him for an unfathomable amount of time.

He smiled a bit, not showing any teeth, and repeated his earlier statement. "It's flat. I can change it," he said calmly.

"Uh no . . . I can call AAA . . . or my sister or . . ." Before I could say another word, he was opening the truck of the Chrysler and removing my spare. For a moment, I wondered if he were a magician. I plunged my hand into my purse, searching for my keys. Then I realized that he had picked them up when I fell.

"You really don't have to do this. I can take care of it in the morn . . ." His head had been buried inside of the back of my car. Then suddenly he rose, like a phoenix, with my jack handle in his powerful fist. It was raised above his waist as if he were about to strike me. I took another step backward, pulled out my cell phone and hit the speed dial. He slammed my trunk shut and stepped toward me. The sound of the trunk closing echoed like a sonic boom, and in my fear, I dropped the phone. It went spattering in five different directions across the asphalt.

"Shit!" I breathed.

"Relax," he said, "this won't take long." God help me! I was making myself crazy! I had to calm down. I stood as still as a stump as he turned his back to me and knelt down. Very methodically, he removed the hubcap and loosened each lug nut with surgical care. I stood there, trying to pull myself together. Standing at least eight feet behind him, I tried to peek over his shoulder to get a better look at his face. There was little of him visible to me, but I watched with great intent as he moved. His hands and fingers were massive, and the muscles in his thick neck spilled over the tight collar of his shirt. His shoulders were broad to the point that his suit was ill-fitting, and even his shoes seemed too big for his stocky frame. As intently as he worked, he was very aware that I watched him. Even though his back was to me, I knew he was watching me, too.

"You don't have an accent," I said, not knowing what made me say it. I immediately wished I hadn't. How stupid was I?

His hands went perfectly still, and the huge muscle in the back of his neck twitched. My heart was racing! The last thing I wanted to do was piss this guy off. I looked up and down the M street alley. There were no signs of life. Then to add to my panic, the street light above our heads made a "pop pop sizzle" sound and slowly faded to black. The only light that remained now in the small lot was from the neon pizzeria sign across the way, blinking red and blue. He stood up, rising to his full height and in three strides erased all the distance between us. The jack handle was still clutched in his hand.

"You should go back inside," he said quietly. "When I am finished, I will come get you," He leaned forward, reaching past me, pressing the release bar on the door. The door opened, and he waited as though he were giving me a choice. But everything else about him said that there were no choices. Since I couldn't go past him or through him, I went back into the building. There were studio chairs in this hallway that was used as a smoking area. He pointed to one of them, bidding me to sit. I smiled hesitantly, and we both watched the double doors close between us, leaving him outside and me safely in.

As soon as the metal doors clanked shut, I hauled ass back upstairs to my office, locking my office door behind me. I was shaking like a leaf, but I was feeling more confident—now that I had half a mile of hallways between me and that man. I didn't know if my fear was real or imagined. I just knew I was scared to death and had to get out of here somehow. I sat down and laid my head on the desk trying to collect myself. My brain almost exploded when the phone rang again.

"Hel . . . hello?"

"Hey mom, this is your son." It was Rakim, sounding strong. My tension ebbed enough to notice.

"Ohh, hi baby," I breathed, trying to instill some calm in my voice.

"You didn't call me tonight, and you left so early. You okay?"

Was I okay? Hell no, but I didn't want to worry my child with that. "Rakim, don't worry about me. All I want you to do is get better, baby," I said practicing my Lamaze breathing.

"What did you think of my girl? You know, Sierra?"

Oh Lord, I really did not want to discuss this now. Rakim started talking a mile a minute, and I didn't hear a word he said. He sounded so excited, but all I could do was look at the clock. It was nearly eight and dark as pitch. With the receiver in hand, I walked over to the south window that overlooked the lot. I peeked through the hand painted Moroccan blinds and looked down. Varying hues of red and blue blinked against the wall. I saw my car, but there was no man kneeling beside it. Again, he was gone! And this time, he had my keys.

"Mamma, you still there?"

"Yeah, yeah" I stammered. "Look, baby, I gotto go! Zeta is waiting for me at home. It's still her birthday, you know."

"Alright. Call me back. I am bored to death in here. I'm ready to go home."

"Not yet, Rakim, in a few more days," I said. Although I understood his impatience. I was ready to go home too!

"Okay, mamma. See ya soon."

"Okay, bye, baby."

I hung the phone up and rushed back to the window. Where the hell had he gone? Then I remembered. I had just spent the day watching more than a dozen workers install one of the world's best security systems. All I had to do was activate the code, and it would lock the whole place up tight. But I didn't know the real code; we had used a test code earlier. Only Dennis and the head of security had the real one. Where the hell was Dennis? I tried to regroup as I picked up the phone once again, dialing frantically.

I tried the number at his penthouse, and no one picked up. Try his cell again, the little voice of reason in my head said. I started dialing, but after the first three numbers, the strangest thing happened. The building began to "clink"—hundreds of little clinking sounds, above me, below me and all around me. The building was locking down! I cried with relief, finally feeling safe. I wasn't sure how it had happened and didn't care. This terrible night was coming to an end.

I flopped down in my over padded chair and finished dialing Dennis' cell phone number. I didn't care if he answered or not. I wanted to leave a message letting him know that I had mastered his big-time security system. I closed my eyes as I waited for the beep. As I sat there, allowing my adrenaline level to stabilize, I heard a familiar chiming sound outside of my door. It was a cell phone, and the ring sounded a lot like Dennis'. He did not pick up, but I dialed it again as I walked over to my closed office door. I pressed my ear to it and heard "The Minute Waltz"—Dennis' ring tone. Was he here in the building? Thank God! I swung the door open wide.

But God had nothing to do with it! The dark man, the creator of this nightmare, was standing at the threshold on the other side. He was smiling; but if a smile could be considered evil, if a smile could evoke fear of the worse kind, then I was faced with it now. Jaw tight, eyes narrowed, he almost looked demonic. And as he stepped toward me, from his trouser pocket came the last few notes of "The Minute Waltz."

He opened the phone then snapped it shut. When he did, I noticed the immaculate seams in his pants and expertly starched cuffs—on a man that wore shoes that were too big. These details were clanging together in my head making no sense at all. Then, suddenly, it was all too clear. I was familiar with the cell phone, and the shoes and the Italian suit that still carried the scent of the man I knew so well. But it was this man who wore them now that was a stranger to me. My heart stopped beating! If this man had stepped into Dennis' life, then where was Dennis?

"*Who are you?* Where . . . is . . . what have you done with Dennis!" I asked, already afraid to hear the answer. He opened his mouth but not to answer me. He looked offended that I would dare question him. A fraction of a second later, his powerful fist was around my neck, and he was dragging me down the hallway like a rag doll.

"Please." I managed to squeeze out.

"Shut up," he barked pulling me down the first flight of stairs.

"Who are you?" I cried, holding on to his wrist with both hands. My feet were barely touching the stairs as he held me adrift.

"I said shut up!" He commanded again, and to emphasize his point, he pushed his fingers into my neck even further.

He dragged me down two more flights of stairs and then pushed open the basement door with a vengeance. He checked the hallway, making sure it was empty, and then maneuvered through the dark building. He moved as if he knew it well. He had obviously been studying it and all of us all day.

"Where . . . where are you taking me?"

He snarled! I had asked another question, and he was not pleased.

When we got to the vault, he slammed my back against it so hard that I thought he had broken me in two. My legs felt numb, and my throat hurt where his fingers gripped me. He relaxed his hold a bit but came closer to me, pinning me against the wall. His hot breathe stung my face, and the heat from his body melted mine.

"Open it," he said.

"Wha . . . what?" I croaked.

"I said, open it, bitch," and he pushed my shoulders flat against the metal door.

"The vault?" I asked incredulously. "I don't know how!"

"Don't lie to me!" He snapped. He stared at me hard, and I could only imagine it was to give me a moment to comply. Then he seemed to soften, running his fore finger lazily down my cheek. That awful smile returned!

"Gina." He tilted his head a little. "Regina," he said in a sing songy tone. "Shit, you must be something else." He laughed to himself.

Gina. Regina.

"Niggas just fallin' all over you. You got it like that? You all dat, bitch?" His forefinger traveled the length of my neck and coursed its way down to my breast bone.

"You're a convict . . . from the prison," I said, now realizing I had heard that voice somewhere before. The day of the riot! My eyes widened in disbelief. There were three men in that smoke-filled room with me—Thomas, Ray and . . .

He smiled again as if reading my thoughts. "No, baby, I ain't Ray."

"Shaka!?" The name passed over my lips in agony.

The realization that I was trapped in an empty building with a murderous convict made me lose my mind. I began to kick and flail wildly, trying to break free. But Shaka proved to be as powerful as the warrior he was named after. Effortlessly, he pulled me into him, making my struggling useless. Then the worse thing imaginable happened. Shaka pressed into me, and I felt his arousal.

"Oh God," I moaned. "Please don't . . ." Slowly, very slowly, Shaka eased his big hand into my blouse, and squeezed down hard on my left breast. I cried out in pain!

"Why? Why are you doing this?" I moaned as he ripped the blouse all the way open, buttons pinking to the floor. Shaka was pulling my breast out of my bra, rubbing the nipple with his palm when he suddenly stopped. My question seemed to sting him, and he looked me straight in the eye.

"Why?" he spat and then said very deliberately, emphasizing each word, "Because I hate him."

I knew he meant Ray. Dennis had been a pawn in their game from the very beginning. Now we were both going to pay! Defensively, I closed my legs tight, sliding my lose hand down in front of me in an effort to protect myself. Shaka laughed, a sadistic sound that made my blood curl. Then he howled so loud I thought I would faint. He looked at me mockingly.

"I'm just playin' wit you, girl. I'm not gonna fuck you," he said as he continued his assault on my body. "I told Beauty Queen I wouldn't hurt you. Make you suffer"

I did a terrible thing. I'm so sorry.

Shaka lowered his head, running his tongue down the length of my face. It felt nasty and coarse. "Hear you got a pretty little girl, though. Fresh and pink! I ain't makin' no promises there."

I told him everything.

Oh my God! Not my baby girl! I screamed in his ear and the piercing sound drove him over the edge. He smacked me hard, and the taste of warm blood filled my mouth.

"You listen here, bitch! You gonna get me into this damn vault; Dickerson fucked up my trade, and now I'm gonna get me some of his art shit. You betta hope it evens the score."

Shaka started grinding into me hard, "Because if it don't, I'm gonna kill you."

Panic turned into total hysteria. I fought back with all of my might, pushing, clawing, and screaming my lungs out. But when all my energy was spent, he simply laughed at me, shaking his head.

"Please . . . please," was all I had strength to say.

"Got to, baby! Can't be no other way." Shaka kissed me sweetly as if to console me. "You got messed up in some shit, that's all."

I cried pitifully, sinking into the metal door at my back. He could have everything in that damn vault, including the necklace. I wanted this predator to leave my family alone.

"You're not going to get away with this," I said. "Get out of town while you have your freedom."

"Later. I got business."

"Getting even is more important than getting away?" I couldn't believe that someone could be so full of hate.

Just then, he pulled a crude knife out of his pocket. The blade was about five inches long, and the makeshift hilt was wrapped in fabric to protect his hand. He tightened his fist around it, crushed his body against mine, and then held me still with his other hand. Broken, I allowed myself to think this was the end. But in some far corner of my mind, there was still hope. I said a silent prayer for my children, knowing my love for them was far greater than any hate this man could have. Shaka tilted his head as if he were seriously considering my question.

"You see, me and Ray go way back, and he ain't easy to get rid of. I've tried! But this time I got a betta idea." Shaka gripped the waistband of my skirt and pulled. The closure tore open, and his hand ventured inside.

"You see, I know what makes him tick." I felt the knife poised at my side, the tip pressed against my skin. "I know what keeps him going." He ran the blade underneath my breast then Shaka leaned his head toward me as if to say goodbye.

"This is how you kill a man like Ray Boden," he hissed. "You kill what he loves."

CHAPTER 14

◆

Love Locked Down

I expected to feel cold steel slicing me to bits. Instead, there was a dull thud, and Shaka collapsed to the floor in front of me. Towering over his limp body was Dennis, wearing a hideous golfer's pullover, paisley Bermuda shorts, and flip flops from the dollar store. He was holding my lug wrench in one hand and the building entry key card in the other. I had never been so happy to see anyone in all my life.

"Regina, are you alright?"

"Dennis, oh God, where have you been?" I asked trying to throw my arms around his neck.

"Locked up at Montgomery! And I do mean locked up."

"In the prison?" I asked.

"It's a long story," Dennis' eyes scanned my body from top to bottom. He stroked my arms with loving care and concern. Anger darkened his face when he saw the dried blood on my lip. "Baby, did he hurt you?"

"I'm fine," I said, so glad to be in his arms. "Everything is fine now."

"After I called the house and Roz told me you were still at work, I tried your cell. When I didn't get an answer, I took Beau's car and broke all speed records trying to get here. Don't worry; the police are on their way," he said.

I was so happy I could have cried. Dennis had found me, and I was being rescued from this nightmare. He held me in his arms.

But seconds later, my happiness would be replaced with dread; it wasn't over! There was movement around my feet, and I heard Shaka's voice once again rise out of the dark.

"You shoulda killed me when you had the chance," and in one swift move, Shaka pushed himself up with one hand and plunged the knife into Dennis' right thigh with the other. Dennis' legs buckled under him as he fell to his knees in excruciating pain.

"Get up and open that damn vault now!" Shaka demanded.

Dennis coiled, and a stream of blood flowed from his leg. He covered it with his hand, trying to put pressure on the wound. I made a move to help him, and Shaka's arm swung out to separate us. Afraid he would come after me next, Dennis braced himself against the wall, trying to pull himself up. He left a trail of bloody hand prints on the wall.

"Hurry up, Dickerson! I'm sicka playin' wit you niggas!" he shouted and kicked Dennis in the ribs. Determined, Dennis staggered to his feet and reluctantly, pressed the entry code into the mounted key pad.

The heavy door eased open, and the convict pushed us both in. At first, he seemed confused as if he expected to see pots of gold and silver piled up everywhere. Then his disappointment led to anger! Running out of time and knowing that his plan was falling apart, he began to attack the metal room. Shaka thrashed around like a crazed gorilla, knocking over metal containers and spilling their contents. He fought his way through oceans of packaging, then, not finding a pile of money hidden inside, he would curse in frustration. Lucky, none of the printed materials seemed to interest him; he tossed them aside without giving them a second look. Then he spotted the twelve-inch cubed metal box with its own lock.

"What's in there?" he asked.

Neither Dennis or I said anything; that made Shaka go wild. He picked up the box in question and threw it across the room. Metal hitting metal, it sounded like an atomic explosion. I screamed, and Shaka came over to me, again grabbing me by the neck. He held the crude knife to my ribs.

"Dickerson, get me into that damn box or I will kill this bitch now! You got that?"

"I got that," Dennis answered sourly. He limped over to the box and produced a small key from his pocket. He looked at me sadly and then turned the key in the lock. The spring release activated, and the lid rose slowly. Millions of dollars worth of diamonds and rubies seemed to light up the dismal gray vault as the three of us stood there in amazement. The legendary *Blood of the Moor* necklace laid on its soft velvet bed, regal in its brilliance. Its gems sparkled against the stark interior of the room, and I gasped. I had known it was beautiful but tonight, threatened with the loss of it, it was magnificent! Shaka whooped with joy.

"Goddamn! That shit is the shit!" he said, eyes as big as saucers. Dennis and I just looked at each other woefully. It was one thing to lose the piece; it was another thing to lose it to a crude ignorant jackass that could not appreciate its full value. It sickened me to know this idiot might trade five hundred years of history for a few bags of weed!

"Candy for daddy!" He pinged at the red gems like they were dime store marbles. Finally satisfied, Shaka forced the box shut and stashed it underneath his arm. Then, quite unexpectantly, he stepped toward Dennis, knocking him back to the floor. I made another move to help him. Shaka threw me a threatening look.

"Don't move, bitch," he said. His head ping ponged back and forth between us as he thought what to do. He knew his time was running out.

"Ya'll got to be the luckiest fools in the world. I ain't got time to fuck her and kill you, too. I definitely wanted to make you suffer, Dickerson. You caused me a lot of fuckin' trouble," he said.

I looked down at him and the floor as I held my breath. I was so scared and Dennis seemed so surprisingly calm. He must have been counting on the police showing up before Shaka could get away . . . or before he could slit our throats. Shaka knew the clock was ticking, and maybe Dennis was right. Maybe our luck would hold up! After all, neither one of us was dead,

270

the police were coming, and as of right now, the necklace was still here. But Shaka began to back away from us, heading for the door. I could tell that some of our luck was about to run out.

"This should even the score, Dickerson," Shaka said, grinning devilishly as he patted the box under his arm. "Ya'll just be cool . . . and count your last breaths, suckas!" and with that, he rushed out of the vault, pulling the door behind him.

"No! Shaka! Don't!" Dennis yelled as he struggled to get up. But it was too late! We heard the metal tumblers click, locking the door. The last thing we heard was Shaka running down the empty hallway until his footfalls echoed into nothing.

"Damn!" Dennis spat, rocking back on his heels and collapsing to the floor. Red droplets trickled down making ruby-like bubbles on the floor. The bleeding was fairly steady despite his efforts to stop it. We were going to have to get out of here soon.

"Your leg . . ." I rushed over to him.

"It's not that! This vault is an air tight chamber. We'll be okay for now but after a while . . ." he hesitated.

"After a while what?" I asked, trying not to sound hysterical.

"After a while, we will run out of air," he said slowly.

"Run out of air," I repeated.

"Yes, well . . . we'll probably get sleepy first. Then . . ."

"Run out of air," I said flatly, absorbing what that statement meant. I pulled my hair away from my face and ran my tongue along the sore corner of my mouth. Then impulsively, I ran to the door and rammed my shoulder into it. When that didn't open it, I began to kick it frantically.

"You're wasting your time," Dennis said. It will never open! I made sure of that when I had it installed."

I collapsed in frustration. I had been on a crazy emotional roller coaster all day, and now my shoulder was aching. Every time I thought things were getting better, they took a turn for the worse. I squatted down on a tall metal shipping container and replayed the series of events.

"So we lost the necklace, and we are going to suffocate to death in here. Shaka is going to get away, and more than likely, find a way to kill Ray. Does that about sum it up?"

I didn't mean to sound so bitchy, but I'm sure that I did. Dennis pursed his lips and exhaled a deep breath at the mention of Ray's name. While I was sure he was trying to come up with a way to get out of this mess, it was obvious he was frustrated with more than our current predicament. For about three minutes, we said nothing to each other. We didn't even look at each other. Then Dennis started tapping his fingers on the tiled floor, driving me crazy!

"How are we getting out of here?" I shrieked.

"I don't know. Let me think, will you?" he barked.

"That lunatic threatened to hurt Zeta, you know!" I moaned.

"Zeta? Don't worry about her. He doesn't have time. Shaka knows he has to get out of DC. Every law enforcement officer within thirty miles is after him."

I nodded, trying to feel assured. Two minutes later, I started to pace. Dennis let out three much exaggerated sighs while he watched me pace. Then, out of nowhere . . .

"Why is it every time I leave you, you wind up with a convict?!" Dennis asked. I hoped he meant it as a joke, but it rubbed me the wrong way. I walked away from him, trying not to go there. Things were bad enough already.

"Maybe you should stop leaving me, and the convicts would stop seeking me out," I retorted.

That obviously rubbed him the wrong way, and he squirmed down to the floor, putting his back against the wall. It was already getting hot in that big metal box. Our bad temperaments were just going to make it hotter.

"Man's got to work, Regina. Oh, but I guess you like your men *locked down* in one place so you know where they are . . . calling you all the time . . . *listening* to you."

"What's wrong with listening to me?" I snapped. I had to admit I liked that part. Ray always seemed so attentive and interested in everything I did. That might have been part of his game, but I didn't care. Every woman likes to be heard. Why don't men get that?

"Oh, and let's not forget, he's got to feed you poetry! 'The beauty of the night was in her eyes.' Jesus! Regina, I thought you were smarter than that!" he barked.

I did not remind him that he had used poetry and jewelry to do his little mating dance with me. The more he talked, the more I realized that there was not much difference between Ray Boden and Dr. Dennis Dickerson.

"I can just hear him now—'And in her voice, the calling of the dove . . . like music.' . . . *Ha!*"

Dennis was really trying to get to me now! I folded my arms across my chest and took a quick inventory of the vault. If I could have found one thing in there that wouldn't cost me my retirement, I would have hurled it in his face! We were both seething, staring each other down. Then Dennis narrowed his eyes and came in for the kill.

"And we can't leave out the most important part—he's got to make love to you over the phone."

My head popped up on that last one.

"You've done that with him, haven't you?" he accused.

"What?"

"Phone sex. You did it with him, right!"

I ignored his question, looked down at the gash in his leg and tried to keep my mouth shut. I knew he had to be in a lot of pain, and he was losing blood rapidly. Red was oozing into those grotesque lime green and blue paisley shorts. I just had to ask.

"Where did you get those awful clothes?"

"Beau Marshall. His guards found me lying half naked under a pile of sheets in the prison laundry room. It's a good thing they did, or I might be somebody's girlfriend by now." He got quiet, and a lump formed in my throat. He had been through a lot and still, he had made it back to me. It was a miracle he was even alive. Dennis sat there looking kind of ridiculous with tiny puckered Donald Ducks blowing kisses at little Daisy Ducks all over the frightening shirt. A smile tried to creep up to my lips, but I bit it back. Dennis made a very unlikely hero, I thought. No capes, no masks, but a hero just the same. I didn't want to argue with him, so I tried to change the subject.

"Dennis, you could have been killed in that place," I said quietly.

"Yes, I could have!" he spat back at me. He snatched up a piece of my torn blouse and began wrapping it around his leg for a tourniquet. He pulled at the cloth like he was wrestling with it. I could tell that his frustration had little to do with the wound.

"Were you fucking him over the phone? Tell me the truth!"

"Ray . . . Dennis, I don't . . ."

"*Did you call me by that bastard's name . . . again?!*"

"No . . . I . . ." God, he had heard me that first time a week ago! My hands started to feel clammy, and little beads of sweat began to pop out on Dennis' forehead. This was taking an ugly turn.

"Are you in love with Ray Boden? You know they call him Rayboy, the Playboy, don't you."

The hairs on the back of my neck bristled, and resentment snaked up my spine. He was really determined to push this issue.

"*Are you in love with him?!!*"

"*I do not want to discuss Ray Boden with you!*" I screamed.

"Fine!" Dennis was steaming, but he had given me the last word. I should have stopped there, but I just could not help myself.

"Fine!"

"*Fine*!!"

"*Fine*!!!"

"Fiiiiine! Keep your jail house dick!" he snapped.

"At least, he wanted me to know he had a dick!" *BAM*! There it was! The gloves were off now. Dennis looked like his head was about to spin off.

"*And that is another thing*! You women make me sick with that shit! I was trying to respect you. Not rush you into bed until we were both sure. But *noooo*, you have to completely humiliate me by reaching out to a *convict*!!"

"Humiliate you? Why does everything have to be about you?"

"Woman, pleeeaase!"

"That's right. Dennis this! Dr. Dickerson that! 'I want to find the damn blood clot necklace'," I mocked in a Donald Duck voice. "I have had it up to here!" My hand flew to my sore neck.

"It is called *The Blood of the Moor*," he corrected.

"Oh that's right. How could I forget? You only told me about it a million times—over and over again. You know, they say women talk all the time! If I had a dollar for every hour I spent listening to some man, I could retire rich!"

Dennis stared up at the ceiling like he was talking to God.

"There she goes again. Comparing me to every no-good man she has ever known." Then he looked me straight in the eye and said, "You are so obsessed with the past!"

"Me?!" I almost choked, "I can't believe you said that when you are the one spending your life chasing dead crap!"

"What!?"

"You heard what I said! Nothing gets your attention unless it is one thousand years old."

"Oh yeah? And what about you, Regina? All you care about is what you can get. The newest thing coming down the pike! A new car, a house, anything! You switch up men like you do handbags!"

I knew he was talking about my history with Jabari and Stephen and both of my kids having different daddies. Throwing that shit up in my face! That was low! I was so mad I had to bring my finger out to dance for him! I got aaalll up in his face.

"Excuuuuse me? You don't think I know what I want? I thought I wanted you! YOU are the one dickin' around with me!"

"Baby, I want you! I know I do. But I'm saying that you wouldn't know a real man if he came up and bit you on the ass!"

I was so angry I couldn't see straight. I was also tired of being the nice girl. I stood up, turned around slowly and took a good look at where I was. I was trapped inside an air-compressed vault with no food or water with a man who had done nothing but lie to me since I met him. A man who had put me, my career, and both of my children in jeopardy! I had done nothing but idolize and support him, and this is what it had gotten me!? My temperature started to rise!

"*A real man*? You have got to be kidding! Tell me, Dennis, what is *real* about you? I mean, you lied to me, played me for a fool, and then left me hangin' out to dry."

Dennis' eyes glared at me, penetrating my soul. "I never left you, Regina. Never! I am not going to let you put that shit on me. I may have done a lot of things wrong, but I have always been there for you."

I closed my eyes, trying to keep his words out. As always, he was trying to justify the chaos he had created in my life. Not today!

Dennis looked at me wide-eyed. "Now what's wrong!!??"

"Nothing! Everything! You really don't understand, do you? I was doing just fine without you. Then you came along and twisted my whole life up," I said. My voice was a whole octave higher than normal. Dennis' eyes rolled to the back of his head.

"Regina, what is your damage anyway? Pleeeaase tell me," he asked with plenty of man-attitude.

"My damage?"

"Yeah! I mean, obviously you think you've been wronged in some way . . . and it's all my fault."

"You admitted it was all your fault!"

"Yeah, *it was all my fault*!" Dennis spat, waving his arms in the air. "Look, let's just get this out in the open now—all I tried to do was give you everything you wanted. You wanted a high paying career? I *hired* you and *promoted* you! You wanted your kids to have a dad? I stepped into that role with no problem. You wanted nice things? I pulled out my checkbook! And, baby, when you really started tripping . . . when you thought you wanted a thug, I tried to be that, too!"

"WHAT!?" I screeched! My neck snapped so hard I thought it would break. "Just what kind of *man-brains* are you using to think with!?"

"You heard me! I am stuck in the middle of a 112-degree desert—doing business with people who would rather slice me up than negotiate with me—and you are back here playing phone tag with Charles Manson!"

"Black man, are you listening to yourself!!? You have lost your mind! You dragged *me* into this shit! I didn't know what the hell you were doing!"

"Maybe not, but you knew something was wrong," he countered.

I thought back to those nights we spent together after he'd returned from a dig. I remembered all the precious artifacts he would bring to my house to impress me. I knew it was wrong. I knew it was unorthodox. But I let it go on because it made me feel special. I was the Egyptian princess, and he was the gallant warrior who had come to rescue me.

"Baby, you knew what the deal was from the very beginning! Admit that!"

"What are you talking about?!"

"All the trips! All the beautiful pieces I brought back and laid at your feet! The night I came back from the big dig. I was parked in your driveway, on the phone, going through my trunk. You knew something was up then! You didn't ask because you didn't want to know."

I stood up and put my hands on my hips. Yes, I knew something was wrong, but I was not going to let him heap this mess on me.

"You cannot possibly be serious! Are you suggesting that I signed on for this shit?"

"I am suggesting that you signed on to be with Dr. Dennis Dickerson, chief curator and founder of Mirathi. I am suggesting that you signed on for all the parties and the fundraisers and the heightened social circle and the fine cars and any other expensive social-climbing bullshit that happens to come with that!"

"Okay, okay Dennis what do you want from me? You want me to say 'yeah, I knew you were dealing drugs and making deals with murderers and selling your soul for a stupid piece of jewelry?' Is that what you want me to say?"

We were really yelling at each other now, sweating like pigs. Dennis looked so frustrated with me that he could have rammed his head into the wall. "No Regina, what I want you to say is that you *love me* and you *trust me* and that even though you know I'm not perfect, you are still there for me!"

His frustration seemed to turn to desperation, and his tone softened. "I want you to say that you want me—the man—not the job, not the image and all that comes with it. Just me because . . . because I know I love you, and that's the only thing I have ever been sure about."

Dennis waited for me to bite back, but I didn't. Those last three words, said with so much emotion and sincerity, had made all the others meaningless. With me silent, he thought it safe to continue.

"Baby, I don't want to feel like our relationship depends on whatever fantasy you got going on in your head. I want you to see me."

The gift of sight! Sister Dora's advice rang in my head. Then I thought about Aunt Betty and her friends all after the same man. Maybe in this great female marathon to get a man, I had treated Dennis like a prize. That bitch Tina and I had been competing for him from the start, ever since we had applied for the same associate curator job. The first time Dennis bought me coffee, I thought I had won something. After that, it had been a race to get Dennis firmly planted into my life and into my bed.

I sat back down on the metal box, and Dennis looked at me wearily. "Regina, we live together, share a life together and are raising your children together. Now ask yourself—before we go any further—do you love me?"

Is it possible I had never really considered it? Had Dennis been my necklace? No, he was much more than that! Every time I looked at him, I saw my future. And that was the frightening part.

"You make me so crazy! Every time I think I . . ."

" I asked you a simple question, woman." And it was simple—horrifyingly, earth-shatteringly simple. Did I love him?

"Be honest with me and yourself," he said, sounding like my friend and not just a lover.

"I . . . think so. I am just so scared." I said whimpering.

Dennis looked at me like his heart was breaking. "It's okay to be scared. Damn, I'm scared, too. You've been hurt; we both have."

We sat there in the silence, absorbing all that had been said. Then after a moment, I dried my eyes and looked at him. At first, all I saw was a good looking brother in tasteless shorts that stopped too far above his knees. Then I saw the man who came to my house almost every evening to check on me and see if I needed anything. I saw the man that read *The Post* with my children, expanding their minds and made sure their homework was done.

EfforteffortreasonreasonreasonreasonreasonEffortreasoneffortreason

"What's that?" I asked.

"A Bible. More precisely, a Winchester Abbey Bible, inspired by the legendary Gutenberg. It is hundreds of years old."

I walked over to him and helped him sit back down, setting the massive Bible down between us. I touched it, running my fingers over the intricately embossed cover.

"Are we going to read it?" I asked quietly.

"No. Not unless you can read Latin," he laughed. Then I saw him wince. The pain in his leg was getting worse. He bowed his head like he was praying.

"Dennis, are . . . are we preparing to die in here?"

"God, no!" he said a little too emphatically. He reached out to still the pain and checked his makeshift bandage. "At least I hope not."

"Then what are we doing with this?" I laid my hand flat on the Bible, and he covered my hand with his. Dennis looked deep into my eyes.

"I'm going to marry you. Now."

"Marry me? Now? Here? In the vault?"

"That's right and don't worry. When we get out of here, you can still have the church and the gown and . . ."

"I've had all that," I said, laughing to myself. I was dirty and bloody and possibly taking my last breaths. Yet, when I looked into Dennis' eyes, I saw the reflection of a beautiful, confident woman that finally knew what love was. I saw a queen. I smoothed the wrinkles from my ripped stockings and skirt. "This is so much better. I am ready now."

Dennis grinned and began kissing me gently—my lips, my cheeks and up to my eye lids—as if he were giving me his greatest treasure. I sat there letting him just love on me, feeling his warmth, accepting his peace. He was giving me comfort—an intimate touch that was more exciting than sex. An intercourse of the spirit! The kiss felt platonic yet sensual. Then he slid his tongue into my mouth for a more erotic experience. I basked in it. I wanted to be with him—just him—and not some ideal of love I had concocted in my head. I wanted to make love to him—without my phantom jailhouse lover waiting in the shadows. Then, I remembered where we were, and how we got here.

"What about Shaka and your necklace? What about *The Blood of the Moor*?"

"Baby, I don't care about the past, and I am not too concerned right now about the future. You are all I ever needed, and nothing I find in this world could ever compare to you."

He squeezed my hand tight. "For better or for worse."

"For better or for worse," I repeated, knowing full well what that meant.

Dennis looked down at the Bible, then back up at me and back down at the Bible again. He seemed a little embarrassed. Then, he hunched his shoulders, and smiled.

"I really don't know how to do this," he said.

"I do."

"Good. How?"

"No! I mean 'I do'," I smiled at him, and then he understood.

"Ohhh! Well, damn! Yeah, I do, too, Mrs. Dickerson!" he shouted, and with that, our vows were said.

"I do love you, Dennis."

"I love you, too, baby . . . and those big phat pretty thighs."

We fell into each others arms laughing, and I cried tears of joy into the ugly golf shirt while he tried to piece my blouse back together. Then, we settled in as husband and wife. Dennis held me in his arms, and we talked about all kinds of things. We shared secrets we had never told anyone else and unspoken dreams we promised we'd help each make come true. Hours later, we were all talked out. I laid my hand across his chest and rested my head on his shoulder. I listened to his steady breathing and felt his heartbeat under my palm until sleep finally came. There was no panic and no worry. No tomorrow! Just peace!

"Did I mention that I love you?" he asked sleepily, eyes still closed as if he were dreaming.

"Yes, you did," I answered, feeling as if we were in a dream.

Eventually, my eyes got weary, and it was harder to breathe, and just like Dennis predicted, sleep came easy. Dennis went to sleep first, probably because he had lost so much blood. That left me alone to wait for the end. I held fast to his hand, still resting on the giant Bible, and considered the life I had lead. It was a good one, I thought, and for the most part I was pleased. I had worked well, played well, raised two wonderful children and been loved by a good man. What more could anyone ask?

Just then, It occurred to me that I had contemplated my life in this manner once before. It had been in a dream where I was in a box, locked down with no escape. In the dream, I was trying to get out before I fell to my death, and the world kept pushing and pushing and pushing me around. Cars racing! The Potomac! Ray had saved me! Ray had saved me! Thoughts were jumbled. Couldn't think straight! I was losing consciousness and a familiar voice rang in my head.

"Regina? Regina? Are you in there?"

Damn, that sounded just like that bitch Tina. Was I awake or was this another dream? If Tina was here, it must be a nightmare. I inhaled what I thought was my last breath and tried to concentrate on Dennis, my husband. Yes, that would be a nice last thought, making love to my husband—him and only him.

"Regina, are you in there? Is Dennis with you?"

I heard muffled voices, the soft clank of metal, and then the sound of feet rushing toward me.

"Oh God, there they are! Oh my Lord, please don't be dead!" I tried to open my eyes. The world looked out of focus. Suddenly, a hand with red-polished nails, slapped me hard!

"Regina! Wake up, girl!" Tina Benchford and several men in uniform were standing over me.

"Miss, miss, can you hear me? Are you alright?" asked one of the men. I felt Dennis move, and I heard other voices saying "he's alright. What about her?"

I tried to speak, but nothing came out. All of a sudden, that same hand came down and slapped me again!

"Come on, girl, you can do it!" I forced one eye open and willed my mouth to move.

"Tina, . . . you bitch. Slap me again . . . and I will . . . kill you."

Hands poised on her wide hips, she let out a sigh of relief and gestured to the paramedics. "Don't worry about this one, boys. She's tough."Tina grinned and gently patted the top of my head.

"She's going to be just fine."

CHAPTER 15

◆

Tina's Story
Political Prisoners

Twelve hours after our ordeal, Shaka had been apprehended and taken back to jail. Marilyn had actually notified the police right after she called me. Whether it was her conscience or a rise in her self-esteem, she had given Shaka up. Marilyn was beautiful, powerful, intelligent, and wealthy—and none of it mattered. I had no doubt that Shaka had taken her insecurities and twisted them into a way to control her. Marilyn was a loose end I had to tie up. I sighed; Ray was another. But my first order of business paraded before me in red-weaved splendor, rhinestone bracelets, and a plunging neckline.

"Fresh from the bakery, Ms. Lambert! Or is it Ms. Jackson? Or is it Ms. Dickerson?"

Tina all but skipped across the cafe floor, carrying a tray of fresh brewed coffee and lemon tarts. We were back on the job, clad in our high fashion power suits complete with trendy boardroom chic accessories. We wore them like armor. Tina took a seat across from me at the table we had shared not long ago, one week before her dismissal. She tried to cross her legs under the short cafe table, spilling half of my coffee over the edge of the cup. I smiled sweetly, telling her no apology was necessary. Then I dabbed at the liquid mess with my napkin, catching it before it ran onto my lap.

Foster and Dennis were both upstairs, lobbying with the board members on Tina's behalf. Considering her heroic actions from the night before, we were sure the outcome would be a complete reinstatement. For now, however, there were only the two of us at the table, and I felt a bit uncomfortable. It was almost ten o'clock; usually by now I would have sabotaged her car, or she would have pulverized my breakfast treat, or at least we would have traded one snide remark. We were both making an effort to be cordial.

"Thank you," I began.

"For what?" she asked.

"Well, to start, for saving my life. I know we haven't always been friendly. If you hadn't come around when you did, I'm not sure Dennis and I would have made it out alive. How did you find us anyway?"

"Completely by accident! My apartment is downtown, and I was on my way home. I noticed your car, and I know you usually try to go home before dark to be with your family," she said. The way she said it made me think she had no family. It occurred to me that I didn't know much about her, other than she had wanted my job and my man.

"I looked for you. Saw your celly smashed on the pavement. Thought it meant trouble. Turns out I was right! The rest is history."

"Anyway, I'm glad you stopped." We both stared down into our coffee, and then I ventured forth on a hunch. "Tina, something tells me that's not the only reason I have to thank you."

She looked up and tilted her head. I could tell that she thought about blowing me off, but I wasn't going to let her. I'd seen Tina in the building too many times since she'd been fired not to know something was up.

"Tina, were you covering up for Dennis? The paper work and when you were cozying up to Foster—were you protecting him?"

"Yes, I knew the numbers did not jive. I knew that Dennis was into something covert. But I also knew that he was trying to build something marvelous, and that men often do unscrupulous things for noble reasons."

"You knew about the mess at the prison?" I thought back to the day Tina was reciting prison statistics to us at that very same table.

"No, but I did know that Foster was on to him and would stop at nothing to find the truth. Mirathi would become just another good idea that went bad, and we would have all been just another group of unemployed black people. Besides, Foster gets a kick out of trying to look up my skirt. I thought I would give him the thrill of his life!"

"No you didn't, girl!" I teased.

"No, but I would have. I just wanted to distract him a bit. He is kinda cute." she laughed, a high pitched sound that probably drove dogs crazy. I changed the subject just to make it stop.

"I'm glad the board has decided to pull out of the prison program," I said. "They say they want to reevaluate its purpose." Tina's smile disappeared, and a look of solemnity replaced it.

"Yes, they have asked me to help coordinate the breakdown tomorrow because I helped to pack that stuff up for Montgomery in the first place. I understand their decision. Still, I wish they would reconsider."

"Why? I thought you hated the idea of Dennis going to Montgomery."

"I did, but more than that, I hate the idea of so many black men being there, so many forgotten names and faces. It's kinda sad, and it's hard out here for a sistah alone."

Tina began to fidget in her chair and play with the salt and pepper shakers. I had said something to make her uncomfortable. "Tina, do you know anybody locked up at Montgomery?"

"No. Not in that prison." Tina hesitated. "But there was a man once. It was a long time ago," she looked up from stirring her coffee, checked her watch, and looked around nervously again. Tina Benchford obviously was not accustomed to this kind of frankness. I had watched her enough in the halls of Mirathi to know that she did not mingle well with her peers. And that "sista-girl" thing that she tried to do often came off biting and bitchy. She was reaching out to me and that was not normal for her.

"Regina," she began. "Did you know I use to work in the Peace Corps?"

"You?" I asked with way too much astonishment in my voice. I could hardly imagine Tina serving rice to orphans in the jungle wearing acrylic nails and five-inch stiletto heels. She laughed again, piercing my ears, and I thought the Hebron glass exhibit on the second floor was a goner.

"Yes, me! It was just after college. We were so young. His name was Oliver Mutanga, and he was Angolan. He had come to the United States for an education. When he went home, I went with him."

I tried not to stare at her. I had never even considered Tina as a real person with any kind of depth or dimension. She had always been "that bitch Tina" to me. She smiled shyly. Tina was obviously sharing something with me that she didn't tell most people. I put the tart down on my plate and listened to her. I wanted her to know she had my undivided attention.

"In the years Oliver was gone, the government in his own country had changed hands. His family was embroiled in the great conflict, and he had to take a stand. Oliver was idealistic and full of that American bravado that foreigners hate. That John-Wayne-America-the-Beautiful crap will get you killed, you know." She frowned as if she were reliving this episode of her life.

"Oliver was brave, brilliant, and rebellious. He was a man of vision. The people loved him and . . ."

"And you were in love with him," I interjected. Tina looked up, startled.

"I guess I was," she admitted. "But it didn't do any good. My love couldn't save him. It couldn't guard him against his own stubborn inclinations. He was a revolutionist."

"He sounds great," I said sincerely. "Where is this dreamboat of yours?"

"Gone," she answered.

"Gone? What happened to him?"

"They took him. They, meaning the corrupt military. They dragged him out of our bed in the middle of the night and put him in prison." She looked up at me. "And I never saw him again."

"Never?"

"Never," she said.

"Surely there must have been channels you could have gone through. Procedures that could have gotten you through to him! You just can't lock up innocent people because they are loud and have different opinions, even in Angola."

"You would be surprised. It happens all over the world. Even here."

I put my tart down again. Surely she didn't mean that!

"This is not Angola, Regina, but we do have thousands of people behind bars because they chose to stand against a dysfunctional government. It could be the tax system or the welfare system or the child protective service system—it doesn't matter. They may not be snatched in the middle of the night, but they are gone just the same. Women left with no men, children left without fathers."

Tina took the last bite of her tart and licked the access from her manicured fingers. I handed her a napkin, afraid she was about to wipe her hands on her Chanel suit. She accepted the napkin as she slurped her coffee with pinky extended.

"Poverty and injustice will make the best of men do wrong," she continued, "And before you know it, they are 'political' prisoners just like my Oliver, fighting systems designed to make them fail."

A lump formed in my throat as I heard the painful truth behind her words. Dennis was a man of vision like her Oliver. A good man who, for whatever reason, had made a series of wrong choices! Oliver had gotten caught up and locked down. I needed to know that there was a future for Tina and this lost lover in Africa.

"Did Oliver write to you?" I asked.

"No . . . well . . . I'm not sure, but I wrote to him. I still do."

"Even now? How long has it been?"

"Oh, about twelve years! I write a letter to Oliver on the fifteen of every month. I send cards on holidays and on his birthday, of course."

"Twelve years! Does he get them?"

Tina looked at me with a sad smile on her face, the ache in her heart as painful as the day they dragged Oliver away. "Regina, I don't even know if he's alive."

"Then why do you continue to write?"

"Because he might be alive! Because my letters might be the only thing that keep him alive!" Tina picked up the little aluminum tin and licked it clean. Yellow lemony ooze clung to one corner of her mouth.

I looked at her in total amazement. I am not sure if I had ever heard of anybody doing anything so selfless. This was Tina Benchford—a totally classless woman with a heart of gold. We finished our coffee and talked about hairdos and hemlines, all the things she was known for boring people with. Our coworkers called her a gossip and a showoff, and she was both, but there was also so much more to her. I made a promise to myself to get to know her better.

Moments later, we were standing in Dennis' plush corner office. He was sitting back in his overstuffed executive chair with his bandaged leg propped up on his desk. Tina and I both had suggested that he not come in today, but he had insisted. We all knew that Mirathi was more than a place we worked; it was like our child. We were dedicated to it, its growth and maturity, and like most parents, we would do just about anything for her survival.

Dennis looked at me, and we burned holes in each other with our eyes. Last night's episode in the vault had supercharged our relationship. When we got home, we practically threw everybody out of the house so we could make love like animals all over the living room floor! He was insatiable, and by the look in his eyes, he was still hungry for more. Tina could smell our sexual appetites rising. She threw her arms in the air.

"So do I have a job or what?" she snapped.

"Yes, you have a job, and you can start by supervising the pack up tomorrow at Montgomery." Dennis never took his eyes off of me.

"Hi, baby." *My wife*, his eyes seem to say!

"Good morning again," *My husband*, I mouthed silently, leaning over the desk and planting a big kiss on his waiting lips. I knew my behind was all up in Tina's face, but I didn't care.

"Uh hmm," came a voice from behind us. I straighten up just in time to see a distinguished man in a black double-breasted suit standing behind the door. Tina and I had walked right past him when we entered.

"Who is that?" I whispered to Dennis.

"This is Mr. Morris. He is an international courier. I hired him this morning to perform a very important task."

"A courier? What is he 'couriering'" I asked playfully.

"This," Dennis opened his Brooks Brothers leather bound briefcase, and Tina and I peered inside. All we saw were ledgers, his palm pilot, a copy of *The Post* and Dennis' '8-out-of-10-doctors-recommended' toothbrush tucked inconspicuously in a side compartment. We were not impressed.

"I don't get it," I said.

Dennis took the newspaper out and leafed through to the financials. He carefully unfolded the section and out came the familiar gleam of priceless diamonds and rubies strung on the purest gold.

"Is that . . . that looks like . . . no way!" Tina eyes were as big as the gems themselves.

"Yes, you got it! The largest rubies ever mined out of Sri Lanka enhanced by the finest diamonds in all of Africa. The adornment of queens," Dennis said proudly as he looked straight into my eyes.

I stared at him, shaking my head in disbelief. "The Blood of the Moor?"

"The Blood of the Moor," he echoed.

"You got it back? How?" I asked.

"Never lost it! The one Shaka took was a fake," he said fondling the priceless necklace. "Imagine, not being able to tell the difference between a masterfully crafted original and a synthetic reproduction. That idiot."

"Yeah, that idiot," I said sarcastically, knowing I had not been able to tell the difference either. I grinned. Dennis could be such a nerd—but he was my nerd. Then, realization hit!

"Dennis, you mean to tell me you stored a worthless copy in our expensive new vault and hid a priceless piece of history in your briefcase wrapped in *The Washington Post*?"

He shrugged his shoulders helplessly, and I grew horns! "Are you crazy? Do you know how liable we are?"

"I know, I know, it was stupid. But there were so many workman in the building and so much publicity around the piece. I didn't trust it out of my hands."

I just stood there for a moment with my hands firmly planted on my hips. Was he nuts!? Sure, it worked out this time, but anything could have happened. It was this same kind of bad judgment that made him bring precious relics to my door step and deal drugs in a prison! Tina looked at my face and saw the explosion about to happen. She gently patted me on the back.

"You know, Regina, men sometimes make foolish choices for the right reasons. That's why they need smart women around them—all the time—*to keep them from screwing up!*"

My head ping-ponged between Dennis and Tina, and I decided to pull in my fangs. He was so obsessed with this thing, he could not be held responsible. He had totally lost his mind. Dennis was stroking the necklace like it was a sleeping baby. At any moment, I expected him to place it over his shoulder and burp it! He was too far gone for me to be angry.

"Dennis, what are you doing?"

"I am saying goodbye to her," he said. "Mr. Morris is taking the necklace back to the museum in Paris."

"Dennis, why?" I asked in horror.

"Because we cannot afford it," he said sadly. "At least not right now."

I knew it had taken a lot for him to let it go. This necklace represented a lifetime of struggle and achievement to him. But the last month had been a learning experience he would hardly forget. He would take it slow and do it right. I looked at him with pride.

"We will find the funding to get it back—for good next time," I chimed.

"That's right Dennis, we'll mount that exhibition in a year or so," said Tina, encouragingly.

"When we can better afford it. We'll work together to make it happen," I looked at him with love.

"Together," Dennis repeated. "I like that."

"Absolutely! Foster and I will spend *countless hours* doing grant research. We will do *whatever it takes* to get that necklace back here at Mirathi," Tina winked at me, and I elbowed her in the arm.

Mr. Morris came forward and secured the necklace in a very ominous looking briefcase and swiftly handcuffed it to his wrist. Then, he looked at Tina and me.

"Ladies, excuse us, but Dr. Dickerson and I need a moment alone," he said in a deep baritone men-in-black sort of way. It was almost comical. I half expected him to whip out a pair of dark glasses and a ray gun.

"I get it," I said jokingly. "We could stay, but you would have to kill us." Morris didn't crack a smile.

Dennis winced at the joke and pointed us toward the door. "See you tonight," he said placing a kiss on my forehead.

"Late tonight. It's Friday, remember? Cards and curried chicken with the girls over at my mother's this evening!"

"Hey, that sounds good," he said.

"No men allowed!" I teased. "And Zeta charmed Righteous into letting her come, too, since she is almost thirteen."

Dennis and I laughed while I noticed Tina bowed her head quietly. Then I did something totally unexpected. I don't know what came over me.

"Tina, if you're not busy tonight, maybe you would like to hang out with us. I mean, it's just my mother's regular Friday night hen party but . . ."

"I would love to!" she shouted, flitting pass me through the door and into the hallway. "Gotta go! I've got a million things to do if I'm going to a party tonight. I've got to pull my office back together, get an update from my assistant. She still is my assistant, isn't she? Got to speak with Patti about my schedule and drop in on Foster," she stopped long enough to look me up and down. "And I've got to go home and change. You're not wearing that thing tonight, are you Regina?"

Now that was the old Tina. I shook my head and laughed as she sped down the hall. Tonight should be interesting. I just hoped I wouldn't live to regret it.

The sweet smell of fried plantains and hot buttered yams met Tina and me at the elevator of Righteous' third floor apartment. When we sailed through the door, the party was already in full swing, the shrill voices of many women raised in overlapping conversation. Roz met me at the door, ushered Tina in, and then after quick intros, pulled me aside.

"Reggie, you didn't tell Righteous, did you?"

I knew exactly what she was talking about. Linwood Pride. I had had plenty of time to think about this asshole and the way he was using my sister. I remembered our high school days. Linwood was smart and very manipulative. He would never give up a woman that was such a fool for him. He was probably dangling Roz like a fish on a hook, giving her just enough affection to keep her hanging on. And I knew my sister, the eternal optimist. In her mind, she probably hoped to be the next Mrs. Pride.

"Let me help you out of the mess, Roz," I pleaded

"Reggie, there is no mess. I know what I'm doing. I love Linwood, and I always will. We'll work this out. I promise."

I didn't believe a word of that, but I knew she did. Looking around at all the happy faces in the room, I sighed deeply. I didn't want to make a fuss, so I gave my sister an ultimatum.

"Roz, I will give you one year. *One*! If you don't get this situation with Linwood and that money straight, I'm sicking Mamma on the both of you! Got that?" I whispered hotly.

She hugged me tight, promising to love herself enough to do the right thing. I prayed that she could.

When I walked into the kitchen, Tina had already been handed her first plate of hot n' spicy curried chicken and Cajun style greens. Righteous was standing over her, giant spoon in hand, waiting to hear Tina's critic of her cooking.

"Now, unless you just want to be single all your life, you learn to cook like dis!" Righteous shoved a heaping spoonful of greens into Tina's mouth. "Dis will get you a man."

Tina's eyes were watering like she had swallowed a three-alarm fire. All she could do was nod. Righteous glowed and chalked Tina up as another satisfied patron. Never far behind, Sister Dora was slicing big hunks of cornbread which she was serving to everyone with a gin and tonic chaser.

"This is what every single workin' girl needs," she giggled as she handed me a glass. "Bottoms up!"

Zeta was standing at the stove tending the piping hot cast iron pots, wearing Righteous' apron that came down to her ankles. Her curly bangs were flopping down in her face because of the rising steam.

"Mamma, I have got to get rid of these things!" she complained. "I'm too old for bangs. I'm practically a woman!"

"Take your time, Zeta," the women chimed in from all corners of the room.

"Growin' up is like stirrin' dat pot," Aunt Hazel said, "You gotto do it slow and steady for it to come out any good," and she held out her arms as if she were driving a car.

"You gotta simmer and mature," added Aunt Betty.

"Bubble and churn," said Dora, swishing her hips.

"Till you ready to be tasted," Roz said slyly, giving Zeta a squeeze.

"And one day some man will come along and *put you right back in front of dem pots*!!" Righteous shouted. We laughed riotously, teasing each other about the men in our lives—or the lack of them. It was the most fun I had had in weeks. We sat down at the table, passing gossip, good spirits, and brimming bowls of soulful goodies. And once again, the deck of cards sat conspicuously undisturbed in the middle of the table.

After several hours, I left the others, walking into Righteous' bedroom to seek some privacy. I wanted to call and check in on Rakim. He was coming home tomorrow afternoon. I couldn't wait to see him back in his own room. He had informed me that his girlfriend, Sierra, would be helping with his therapy. What therapy!? Rakim knew he was just fine, healthier now than when he went in to the hospital! I went into my purse and took out my wallet. A gallery of pictures spilled out, all of my children. I smiled with pride. They had grown so much, and so had I.

"I'm so glad you are settled, girl," came a familiar voice. Righteous stood in the door frame watching me.

"I'm happy," I said, simply.

"I know, and I'm blessed by it. I didn't want you to live de life I had."

I looked at her, puzzled. My sister and I had had a great life. When we thought back on our childhood, we remembered the good things. Like most children, we were seldom aware of the struggle and pain that parents endure just trying to keep our heads above water. Thoughts of my father tiptoed across my head. Maybe our lives could have been better. Her life could have been easier if he had been around.

"You did okay as a single mother, Righteous. Roz and I had everything we needed."

"I ain't talkin' about dat, girl. I'm talkin' about you and de good doctor. A daddy in dat house of yours would be a good thing, but I know you can raise dose children and be fine. The Lord will see to dat. What I am saying is, I didn't want you to live your life afraid to love. Always lookin' over your shoulder and afraid to trust a man. Walkin' away from affection 'cause you know you don't need no more hurt in your life."

"Dese are backward times we livin' in, chile. World has it lookin' like women be better off without a man, and you been lookin' for a good man for a long time. You young gals got it hard. Man make less money than you, some women shamed. He ain't finish college—or high school—she don't want him."

I had heard this all before, and I didn't like it any better now. "Righteous, women are just tired of settling for whatever they can get. Do we always have to settle?"

"I ain't sayin' settle—I'm saying, solve it! Save it! Make it work. All the government reform in the world can't do what a little hard love can."

She sat down beside me and patted my hand. Strangely, I had a flashback from when I was a girl, and Roz and I would see our mother sitting on the side of her bed, crying. She cried all the time when daddy first went away.

"Can't get no decent welfare check with a working man in your house. Less government assistance! And men have it rough, too. Dis country look at the black man like he the enemy. He been hated and feared so long, he startin' to hate himself. Then *we* startin' to hate him. Men and women just as locked away from each other out here as they are in the prison. We all locked down, baby. Buildin' up our own walls."

Righteous stared in the mirror at her own image. She ran her palm along her face, conscious of the lines that life had put there. She may have started this conversation talking about me and Dennis, but now it was all about her.

"Almost like the government wants to keep you broke and alone. I had to go on assistance a few times to keep food in your bellies. I know Lambert wouldn't have liked that."

"He wasn't here," I said accusingly.

"No, he wasn't here," she repeated more to herself than to me. She knew I didn't like to talk about daddy, so she tried to change the subject. Her face brightened.

"I'm glad you put away all dat foolishness with dat inmate. Prison ain't no kinda place for a man, sweetie. You keep a man from his woman, and what you get? Somethin' less. Now you go on home to dat good man you got!"

"I'm going. I've got to drop Tina off and get Zeta home to bed. Tomorrow's a big day. Rakim comes home from the hospital, you know, and I need to take Roz back to the airport. I'd better go."

Righteous gave me a huge hug, and we said our goodnights as we had when I was a girl, standing in her room at the foot of her bed. As I held her tonight, she seemed so much older but not in that flesh and bone way; rather, she had become classic. Even monumental! The neophyte of the seven wonders! I was so grateful that she was mine. Just as I began to pull away, I spied a gray hair corkscrewing from her left temple. I plucked it out with the quickness of a viper!

"Ouch!" she howled, rubbing the spot that was violated. "Why you do dat? You know, when you pull one out *two* grow back in its place!"

"I know," I said, giggling, "but I couldn't help myself."

"And you da one put it there in da first place," she said with a wink.

"I know that, too," I said more seriously. "I . . . I love you so much."

"Then go home to dat man. Now."

Back at the house, Dennis had fallen asleep on the sofa, probably having very sweet dreams of our escapades from the night before. I decided not to disturb him. Zeta, Roz, and I tiptoed past him, heading up the stairs. Exhausted and stuffed, we said goodnight and stumbled into our rooms.

As soon as my head hit the pillow, the phone rang, and I knew—I just knew. I approached it timidly as if it could bite. I anticipated each ring knowing that he was counting each ring, wondering whether or not I would pick up the phone. The third ring! Perhaps it would be easier not to answer it at all. Let him call until he got tired of calling. Until he stopped calling! The fourth ring! Excitement and fear moved through my body like a jolt of electricity. It was the rush that was Ray Boden. He still titillated me, jump starting me like a race car unleashed on the open road. The fifth ring—the final one. I leaped for the phone.

"Hello?" There was the drone of the operator.

"You have a collect call from the Montgomery County Correctional Center. Do you accept the call?"

"Yes, I accept."

Click, click, click, Pause. Silence. There was just dead air for almost thirty seconds, but I knew he was there. And he knew I was there waiting for him.

"Hey, Gina," Ray said softly. There was music from the little radio. It sounded like an old Marvin Gaye and Tammy Terrell tune.

"Hi Ray, how are you doing?"

"Oh it's cool! It's cool! Look, I was just wondering."

"Wondering what?"

"Well . . . if you had fifteen minutes . . . just for me."

My heart broke just a little bit. "Sure, I do, Ray. I got fifteen minutes." We were back where we started, unsure and afraid.

Another dead silence. We were both breathing a little harder than normal, struggling to keep the avalanche of questions and accusations at bay. This was killing me, and part of me just wanted to hang up. Still, I knew he deserved better than that.

"Ray, Dennis and I . . ."

"Oh, and don't worry about Shaka Blu squealing on Dickerson." Ray laughed a little bit. "Gina, he was mad as hell when he found out that necklace was a piece of junk. But he can't rat out Dennis; he needs his clients to think everything is still cool. Like he still in control."

"But he can still have Dennis arrested. He can still tell the police," Ray heard the fear in my voice.

"Gina, we don't handle things like that in here. We are cons, remember? We don't call the police."

I remembered. Ray was a convict, locked away from me, and somehow a small piece of me was locked away with him. I had to at least give him the truth.

"Ray, I should tell you that Dennis and I . . ."

"I know. You know I already know that shit, too, Gina, and it's cool. It's all cool with me." The words came out in a rush like he had practiced them in his head.

"You know what happen with Shaka in the vault?"

"Yeah, and I know he hurt you," Ray swallowed hard as if he were still angry. "Me and him got a lot to settle, and it's gonna happen. All I gotta do is wait. He's in solitary now—the hole—but that ain't forever. When he gets out, it's gonna be just like the Moors. A fight to the death!"

An image of Ray and Shaka squaring off like gladiators in some dark corner of the prison flashed inside my head. It was gruesome and bloody, and not the way any sane man would want to die.

"Ray . . ."

"Gina, I didn't call to talk about that. So you and your man all straight now! Right?" Ray got right to the point.

"Dennis and I are getting married," I said, not wanting to explain what had gone on in the vault. I prayed he would just accept that. I prayed he would understand that this was goodbye. He didn't react immediately. For a moment, I thought he had walked away from the phone. Then, the music got louder. He had turned it up; maybe he didn't want to hear what I was saying at all.

"Married! Hey, that's great, Gina. Dickerson is alright with me. I mean, he was there when you needed him. He fought for you. That has got to be alright with me, you know?"

Thank God! Ray was trying to make this easy for me.

"I mean, no harm, no foul, right? Shaka is out of my face; niggas ain't warring in here no more. Everybody got what they wanted, right?" he asked.

Silence again, and then a whole other conversation took place. Whatever had drawn us together was still alive, pushing the issue, wanting to be satisfied.

I didn't get what I wanted. I didn't get you. I didn't get to love you like I wanted to.

"Right. Then I guess that's it," I said, *but I didn't get to lie in your arms, listening to jazz in the moonlight.*

"Like I said, Shaka is in solitary. Drugs ain't movin' so hard in here, at least for a while. Things have calmed down." *But I didn't get to move inside you and make you moan for me. I didn't get to feel the heat from your body pressed under mine.*

"We are looking at more legitimate ways of funding the museum. Less dangerous," I tried to laugh and shut off the voice in my head. *I didn't get to love you, not like I wanted to.*

"Ray, it's getting late. I better go."

"I need to see you," he blurted.

"What? No, I . . ."

"Tomorrow. Come tomorrow."

"No, Ray, I can't."

"Please. I know you can; you have clearance. I know they are packing up tomorrow morning. There will be a truck. You can come."

I hesitated. I needed to say no. I had made a commitment to Dennis, and I had meant every word. I loved him, and I was devoted to building a good life with him. There was no room in my life for Ray Boden anymore.

"Gina! Just this one time! This last time!"

I should say "no" and end it now. That was the right thing. Cut it off clean. Just say goodbye and hang up.

"Baby, please . . . I got something for you."

"Something for me? What is it?" I asked.

"Something I wanted to give you that very first night. Something to make all your nightmares go away. Trust me, you'll like it. Please come, Gina. Please, baby."

Say yes! Say yes!

"Yes, alright! Ray, I'll come."

"Good! Then I will see you tomorrow. Ten o'clock. You'll get your present. Goodnight, baby."

"Goodnight."

I held the phone in my hand long after Ray had hung up. I needed to let go. I needed to let go.

CHAPTER 16

◆

Love Set Free

I could not remember ever being this nervous in all my life. I woke up before sunrise, got completely dressed and was sitting outside in my Chrysler long before anyone in the house had stirred. I didn't want to face any of them, afraid they would see right through me. Especially my sister! I didn't want to hear her mouth. After all, I had lectured her about her locked-down relationship and had not told her one thing about mine!

And my daughter—I was petrified that Zeta would ask me something mundane like "Mamma, why are you dressed for work so early?" and I would say something really stupid like "because I am going to visit the convict that I have been having sexual fantasies about. Be back in time for dinner, honey."

All I could think about was seeing Ray.

On the long drive out to Montgomery, I thought about him and what drew us together in the first place. What had made him choose me? Ray was charming and attentive and funny and smart—like a lot of men. The real question was why was I drawn to him? What was it about me that made me fall so hard for a con? I counted down the possibilities—

#1—   I was available: not in a committed relationship.

#2—   I was insecure about my past relationships, feeling that everything was my fault.

#3—   I was lonely. Just that simple!

#4—   I had no idea what a healthy relationship looked like.

#5—   I was ready for adventure! I needed someone else to make *me* less boring.

#6—   I wanted something that was just mine—exclusive and illusive.

#7—   I had abandonment issues. A locked-down man could not leave me.

#8—   I needed to be needed.

#9—   I thought that love was suppose to feel difficult and frustrating.

#10—   I was desperate, not for a man, but for something or someone who could make me feel special.

I thought back to all of the women I had met in the past few weeks who were in their own locked-down relationship. Trisha, CeCe, Sophia (over the Internet), Anna, Marilyn, and Carmela. Even my own family and friends—Aunt Betty, Sister Dora, and Roz—all of these women had one or more of these things in common. Did it make us suckers? No, but these reasons did leave us vulnerable to men that were *just as vulnerable as we were*. I shook it off vowing to choose men with my eyes wide open and not dreaming with my eyes closed shut.

Moments later, I pulled into the Montgomery prison compound. I checked in at the gate, spying Tina with a group of men at the dock. Some of them were guards, but a handfull of inmates had also been selected to assist with the packing. One inmate, carrying a box of framed reproductions, caught my eye. Tina was barking instructions at him, warning him to be careful not to drop the box. He stumbled, and the box nearly hit the ground. Tina was livid, and she rushed over to him, ready to chew off his arm. He was older, but very attractive with a smile that would melt ice, and Tina was instantly charmed. After a short exchange, she left the packing to them, and she walked over to me.

"Cute but clumsy."

"Got that right," she said, "But damn, the girls in the cafe are right. All the good-looking men are locked up. Have you taken a look at these guys?"

"Stop drooling, Tina. We've got work to do," I said, anxious to see this job completed so she could be on her way. I didn't want her to know about my little rendezvous.

"I'm just saying—damn! They are fine, all three of them. Maybe we can get the board to reconsider. I would teach a class here any day."

"Tina, these men are locked away for a reason."

"I know, I know. I'm just saying—damn!"

The men were coming past us again with the last load of boxes, and suddenly, I was knocked from behind by an elbow trying to squeeze through.

"Excuse me, gorgeous. I didn't mean to hurt you," he said. I turned around just in time to see "cute but clumsy" smiling at me.

"No problem," I said as I moved out of his way. The inmate walked on, stepped into the back of the truck and began to arrange the boxes so they wouldn't fall out. They were almost finished, and I was glad of it.

I looked at my watch. It was getting late. I had a lot to do today, and I still had not seen Ray. Then Tina spoke to the driver, who handed her some paperwork from out of the window. A moment later, the truck pulled away.

"Well that's that," she said. "The fellas are going to stop for gas, then be on their way. They are going to take this stuff to a boys' home upstate. I'll head back to the museum. Would you mind checking in with the guards in the book room? Let them know we are gone."

"Fine, I can do that. I'll also give it a last look to make sure we haven't left anything behind."

"Oh, I almost forgot! The driver handed me these papers. Just prison stuff you have to sign off on." Tina handed me the sheets. "See you by lunch?"

"I'll try! You better get going," I said, knowing that I would want to spend as much time as I could with Ray.

I waited till both the truck, and Tina's car was well out of the prison compound before I asked the guard to escort me upstairs. I went through all of the security checks in a daze. Every time I passed a bulletproof window, I checked my lipstick or straightened my blouse. I can't explain why, but I wanted Ray to like what he saw. Even though I had made my choice and would never turn back, I wanted this first and last meeting to be unforgettable.

"Where to, ma'am?" the guard asked. I wanted to say "the visitation hall" but first things first. I needed to look over these papers, get them signed and eyeball the book room like I promised.

One elevator ride and a long hallway later, the guard and I entered the book room where Dennis had held his lectures for the prisoners. It was smaller than I expected, bland now because of all the things we had taken away. The chairs were bolted down, and there were big metal rings popping out of the floor.

"What are they for?" I asked the guard.

"Them? Oh, sometimes we gotta shackle the rough ones down to make them shut up and listen," he said.

Yikes! I thought. "You're not expecting any of them today, are we?"

The guard laughed, "No ma'am, just you and the old man." He pointed to the inmate in the far side of the room. "He's harmless."

I sat down in one of those extremely uncomfortable metal chairs and quickly filed through the papers in my lap. Suddenly, an envelope fell out from between them, landing by my foot.

"G.I.N.A" it said, in all capital letters. My breath caught! It was from Ray and suddenly, I knew. That was him! The hot-looking inmate I had bumped into, the one that had spoken to me. I saw when he got into the back of the truck, but I never saw him come out! My head pivoted in the direction the truck had taken. *If I run to my car, maybe I can . . .* But it was too late! It would take me forever to get back out through security. By now, the driver would have already passed all of the security checks, and the last gate would have closed. That truck was on its way up Highway 95.

Ray was gone. Gone! My feet felt like lead, weighed down to the pavement as reality set in. Again, I had been close enough to smell him, touch him, and taste him if I had only known. I tore the envelope open like a wild animal, and of all things, a lottery ticket fell out of it, floating to the floor. I left it there and read the letter through watery eyes.

Hey Sweet Girl,

If you are reading this, I made it out on the truck. Sorry we didn't get a chance to talk, but you are as soft and sweet smelling as I remember.

A wise man once told me that when you truly love a woman, you give her what she really wants. Do you know what you want, Gina? I figure you want what everybody else does—redemption. Somebody to rescue you! Somebody to set you free!

Enjoy your freedom, baby. It's only a blue note away.
P.S.—Thanks for accepting my call. You're one in a million!

I retrieved the ticket and held it in my hand as if it were the man himself. For whatever reason, he had not wanted me to see him leave. He had not wanted to implicate me in his escape. He had cared for me even to the end. Deep down, I knew this was for the best, but why did I feel so bad?

The old man watched me read Ray's letter and was standing across the room, packing books in a box and straightening the library shelves. He wore no handcuffs or shackles which meant he was well trusted and was probably afforded more privileges in the prison than most. That explained why he worked so leisurely, listening to the small radio that sat on the table by his side. I approached him slowly, not quite knowing what I was going to say.

"Excuse me, sir. Rayboy! Ray Boden. Do you know him?'"

"Ray? Yeah, I know him," he replied. "Better than most. What you want with him?"

I didn't quite know what to say to that. I didn't want to ask to see him; that would alert everybody that he had escaped. The old man stared at me for a long time, waiting for me to answer.

The tinny sound of the radio reminded me of the one I had hear so many times over the phone with Ray, and the station was the same—smooth moody blues. The old man hummed along as he worked. I watched him for a while, for no real reason except for the fact that I felt a little empty. The man I had come to see had gone, and all that was left was this old man and a stack on moldy old books.

"Geography," he said, not looking up at me, still tending to his task.

"Excuse me?"

"These books! They about geography. I saw you lookin' and I thought you were wondering."

He obviously wanted to talk, and I certainly had the time. Perhaps he could tell me where Rayboy had gone. I walked toward him.

"You like geography?" I asked.

"Yeah, well, it has always been a passion of mine," he said,

"Travel much?" I asked, partly as a bad joke. He wasn't going very far in this place.

"Nah, never been much further than I am right now. But I liked moving around. I useta work on the DC Metro back in the day. I was one of their first colored drivers."

"Really?" I said suddenly very excited. "My daddy use to drive for the metro, too." I was amazed by my own enthusiasm. I never brought information about my father into conversation. I didn't know what made me do it then.

"Yeah, back then, it was hard for a black man to travel anywhere 'less he was carrying a gun for Uncle Sam. I always dreamed of going places—Paris, London, the Ivory Coast—but it never happened."

"Why?" I asked.

"Got married young, had children, then wound up in here."

"What got you here, if you don't mind me asking."

"Don't mind at all, pretty lady," he smiled, and a shiver went through me. "Walking home one night, white man thought I looked at his woman too long. He pulled a knife on me; I defended myself, and next thing I know, he lying dead on the pavement."

"Oh my God! That was terrible!" I said.

"Yeah, my wife was all broke up over it. 'Specially after his woman testified against me. Said I came after her. My wife never trusted me after that. They tried me on assault and first degree murder. I been in here ever since. But I dream of going places, exotic places, and I do from right here."

He picked up a book and held it in front of my face. "With these, the world comes to me, understand?"

"Yes, I do understand," I said, and I did. When I walked around in the museum, I felt like the world was at my feet. I didn't have to leave my office to feel like I had been somewhere. Rakim was the only other person who understood that—until now.

A silky Sarah Vaughan tune flowed like a river around us, and both our heads began to sway. It was relaxing, and I was enjoying the company, then a guard came through the door.

"Miss, you about through? We gotta lock this place down in a minute."

"Oh, yes sir, I'm just leaving," I said, but I wanted to stay and not only because I had questions about Ray. I wanted to know more about this man;

I felt strangely content in his presence. The guard cast a stern eye at me, and I started to turn for the door.

"Hey, you like to write letters?" the old man asked.

"Yes, I do," I answered.

"Wanna write one to me?" he asked with a wink.

I frowned at him. "Are you making a pass at me, old man?"

"Who me? Oh no! I got daughters your age, two of them!" He laughed, and it sounded like an old familiar song, like those blues. His eyes seem to dance with a rekindled memory.

His eyes!

The guard gestured to me again, and I stood motionless, frozen in that one spot. Those eyes! I had seen them before, a thousand times, staring at me from photographs plastered all over my house that were yellow with age. The same eyes I had seen in the faces of my children!

Give her what she really wants!

The guard was growing impatient as I stood there in amazement. Could it be him? After all these years, "Could this man be my . . ."

"Ma'am, I have to ask you to leave." The guard was standing right on top of me now, his hand on my elbow ready to escort me out. But I had to know, I had to know! Another guard came through the door. The old man picked up the box and walked toward him. He was leaving me.

"Sir!" I screamed, tears streaming down my cheeks. "You didn't tell me your name."

He looked back at me, pain and joy both reflected in his face. This had been no chance meeting. He had known who I was from the very beginning, and he had waited for me to come to him.

Redemption. Somebody to rescue you. Somebody to set you free.

The guards were pulling us further apart. In a moment, this man would be on the other side of the door, prison walls, locks and gates separating us again forever. In my heart, I knew there was one word—one word—I could say that would make all the walls in my heart break away.

"Come on, get that last box and let's go, Lambert," yelled the second guard.

Lambert!

Our eyes held each other, as he waited for me to end years of heartache and emptiness. I shook the guard's hand away and took one step toward him, then another. I wanted so badly to feel whole, and to know love from the first man in my life, the one who gave me life. The hurt little girl in me wanted to continue to hate him, but a bigger part of me needs to forgive him.

"Daddy?"

The man dropped the box. "Regina, my sweet baby," he cried and walked straight into my arms. And without hesitation, I embraced him, weeping into his chest, releasing all of the pain I had held in for so long. He stroked my back and shoulders, comforting me in the way only a father could do. His tears mixed with mine, and he spoke gentle words in my ear, asking my forgiveness and proclaiming his love for me.

When you truly love a woman . . . when you truly love her . . .

Ray had done it. He had kept his promise made to me from the very beginning and made all my bad dreams disappear. He had released all the ghosts locked away in my head and left me free to love.

As my father held me, I thought of the man who had made this possible. I ran my fingers over the surface of the ticket as if I were reading it in Braille.

"What's this?" my father asked, taking the old lottery ticket from me.

"It's from Ray," I smiled. "He wanted me to have it."

Lambert squinted, giving it a closer look. "Wow," he said. It's not from DC. This is for the New York State lottery!" he beamed, "I hope it's a winner!"

New York? I shook my head in amazement. Ray had left me a clue to where he was headed, letting me know where I could find him. Suddenly, I felt that same hot jolt of electricity course through me. Ray might as well have been standing beside me. Inside me! This wasn't just a lottery ticket. It was a ticket to endless possibilities.

And then it hit me—the wrong man for me might just be the right man for me.

Lambert saw the smile on my face, and he smiled, too. "What you thinkin' about, girl?"

"Bright lights and smooth rhythms," I said out loud, and laughed as I envisioned Ray sipping smooth gin, his hand on the thigh of a big-legged woman. Ray Boden was on his way up north to the things he loved. I looked at the ticket and then back up at my father's face.

"Take a chance," he whispered, his old eyes full of renewed hope. "It might be a winner."

"Yes," I nodded, dazed by all the possibilities. The hot steamy sexy possibilities! "Yes, I know it's a winner. It's got to be. It's one in a million."

Epilogue

Patti sat liesurely at the big mahogany desk slowly sipping her coffee and filing through the pile of mail that was gradually accumulating. With Regina and Dennis on vacation, Patti was in charge and loving it!

From the Desk of

Regina Jackson
Researcher and Curator of African Art
Mirathi Foundation of Fine Art

A Birth Announcement from Trisha

Little Lamont Samuel Reynolds was born three days after Cowboy's parole. The couple is already expecting another child. Sam is looking forward to a life on the outside.

A Wedding Announcement from Anna

Anna and her man decided on a prison wedding. Her family and church members did not attend.

A Postcard from Marilyn Marshall

Marilyn and Beau have decided to get out of the corrections business. They are currently vacationing in the Bahamas. Beau wants to invest in tropical spas and resorts, and Marilyn wants to start an escort service.

A card from CeCe

CeCe decided to go back to junior college last fall where she met a nice accounting major. They moved in together in a small apartment in Suitland, Maryland. They do not own a home computer or have email addresses.

News Clipping about Sophia

Sophia and Wildbuck were finally caught by police in a small town in Tennessee. Wildbuck was sent back to prison, and Beverly was sentenced to three years in prison for aiding and abetting.

A Wedding Announcement from Betty

After his release, Aunt Betty and her Elvis impersonator started their own church in Las Vegas, Nevada. Their prison pen pal ministry is a blessing to over two hundred inmates all over the country.

A Change of Address Notice from Roz

Roz bought a beautiful home in Northwest DC near her Righteous. She and Linwood's ex-wife are friends again. Linwood is working three jobs to pay child support and to repay the $1.5 million!

Invitation to a Restaurant Opening from Carmela

Carmela and Hernando have opened a combination restaurant and amateur boxing arena in Barcelona. Hernando does the cooking while Milli manages the business. Carmela manufactures a sports remedy that has made them millions!

Death Announcement from Tina

Unfortunately, Oliver died in prison six years after he was arrested. The news was delivered to her by his cell mate, Mustafa, who continued to read Tina's letters for the next six years. He says they kept him alive during his terrible incarceration. Tina and Mustafa are living happily together in her luxury apartment in downtown DC. They both volunteer for Amnesty International.

About the Author

R. Satiafa is a writer and philanthropist who works in the fields of African American Folklore and Women's Studies. She is the author of two books, *Broom Jumping: A Celebration of Love* (1992) and *Grandmother's Gift of Memories* (Broadway Books1997). *Love Locked Down* is her first novel. While conducting workshops on legacy building and restorative traditions, Ms. Satiafa remains a successful entreprenuer and speaker. A native of Richmond, Virginia, she is the mother of three dynamic sons, and is affectionately known nationwide as The Broom Lady.

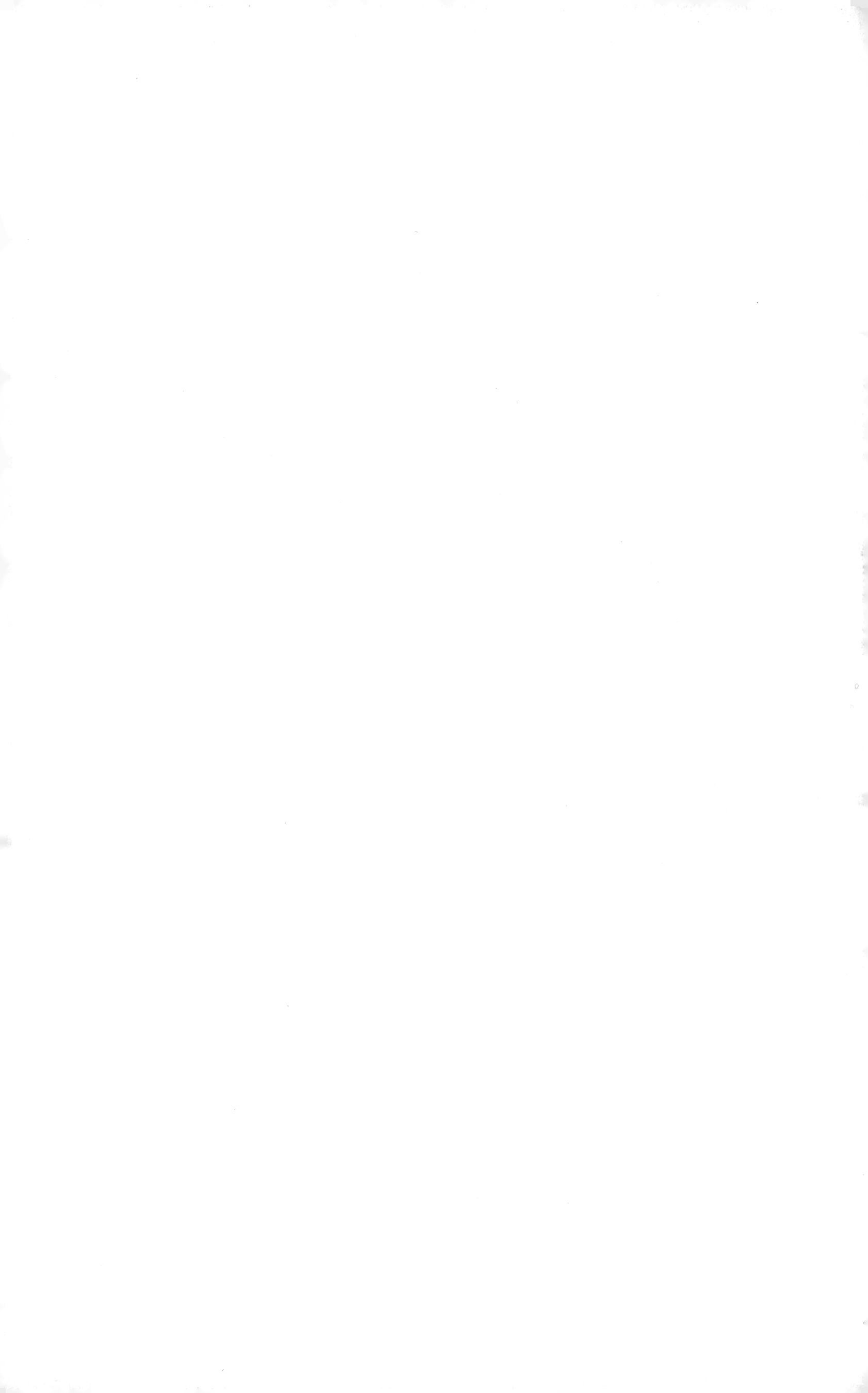